Signed Language Interpreting in the 21st Century

LEN ROBERSON AND
SHERRY SHAW, *Editors*

Signed Language Interpreting in the 21st Century

An Overview of the Profession

GALLAUDET UNIVERSITY PRESS
Washington, DC

Gallaudet University Press
Washington, DC 20002

http://gupress.gallaudet.edu
© 2018 by Gallaudet University
All rights reserved. Published 2018.
Second printing 2019.
Printed in the United States of America

Library of Congress Cataloging-in-Publication Data

Names: Roberson, Len. | Shaw, Sherry, editors.
Title: Signed language interpreting in the 21st century : an overview of the
profession / Len Roberson and Sherry Shaw, editors.
Description: Washington, DC : Gallaudet University Press, [2018]
Identifiers: LCCN 2018020068| ISBN 9781944838249 (hard cover :alk. paper) |
    ISBN 9781944838256 (e-book)
Subjects: LCSH: Interpreters for the deaf—United States. | Sign
language—Study and teaching—United States.
Classification: LCC HV2402 .S547 2018 | DDC 331.7/6141970802—dc23
LC record available at https://lccn.loc.gov/2018020068

⊗ This paper meets the requirements
of ANSI/NISO Z39.48-1992 (Permanence of Paper).

CONTENTS

CONTRIBUTORS

Carolyn Ball
  VRS Interpreting Institute
  Salt Lake City, Utah

Robyn K. Dean
  Department of American Sign
  Language and Interpreting
  Education
  National Technical Institute
  for the Deaf
  Rochester, New York

Carla M. Mathers, Esq.
  Hyattsville, MD

Robert Q Pollard, Jr.
  Administrative Council
  National Technical Institute
  for the Deaf
  Rochester, New York

Len Roberson
  Department of Exceptional, Deaf,
  and Interpreter Education
  University of North Florida
  Jacksonville, Florida

Debra Russell
  Department of Educational
  Psychology
  University of Alberta
  Edmonton, Canada

Sherry Shaw
  Department of Exceptional, Deaf,
  and Interpreter Education
  University of North Florida
  Jacksonville, Florida

Linda K. Stauffer
  Interpreter Education Program
  University of Arkansas
  Little Rock, Arkansas

Laurie Swabey
  Department of American Sign
  Language and Interpreting
  St. Catherine University
  St. Paul, Minnesota

Anna Witter-Merithew
  Project CLIMB
  University of North Colorado
  Greely, Colorado

1

Interpreting: An Overview

LEN ROBERSON

DEFINING TERMS: WHAT IS IT WE DO?

An interpreter conveys what is said or signed in one language into another language while maintaining the original intended message. *Interpreting* allows two or more individuals who do not share a common language to engage in a communicative interaction through a person who is bilingual. Signed language interpreters render "a spoken or signed source language message into a spoken or signed target language in real time" (International Organization for Standardization, 2014, p. 1).

Within the field of signed language interpretation, interpreters not only work between two or more languages, but also between different forms of the same language. This process, working between different forms of the same language, is referred to as *transliterating.* According to Winston (1989), transliterating is "a specific form of sign language interpreting." It is the process of changing one form of an English message, either spoken English or signed English, into the other form. *Translation,* although often confused with interpreting, is a unique, albeit closely related, linguistic discipline. *Translation* is the process of converting a message in one printed language to the same message in another printed language while retaining all of the original meaning. Translators, like interpreters, work to not only maintain the integrity of the message itself, but also to include cultural understanding in the translation. There are times when signed language interpreters perform a similar task known as *sight translation,* working from a printed text into sign language. For example, an interpreter may have to translate an intake document in a doctor's office for a Deaf consumer who

1

prefers to have the form signed. In essence, the key difference between these two linguistic processes is in the medium of the work; translation involves a written text, whereas interpreting occurs between spoken and/ or signed languages.

SERVICE DELIVERY

Interpreting can be done in a number of ways, but it is typically accomplished either in person or via some form of technology. In-person interpreting is by far the more common method of interpreting and certainly, for many Deaf and hard of hearing individuals, the preferred method. However, recent advances in technology have created opportunities for interpreting to occur without the physical presence of an interpreter. For the field of sign language interpreting, this is a rather new occurrence. The availability of high-definition video technology allows interpreters to be in one location while the individuals who are communicating are in two different locations. Although interpreting services using technology are constantly improving and serve a general purpose for non-urgent interpreting, there is still a need for research on the effectiveness of technology-based interpreting in the areas of high-risk interpreting (e.g., medical and legal interpreting). Although many deaf and hard of hearing individuals enjoy the use of technology-based interpreting for everyday tasks, such as calling a friend, ordering a meal, or making an appointment, these same individuals often prefer a live interpreter to be present with them during other interpreted events.

In-Person Interpreting

Interpreters who work in a live setting have direct and in-person access to all parties engaged in communication. Often, this means managing the physical space and environment as well as the discourse exchange between speakers. For example, when interpreting in person, an interpreter is often the individual who ensures the arrangement of all parties in the room is supportive of full and equal access to all as well the general management of such environmental factors as lighting, seating, and audio/visual materials. Interpreters working in a live setting have an easier time with turn-taking, the volume of the spoken message, and visual access to extra items and people present that may not be easily accessible via technology.

Signed language interpreters work as *independent (freelance) contractors*, or as *staff interpreters*. Independent contractors provide their services to many different people. They can obtain jobs through a signed language interpreting agency or by contracting directly with companies and people in need of interpreting services. These interpreters work on a fee-for-service basis, and they are paid by the hour or by the day or week. They can work for more than one company or person at a time, but they are not employees of any one agency or company; they are self-employed. As such, they are responsible for paying taxes on a quarterly schedule.

Staff interpreters are salaried workers in an organization, and they provide interpreting services for employees, visitors, or customers. Many businesses, organizations, and agencies (e.g., K–12 and postsecondary school systems, government agencies, hospitals, state and federal court systems, and private corporations) hire full-time interpreters. According to AIIC, "career paths of staff interpreters vary widely" with many staff interpreters remaining with a single organization for many years (see International Association of Conference Interpreters, 2011). Staff interpreting positions may include other responsibilities (e.g., managing interpreting services for the organization, administrative support services, providing accessibility consultation and training, etc.), and often build in time to prepare for specific assignments and other duties. Staff interpreter positions are usually salaried, include benefits, and often provide for regular salary increases, opportunities for professional development and training, as well as advancement opportunities. Another benefit of a staff interpreter position is the development of collegial relationships with other employees, both Deaf and hearing.

A staff interpreter may also be a *designated interpreter*, that is, hired to work alongside a Deaf professional to interpret all of the individual's interaction with nonsigning individuals (e.g., customers, patients, and coworkers). Designated interpreters have been hired to work with Deaf doctors, lawyers, engineers, real estate agents, artists, educators, and corporate administrators, to name a few. Designated interpreters must have excellent linguistic and interpreting skills, expertise in a particular field or profession, including terminology, and a strong partnership with the

Deaf professionals with whom they work. The book *Deaf Professionals and Designated Interpreters: A New Paradigm* is an excellent resource for understanding the work of designated interpreters.

Interpreting via Technology

Interpreting, in a fundamental sense, is about access. From the time the telephone was developed, technology has had a part in providing access. Although deaf people could not use the telephone themselves, they would ask a hearing family member or friend who signed to make the call, so they could engage in conversation with someone. With the advent of telecommunications devices for the deaf (TDDs), deaf people could call each other over the telephone lines and type their conversations. Access to the telephone became more widely available when the Americans with Disabilities Act (ADA) required (see Title IV of the ADA) telephone companies to provide relay services across the United States. The early relay services used a TDD and involved a hearing person, a deaf person, and a communication assistant (interpreter) to relay the messages back and forth. All of the parties involved in the call were in a different location.

New video technologies have made it possible for interpreters to work in one location for an entire shift and to handle calls from many different locations. The newest forms of technology-related interpreting are video remote interpreting (VRI) and video-relay service interpreting (VRS). Both types rely on computers or other similar devices with video capabilities and broadband internet access to connect Deaf and hearing individuals with an interpreter. The interpreter can then facilitate the communication between all parties.

There are fundamental differences between these two services. Video-relay services are provided by companies who specialize in this form of interpreting. The Federal Communications Commission (FCC) reimburses the companies and requires that the parties (the Deaf person, the hearing person, and the signed language interpreter) cannot be in the same location.

VRI services are often used when two of the parties (e.g., the Deaf and hearing person, the Deaf person and the interpreter, or the interpreter and the hearing, nonsigning person) are in the same room. The VRI service provider usually has a contract with the individual or organization requesting the interpreting services. Both VRI and VRS allow interpreters to work from remote locations that may be far from the physical location of the assignment. Although this seems to be an excellent solution for access, often the communication may prove to be ineffective due to limitations in bandwidth, difficulty in viewing a multidimensional language on a flat screen, and the challenges of interacting with all parties and the environment via video technologies. VRI may not be the right solution for all situations or all individuals involved, and its use should be carefully considered and the benefits and limitations weighed before using.

SETTINGS

General

Signed language interpreters have many opportunities to work in a variety of settings with diverse groups of individuals. Some of these settings require specialized skill sets, training, and experience. This is especially true for educational, medical, and legal interpreting.

Although a list of potential settings can be considered and presented, in reality, an interpreter *could* work in any situation in which a Deaf person interacts with others who cannot communicate on their own with the Deaf person. This suggests endless possibilities for where an interpreter *could* work. Such possibilities might include any of the following:

- working as a full-time staff interpreter for a company, corporation, or organization
- health care (i.e., doctor's office, hospital, surgical center)
- educational (i.e., preschool–12th grade, college, technical school, continuing education)
- legal (i.e., attorney–client meetings, court, mediation, law enforcement)
- conferences and meetings
- social clubs and activities
- vacation and holiday events (i.e., amusement parks, cruises, travel tours)
- sporting teams, events
- theater and musical performances
- religious services, events
- family events (i.e., funerals, weddings, family reunions)

Educational

Educational interpreters provide services in settings that involve teaching and learning. These settings range from traditional classrooms (preschool through college) to continuing education classes, adult learning opportunities, employee training within work settings, and even postsecondary training programs. Interpreters have been used in schools and educational environments for many decades; however, the field of educational interpreting has experienced significant growth thanks to federal legislation, particularly the Education for All Handicapped Children Act of 1975 and its reauthorization as the Individuals with Disabilities Education Act (1990, 2004). Although residential schools for the deaf have had a long history of educating both deaf and hard of hearing students, the recent and current focus on inclusion as an educational practice has significantly increased the number of deaf and hard of hearing students being educated alongside their hearing peers throughout the public schools of the United States. This increase in placements has necessitated the growth of the number of educational interpreters employed by school districts.

Educational interpreters can expect their duties and responsibilities to vary, depending on the school system in which they work. Some schools require interpreters to interpret not only for academic classes, but also for extracurricular activities, which can include athletic events, student organization meetings, student clubs, and even on-the-job training work experiences and internships. They may also expect the interpreter to fulfill other responsibilities as a staff member within the school. A growing trend in the area of educational interpreting is that interpreters are hired predominately for interpreting work and less frequently for other responsibilities, such as general classroom assistance, administrative support assistance, or in other noninstructional duties.

Qualifications vary dramatically from school system to school system and even among schools within a school system. Although some educational institutions or systems require interpreters to have national certification, many school systems or institutions do not require any certification at all. Although some school systems and schools do require advanced preparation, experience, or degrees related to the work of an interpreter, many often classify signed language interpreters as *paraprofessionals* or other general educational staff members and as such may require only a high school diploma and other minimal skills. In some states, licensure as an interpreter is required, which often requires national certification as an interpreter. In her chapter on "Credentialing and Regulation of Signed Language Interpreters," Witter-Merithew (this volume) addresses interpreting credentials in greater detail, including the Educational Interpreter Performance Assessment (EIPA). This has been extremely controversial over the years, because professionals who work within the field of deaf education as well as families and parents all agree that deaf children deserve the best skilled and experienced interpreters as possible. Often well-meaning individuals who know sign language get hired as educational interpreters despite the fact that they do not have the necessary language or interpreting skills to provide effective, efficient, and accurate interpretation to the students they are hired to serve. This jeopardizes deaf students' access not only to education, but also to the future.

For many deaf children whose families do not use sign language themselves, access to language comes most often through the hands of their educational interpreters. Similarly, deaf students who are educated entirely in a mainstream situation can gain access to education only through the hands of their signed language interpreters. This is a significant responsibility, and one that should not be taken lightly. Deaf students' access to education and language will have a lasting impact on their lives. Like teachers, educational interpreters must continually further their language skills, subject-area knowledge, and understanding of students' needs at various stages of their education.

"Interpreting in the educational setting requires additional knowledge and skills relevant to children" (Registry of Interpreters for the Deaf, 2010). Interpreters in educational settings should have a degree from an interpreter education program and have taken courses in educational interpreting, child development, and generally in the education of deaf children. Interpreters in educational settings should hold certification as a signed language interpreter preferably at a national level and should also hold an undergraduate degree in signed language interpreting or the educational field. According to data collected and shared by the Distance Opportunities for Interpreters and Teachers Center at the University of Northern Colorado, 42 states use the EIPA as, or as part of, their standards for educational interpreting (Johnson, Bolster, & Brown, 2014).

Healthcare

Everyone needs access to medical services and healthcare; however, without an interpreter, many deaf people are denied this access. Medical, or healthcare, interpreting can occur in a variety of settings, including, but not limited to, physician offices, hospitals, urgent care centers, mental health counseling, school healthcare clinics, and surgical care centers. Although providing interpreting services in any situation deserves attention and best practices, healthcare interpreting involves relaying extremely sensitive and personal information between the deaf person and the healthcare professional. As one might expect, the deaf patient may be worried, concerned, frightened, or in pain. All of these emotions can affect an interpreter's ability to communicate effectively; therefore, interpreters should take special care in providing adequate and effective communication in medical settings.

Although there are currently no national standards or special certifications for medical interpreting, as is the case with other forms of specialized interpreting (e.g., legal interpreting), interpreters working in healthcare settings must be highly competent, with both the skills and experience to effectively interpret in complex situations. Healthcare interpreting assignments are filled with special terminology, processes, and procedures that may have a high potential for risk and complications. Interpreters should be aware of their role in the communicative interaction between doctor and patient, their placement during medical assignments, and the potential for specialized vocabulary knowledge and skills necessary for the assignment. In her chapter on healthcare interpreting, Dr. Laurie Swabey (this volume) presents additional details on interpreters working in healthcare settings and suggests that the ability to recognize when an interpreting specialist is needed is a necessary skill for competent interpreters. Swabey also identifies the knowledge and skills needed by healthcare interpreters.

Placement of the interpreter during a medical appointment is often different than that in traditional interpreting assignments. The interpreter, in consultation with the deaf patient and potentially the medical professional, should give consideration to the best place to be during the appointment, to ensure the deaf patient has a clear line of sight to the interpreter at all times. Although this may seem obvious and applicable to all interpreting work, one should realize that it is not uncommon in medical situations for patients to be placed face down on a table or lying on their sides facing the wall; and in both situations, the view of the interpreter may not be adequate. The interpreter should work with the deaf patient and the medical professional to ensure an appropriate line of sight during the assignment at all times.

Special consideration should also be given to the appropriate protocol to follow during a medical interpreting assignment, which may be different from standard operating procedures for other, more general, types of interpreting. For example, while interpreting in a general community setting, it may be appropriate for the interpreter to always be near the deaf participants and available to them throughout the assignment. In a medical situation, however, it may be more appropriate to not be with the deaf patient at all times. There may be times when the deaf patient is asked to change into a medical gown or an occasion where a physical is going to include the doctor's examination of the deaf patient's body, and in both situations, the interpreter should appropriately step out of the room. The interpreter in these situations would need to ensure that the deaf patient understands the instructions of the medical professional and what will occur as part of the procedure prior to stepping out of the room. It is often seen as beneficial for interpreters in medical settings to follow the other professionals in their protocol and apply that protocol accordingly to the role of the interpreter.

One of the reasons interpreting in medical settings is considered a specialty area is because of the necessity for the interpreter to be familiar with special terms, specialized signs, and medical procedures and processes, and be able to effectively communicate the procedures and processes to the deaf patient. Even though an interpreter may be very experienced in personally going to the doctor or seeking medical care, the ability to explain complicated processes and medical terminology in another language is often found to be very difficult. Interpreters who specialize in medical interpreting often spend time studying medical terminology and working with other experts to find the best and most accurate interpretation of the terms. There is often a need to expand upon what might be seen as a simple statement or question, to be fully understood in a second language. Part of an interpreter's role is to help educate the medical professionals as to the interpreter's integration into the medical procedures in a way that is both appropriate and effective. For example, when interpreting for a surgical procedure, a medical professional may not think to include the interpreter throughout the entirety of the procedure until the point that the deaf patient is fully asleep. The interpreter may need to suggest this to the professional in order to ensure effective communication throughout the entire time that the deaf patient is awake.

Legal

Interpreting in legal settings is not uncommon. As mentioned with other areas above, nearly everyone finds themselves in a legal situation at some point. Whether it is working with an attorney on a formal legal contract or in developing a will, attending a hearing as a witness, or being a defendant in a court proceeding, interpreters are often requested for legal assignments. In fact, many assignments that begin as nonlegal situations can become legal situations quickly. For example, you might be called to interpret at a school for a meeting that turns out to be an investigation about possible abuse for which the police are contacted, and you are asked to continue interpreting once the police arrive. As well, an interpreting assignment that begins with a Deaf couple attending an open house may end with a meeting at a real estate office to purchase the home, which necessitates translating several legal documents. Legal interpreting can take place in a variety of locations, including, but not limited to, an attorney's office, a police station, a courtroom, a court reporter's office, a jail, or even in a private home or business. When a Deaf person interacts with a legal professional or engages in a legal exchange or context, and an interpreter is involved, it is legal interpreting.

Legal interpreting should be viewed as a specialty area of interpreting. As such, interpreters who choose to work in legal situations should have additional training and experience above what is necessary to be a competent, successful general practitioner. A legal interpreter must first be an experienced and skilled interpreter with fluency in all languages used and possess a deep understanding of the process of interpreting. To develop the special knowledge and skills necessary for work as a legal interpreter, interpreters should begin by spending time with a mentor who is certified and experienced in legal interpreting. Additional training should be taken that focuses on topics, such as legal systems, court processes and protocols, and legal language, as well as in practices that support the work of legal interpreting, such as note-taking skills, preparation techniques, and working in Deaf-hearing teams.

FORMS OF INTERPRETING

Simultaneous interpreting refers to the process of interpreting from one language into another language while the speaker, or the signer in the case of ASL, is delivering the message (see Russell, 2005; Napier, McKee, & Goswell, 2010). In other words, while someone is delivering a message in one language, a simultaneous interpreter renders the equivalent message in a second language without interrupting the speaker. Simultaneous interpreting is often considered more challenging than other forms of interpreting, as the interpreter must process information rapidly to accurately convey equivalent messages. The interpreter must render the interpreted message immediately and while continuing to process the ongoing message of the speaker. Simultaneous interpreting is able to occur more frequently when a signed language is used, because the act of interpreting between a signed and spoken language can occur without disrupting the flow of communication. It would not be unusual for the majority of signed language interpreters' work to be done using simultaneous interpreting. You can see it in use during typical, day-to-day interpreting assignments, such as meetings, trainings, educational interactions, conferences, etc.

Consecutive interpreting occurs when the interpreter listens to, or watches, in the case of a signed language, the speaker deliver a message or part of a message and then delivers the interpretation in a different language (see Russell, 2005; Napier, McKee, & Goswell, 2010). Consecutive interpreting is not used as frequently in the field of signed language interpreting, but is often used in high-risk interactions, such as legal and medical exchanges. There are benefits to using consecutive interpreting, such as allowing the interpreter to gain a full understanding of the context, intent, and deep meaning of the message and deliver an accurate message. The interpreter can take notes while listening to the speaker and then use those notes when delivering the interpretation.

Sight translation is the process of changing a frozen form of one language, such as English, to either a spoken or signed language. As a signed language interpreter, you may be called upon to interpret into sign language a standard form (e.g., a medical history survey, a legal contract). Often, sight translation occurs without time to review the form or work on a formal translation. An example would be a signed language interpreter being hired to interpret into ASL an apartment lease for a Deaf person seeking to rent an apartment. The lease is a standard document frozen in written English, and the interpreter would interpret each part of the form into ASL.

It is worth noting the differences between interpreting and transliterating. Interpreting is essentially work between two different and unique languages, such as spoken English and ASL. Transliterating is working between two forms of the same language, for example, working between spoken English and signed English.

MODELS OF INTERPRETING

As suggested in the beginning of this chapter, interpreting is really about communicating. When two or more people who do not share a common language wish to communicate with one another, an interpreter who understands both languages is needed to allow communication to occur. As suggested by Wilcox and Shaffer (2005, p. 27), "Although the interpreting situation is a unique communicative event, and the process of interpreting between two languages and two cultures places special constraints and demands on the interpreter, all acts of interpreting can ultimately be reduced to acts of communication." Wilcox and Shaffer posit that in order to really understand the process of interpreting, an interpreter must first understand the process of communicating. Over the years, within the field of both spoken and signed language interpreting, a variety of models of interpretation have been developed. These models of interpretation have provided a framework that examines the role of the interpreter as well as the process involved in the active interpreting. These models of interpretation have suggested a variety of roles that an interpreter plays in the interpreting process. The various models used to frame the work of an interpreter have changed over the years. An understanding of these models will help provide context to future interpreters. As research into the field of signed language interpreting continues, new models of interpreting will more than likely be developed.

The Helper Model

In the beginning, there were family members and friends; there were neighbors and ministers; there were teachers and dorm parents. There were many who were signers, usually because they had family members who were Deaf or worked at a Deaf school, or in a Deaf ministry. These people often came to the rescue when communicative actions without sign were not successful, expedient, or easy. Really, interpreting has been around far longer than the formal field of interpreting itself. These well-meaning friends and family who knew sign were always willing to help out and sign for their Deaf friend or family member when needed. There was rarely compensation, and until the late 1940s, no real preparation or training to be an interpreter. There was, however, a desire to help a friend out or to see a family member not be taken advantage of when engaging with a nonsigner. As Nancy Frishberg (1990, p. 10) states, "Often the interpreters were family members, neighbors, or friends who obliged a deaf relative or friend by 'pitching in' during a difficult communication situation."

An unintended consequence of this helper approach to Deaf–hearing interactions was the spread of the misguided belief on the part of nonsigners that Deaf people were not all that capable of handling things on their own or not able to succeed professionally without the help of some signing friend or family. Although the helper model is probably the earliest model of interpreting, and one that relied on the assistance of family and close friends, it led interpreters to take on the role of assisting and enabling their Deaf friends and family more so than truly help them as Deaf people. Many stories can be shared by Deaf people of the interpreter who carried their bags, stopped by to remind them of their appointments, or answered questions on their behalf. Although more than likely well-meaning, those in the helper mode did not always do the most good for their clients.

The Conduit Model

The conduit model came about after people began to realize that operating within the helper model was not in the best interest of the Deaf people. We saw a shift from one extreme to another, as interpreters began to see themselves only as a communication conduit or link between their deaf clients and their nonsigning clients. The shift in the paradigm coincided with the establishment of the Registry of Interpreters for the Deaf (RID) in 1964 and the new emphasis on the professionalism of interpreting. As Wilcox and Shaffer (2005) suggest, "'Helping' out was no longer always viewed as admirable, but instead as a potential intrusion." So, a new model was born, in which the interpreter was compared with a telephone line that simply transmitted information back and forth between multiple parties. This philosophical view of interpreters as only a conduit influenced not only how interpreters performed their work, but also how people interpreted the recently developed code of ethics for interpreters. Interpreters began to see themselves as not really being involved at all in the situation or exchange and having no impact on the act of communicating. Additionally, interpreters strived to deliver everything they received, in either language, rendering volumes of information without regard for meaning. This model of interpreting led to the use of multiple metaphors of interpreters as a telephone, a robot, or a machine, all of which took the human aspect of the interpreter out of the exchange—often to the detriment of all involved and certainly to the success of the communicative act.

The Sociolinguistic Model

Dennis Cokely developed and published his sociolinguistic model of interpreting in the early 1990s and posited that the process of interpreting includes both a sender and receiver of a message and is a linear process, although multiple processes may occur simultaneously. Cokely's model begins with the reception of a message, hence the assumption of both a sender and a receiver, followed by the processing of that message for intent and equivalency, and ends with the formation, production, and delivery of the interpretation in the target language.

The Colonomos Model

Betty Colonomos, whose work was heavily influenced by Seleskovitch (1978), developed a model of interpreting that focused on ascertaining both the meaning and intent of a speaker's message without necessarily the restraints of the language of the source message. Colonomos' model, originally referred to as a *pedagogical model* or the *Colonomos model*, became what is known today as the *integrated model of interpreting* (IMI). The IMI stresses the receipt of a source message, an analysis of the message's meaning, and the delivery of an equivalent message in the target language while emphasizing the importance of both analysis and compositional factors that ultimately influence the final interpretation. It has been suggested that the Colonomos model is, at its core, a conduit model (see Wilcox & Shaffer, 2005).

The Cognitive Model

A cognitive model of interpreting, similar in basic process to the Colonomos model, was proposed by Stewart, Schein, and Cartwright in 1998 with the publication of their text, *Sign Language Interpreting: Exploring its Art and Science*. The cognitive model developed by Stewart and his colleagues basically shows the process of interpreting beginning with a source message (i.e., the original message from the speaker) and ending with a final interpreted message in the target language (i.e., the language used by the recipient of the message). In between the two messages, the interpreter processes the message by comprehending the message, analyzing it for meaning, encoding it into the target language, and delivering it to the recipient in the target language. The interpreter ends the process by evaluating the target message for equivalency and making adjustments as needed. This model begins with an assumption that the interpreters already comprehend what they are receiving from the speaker.

The Bilingual-Bicultural Model

What the models described above do not take into account, as they describe and focus on the interpreting process, is the connection between language, its users, and the culture from which the language users come. A model first proposed by Arjona and Ingram in the 1990s (see Roy, 1993) made the connection between language and culture, and emphasized that an interpreter works between, at a minimum, two cultures and two languages. In doing so, the interpreter must be able to address cultural differences and be skilled at bridging or mediating these differences, thereby bringing the people who are communicating with one another *together*. Interpreters not only worked to ensure the fidelity and equivalence of the linguistic message, but also focused their efforts on mediating or bridging the different cultures within which the communicative exchange was occurring. Originally referred to as the *communication-facilitator model*, Arjona and Ingram's model later became more commonly referred to as the *bilingual-bicultural model*, and it is the primary lens through which interpreters have been taught since the mid-1990s.

Interpreters operating within this model recognize differences in culture as well as language and strive to achieve equivalence across the interaction by not only mediating language differences (i.e., interpreting between ASL and English), but also by mediating cultural differences as well. In their text, *So You Want to Be an Interpreter? An Introduction to Sign Language Interpreting*, Humphrey and Alcorn state that in the bilingual-bicultural model, interpreters are "keenly aware of the inherent differences in the languages, cultures, norms for social interaction and schema of the parties using interpreting services" (2007, p. 178), and that obtaining an effective interpretation "requires cultural and linguistic mediation while accomplishing speaker goals and maintaining dynamic equivalence" (2007, p. 178).

Other Cognitive Process Models

On the surface, one might assume that the work of an interpreter is fairly straight forward. An interpreter receives (i.e., hears or sees) a message in one language and then conveys the equivalent message in another language. However, the processes involved in this communicative act are both complex and numerous. According to Russell, "interpreting, whether simultaneous or consecutive, is a highly complex discourse interchange where language perception, comprehension, translation and production operations are carried out virtually in parallel" (2005, p. 136). Researchers have examined the process of interpreting over the years and offered rather complex models of what happens with the information received and conveyed by interpreters. Three prominent models of simultaneous interpreting that emerged worth noting are those developed by David Gerver (1976), Barbara Moser-Mercer (1978), and Daniel Gile (1985). Each examined the process of interpreting.

The model developed by David Gerver and first published in 1976, emphasized the memory systems used during the interpreting process. Gerver suggested that the information an interpreter receives (i.e., the message in the source language) is kept in a short-term memory area, or *buffer* as Gerver describes it, whereas previously received information is decoded from the source language, encoded into the target language, and eventually delivered as the equivalent message in the target language. Gerver's model allows for the testing of the encoded message against the source message, as needed. The buffer identified by Gerver is where the incoming chunks of the message are retained while prior chunks are interpreted. This model was, by Gerver's own revelation, a beginning point in modeling what occurs during the interpreting process. Although no mention in the original model was made of the interpreter's understanding of the message, the process did start the discussions and research into exactly what transpires when a person interprets.

Originally based on a model of understanding speech, Moser's model (1978) also emphasized the role of memory in the interpretation process. As with Gerver's model, working memory is, in essence, a storage area for the message received by the interpreter while it is being decoded, analyzed, and encoded into the target language. Unlike Gerver's depiction of the process, however, Moser's view of memory included specific functional purposes or tasks and not solely a structural function of memory. In the Moser model, memory not only stored incoming information, but also worked to process the message, changing the phrase linguistically into meaningful chunks in the target language. This model, like Gerver's, suggests a formal depiction of how information is processed by an interpreter.

In an effort to represent the process of interpreting as a framework for interpreting students, Daniel Gile (1985) chose to represent what occurs during the interpreting process by emphasizing the work or effort that is required. His model identified separate efforts that occur: listening and analysis (L), production (P), memory (M), and coordination (C). The listening and analysis effort focuses on the receiving and comprehension of the original message in the source language as well as the identification of words and the determination of what the message or utterance means. Memory effort is about the storage of the language utterances once received and during the process of interpreting, similar to what Gerver and Moser presented in their models. The production effort is what occurs from the moment the interpreter begins to mentally determine what the source message means and includes the planning of the delivery of the equivalent message in the target language. The coordination effort focuses on the overall effort of the interpreter in managing everything in the process, including focus and self-monitoring. These efforts can then be used to represent simultaneous interpreting as follows:

$$SI = L + P + M + C$$

Models Influencing Consecutive Interpreting

In her chapter on *Consecutive and Simultaneous Interpreting*, Debra Russell presents a detailed review of several models, some of which were discussed above, that have had an impact on both simultaneous and consecutive interpreting. According to Russell, "the value of some of these models to the field of ASL-English interpreting is that they offer guidance in understanding the nature of how communicators structure their messages and how interpreters try to capture that meaning in order to recreate it in a second language" (2005, p. 142). Russell then discusses a model she developed and calls the *meaning-based interpreting model*, which has five steps and

> identifies the need for the interpreter to assess and apply the contextual factors impacting the interpretation, actively using her background knowledge about language, culture, conventional ways of communication in both English and ALS, and to determine whether to use consecutive or simultaneous interpreting within a given interaction (2005, p. 144).

CONCLUSION

In the introduction of *The Interpreting Studies Reader*, editors Franz Pöchhacker and Miriam Shlesinger begin with a powerful statement that expresses "While interpreting as a form of mediating across boundaries of language and culture has been instrumental in human communication since earliest times, its recognition as something to be studied and observed is relatively recent" (2002, p. 1). This text has been developed for students and aspiring interpreters, both Deaf and hearing, who are beginning their own study and observation of interpreting. This book is intended to provide an overview of how interpreters become qualified to serve in a rapidly changing marketplace. The authors seek to give readers a broad knowledge base that encompasses the latest research, addresses current trends, and promotes critical thinking and open dialogue about working conditions, ethics, boundaries, and competencies needed by a highly qualified interpreter (or translator) in various settings. In this first chapter, a foundation was laid for your study of interpreting with the identification and explanation of key words you need to understand as you proceed to learn about interpreting (please see the Appendix). You also examined how interpreting is done and in what settings, including learning about the role of technology in the work of interpreters. The idea of specializations within the field of interpreting was introduced in this chapter, including a review of work as an educational, legal, and healthcare interpreter. Some of these areas will be further expanded upon in later chapters. The two primary processes or forms of interpreting, simultaneous and consecutive, were introduced in this chapter, and some of the key models of the work of interpreters were reviewed as well. These key concepts will provide you the foundation you need to continue your study of interpreting through the remaining chapters of the book.

RESOURCES AND REFERENCES

Americans With Disabilities Act of 1990, Pub. L. No. 101-336, 104 Stat. 328.

Berge, S. (2014). Social and private speech in an interpreted meeting of deafblind persons. *Interpreting, 16*(1), 82–106.

Cokely, D. (1992). *Interpreting: A sociolinguistic model.* Burtonsville, MD: Linstok Press.

Colonomos, B. (1992). *Process of interpreting and transliterating: Making them work for you.* Workshop handout: Front Range Community College, Westminster, CO.

Education of the Handicapped Act, sec. 601(c), 20 U.S.C. 1401 (1975).

Frishberg, N. (1986). *Interpreting: An introduction.* Silver Spring, MD: Registry of Interpreters for the Deaf.

Gerver, D. (1976). Empirical studies of simultaneous interpretation: A review and a model. In R. W. Brislin (Ed.), *Translation. Application and research* (pp. 165–207). New York: Garden Press.

Gile, D. (1985). Le modele d'efforts et l'equilibre d'interpretation en interpretation simultanee. *Meta, 30*(1), 44–48.

Hauser, P. C., Finch, K. L., & Hauser, A. B. (2008). *Deaf professionals and designated interpreters: A new paradigm.* Washington, DC: Gallaudet University Press.

Humphrey, J. H., & Alcorn, B. J. (2007). *So you want to be an interpreter? An introduction to sign language interpreting.* Seattle, WA: H & H Publishing Company.

Individuals with Disabilities Education Act, 20 U.S.C. § 1400 (1990, 2004).

International Association of Conference Interpreters. (2011). *Staff Interpreters.* Geneva, Switzerland: AIIC. Retrieved from http://aiic.net/p/4010>

International Organization for Standardization. *Interpreting: Guidelines for community interpreting.* [Foreword]. Geneva, Switzerland: ISO. Retrieved from https://www.iso.org/obp/ui/#iso:std:iso:13611:ed-1:v1:en

Johnson, L., Bolster, L., & Brown, S. (2014). *States that require or accept the EIPA: Summary.* Denver, CO: University of Northern Colorado, Distance Opportunities for Interpreters and Teachers Center. Retrieved from http://www.unco.edu/cebs/asl-interpreting/pdf/osep-project/eipa-data-summary.pdf

Merriam-Webster Inc. (n.d.). *Interpret.* Retrieved from http://www.merriam-webster.com/dictionary/interpret

Moser-Mercer, B. (1978). Simultaneous interpretation: A theoretical model and its practical application. In D. Gerver and W. H. Sinaiko (Eds.), *Language, interpretation and communication* (pp. 353–368). New York: Plenum Press.

Napier, J., McKee, R., & Goswell, D. (2010). *Sign language interpreting: Theory and practice in Australia and New Zealand.* 2nd edition. Sydney, NSW: The Federation Press.

Pöchhacker, F., & Shlesinger, M. (2002). *The interpreting studies reader.* London: Routledge.

Registry of Interpreters for the Deaf, Inc. (2007). *Video relay service interpreting.* [Standard practice paper]. Alexandria, VA: RID Publications. Retrieved from https://drive.google.com/file/d/0B3DKvZMflFLdNE1zZGRPdDN4NGM/view

Registry of Interpreters for the Deaf, Inc. (2010). *An overview of K-12 educational interpreting.* [Standard practice paper]. Alexandria, VA: RID Publications. Retrieved from https://drive.google.com/file/d/0B3DKvZMflFLdcFE2N25NM1NkaGs/view

Registry of Interpreters for the Deaf, Inc. (2010). *Video remote interpreting.* [Standard practice paper]. Alexandria, VA: RID Publications. Retrieved from https://drive.google.com/file/d/0B3DKvZMflFLdTkk4QnM3T1JRR1U/view

Roy, C. B. (1993). The problem with definitions, descriptions and the role of metaphors of interpreters. *Journal of Interpretation, 6*(1), 127–154.

Roy, C. B. (2000). *Interpreting as a discourse process.* New York, NY: Oxford University Press.

Russell, D. (2005). Consecutive and simultaneous interpreting. In T. Janzen (Ed.), *Topics in signed language interpreting* (pp. 135–164). Amsterdam: John Benjamins Publishing Company.

Seleskovitch, D. (1978). *Interpreting for international conferences.* Washington, DC: Pen and Booth.

Stewart, D. A., Schein, J. D., & Cartwright, B. E. (1998). *Sign language interpreting: Exploring its art and science.* Needham Heights, MA: Allyn and Bacon.

Wilcox, S., & Shaffer, B. (2005). Towards a cognitive model of interpreting. In T. Janzen (Ed.), *Topics in signed language interpreting: Theory and practice* (pp. 27–51). Amsterdam: John Benjamins Publishing Company.

Winston, E. A. (1989). Transliteration: What's the message. In C. Lucas (Ed.), *The sociolinguistics of the deaf community* (pp. 147–164). San Diego, CA. Academic Press.

2

Historical Foundations of a Trust-Based Profession

CAROLYN BALL

IN THE BEGINNING: EARLY RECORDS OF INTERPRETERS IN ACTION

Investigating our heritage as signed language interpreters takes us first to the onset of spoken language interpreting, where someone served as an intermediary between two people who did not speak the same language. As long as there have been different languages between groups of people, it is likely there have been interpreters to assist in communication. The first documentation of the existence of interpreters is an Egyptian hieroglyph, dating the profession's beginning as early as 3000 BCE (Gardiner, 1969). These early historical records were found in Greek literature and related to military interpreters employed by Alexander the Great in Asia and India. Alexander III relied on interpreters to conduct his business and communicate with the different groups of people with whom he tried to conquer and establish alliances. The Romans used interpreters for the same reasons as Alexander the Great: to conquer people and countries. Another early reference to interpreters came in 1248 when Louis IX of France led his army to the Middle East. Many of the interpreters who were used during this campaign are documented in the *Chronicles of the Crusades* (de Joinville & de Villehardouin, 1963) and were very important to the mission of Louis IX's reign (Delisle & Woodsworth, 2012).

Additionally, during Napoleon's conquests in Egypt and Palestine, there are several references to interpreters and translators who could speak both French and Arabic (Roditi, 1982). More recently, in the history of the United States, there is reference to interpreters during the early career of George Washington. As a mapmaker and military officer, Washington went into the forest and tried to maintain friendly contact with indigenous Indians. Washington also appointed interpreters to help him in his work to conquer the French (Delisle & Woodsworth, 2012). All of these world leaders used interpreters to communicate; however, we know very little about whether these early interpreters worked consecutively or simultaneously.

Although we have limited access to historical journals or documentation about the work of early translators and interpreters, the leaders of the Fédération Internationale des Traducteurs/International Federation of Translators (FIT) voted at the Fourth World Congress in Dubrovnik, Croatia (1963) to support the idea of a written "comprehensive history" of translation (Delisle & Woodsworth, 2012, p. xxiii). Dr. Gyorgy Rado (1912–1994) began the work by telling the FIT that "we have to show the way and lay the foundations; in other words, we must create a framework and a method that will enable us to carry out the research and ultimately write the proposed history of translation" (1964, p. 15). Rado's collection of monographs about the experiences of spoken language translators and interpreters led to the FIT publishing the first historical record of translators and the invention of alphabets, development of national languages, emergence of national literatures, transmission of cultural values, production of dictionaries, and spread of religions (Delisle & Woodsworth, 2012, pp. vii–ix). This historical documentation revealed the emerging practices of consecutive and simultaneous interpreting, and we began to see how each method became prevalent in certain situations where effective communication between people could tremendously impact international relations.

EMERGING PRACTICES OF CONSECUTIVE AND SIMULTANEOUS INTERPRETING

Consecutive interpreting, which involves retaining "chunks" of information from the source language before interpreting into the target language, was used at the Paris Peace Conference in 1898 to develop a treaty that would end the Spanish-American War. Each country involved in the conflict had its own interpreter, who would interpret that country's contribution to the peace terms aloud, and the original speaker waited until the information was interpreted before resuming speaking. As a result of the successful use of interpreters during the Paris Peace Conference, the League of Nations was formed as the first international organization devoted to world peace. Thereafter, the need for interpreters expanded into world politics, but consecutive interpreting introduced a time constraint that impeded or delayed negotiations and deliberations between countries (Morgan, 1965).

The practice of "chuchotage," or simultaneously whispering the interpretation to an audience of close proximity, became a viable option for conserving time when interpreters were needed. Chuchotage, which means *whispering* in French, was called "whispered interpreting," and it was effective for small groups of people; however, the work of the League of Nations demanded a solution that was more expedient for all the countries involved in diplomatic conversations. It was during this period that three Americans, Edward Filene, a businessman, Gordon Finlay, an electrical engineer, and Thomas Watson, the president of International Business Machines (IBM), developed equipment that would allow for simultaneous interpreting in large-scale, diplomatic settings (Delisle & Woodsworth, 2012).

Patented in 1926 and permanently installed at the League of Nations in Geneva in 1931, the Filene-Finlay simultaneous translator was manufactured by IBM, allowing interpreters at the League of Nations to talk into a machine that would transmit the interpretation to the listener via a headset. This new invention was considered to be quite remarkable, as anyone who wanted to hear an interpretation in a specific language could tune in to the channel of choice (Delisle & Woodsworth, 2012). The Filene-Finlay system became more popular due to its ease of use and was replicated for use in various interpreting locations. For example, the Filene-Finlay equipment appeared at a 1944 conference in Philadelphia, Pennsylvania, where the earlier practice of interpreters using the equipment in a separate room from the speakers was replaced with the practice of placing the system in the same room as the people in attendance. With interpreters in the same room as the participants who had language barriers, the interpreters were able to observe the interactions and check for understanding between the parties.

During this period, simultaneous interpreting and consecutive interpreting were still in a trial period to determine which mode worked best in which setting.

The United Nations drafted its charter using consecutive interpreting in San Francisco, California, in 1945 (Delisle & Woodsworth, 2012); however, simultaneous interpreting was the most efficient method for the War Crimes Trial of the International Military Tribunal to bring Nazi war criminals to justice (Nuremberg, Germany, 1945–1946). The victorious countries in World War II, known as the *Allies*, included Great Britain, France, the United Soviet Socialist Republic, and the United States, and the war criminals on trial were German-speaking Nazi leaders. The primary languages of the Nuremburg Trial were English, French, Russian, and German, and the proceedings were of great interest to the world and especially to people who were directly affected by the war and the holocaust. Gaiba (1998) emphasized the critical work of the interpreters when he said, "The Nuremburg Trial would not have been possible without simultaneous interpretation" (p. 20). Patrie (2005) calculated that the Nuremberg Trial may have taken more than four years using consecutive interpreting; thus, the use of simultaneous interpreting was desperately needed for such a lengthy process of trying war criminals in an international court.

PREPARING INTERPRETERS TO MEET THE GROWING DEMAND

Following World War II and the Nuremberg Trial, world leaders and diplomatic constituents recognized the importance of qualified interpreters, and with the evolution of professional interpreting came the need for formal interpreter preparation as a priority for the future of international alliances. The advent of spoken language interpreter education programs came during the 1940s at the University of Geneva (Switzerland), the University of Vienna (Austria), the University of Mainz in Germersheim, (Germany), the University of Saarland (Germany), Georgetown University (Washington, DC), and Heidelberg College (Ohio). The number of spoken language interpreting programs multiplied in the 1970s, and since that time, technology, teaching methods, and curricular innovations have been continually improving. Interpreter training programs within the university setting resulted in greater visibility of spoken language interpreting as a discipline that impacted interpreters across, "all religions, cultures and political entities" (Delisle & Woodsworth, 2012, p. 255). The history of spoken language interpreters and global training programs provides a framework for our transition to signed language interpreter preparation within the United States.

LANGUAGE DESIGNATION AS THE BACKDROP OF INTERPRETER PREPARATION

It is not known when signed language interpreters in the United States began to practice as language mediators outside of their own families, but the need for interpreting likely coincided with advancements in Deaf education in the early 1800s. One of the earliest documented examples of formal interpreting occurred in 1818 when Laurent Clerc, a Deaf Frenchman who co-founded the first School for the Deaf in the United States with Thomas Hopkins Gallaudet, addressed the President, Senate, and Congress of the United States using a signed language (not yet evolved into American Sign Language, or ASL). While Clerc signed, Henry Hudson spoke his words aloud. One of the earliest known articles regarding what would make a good interpreter is found in the *American Annals of the Deaf* in 1948. Elmer (1948, pp. 545–546) states the following,

1. The interpreter must have a three-track mind.
2. The interpreter has an excellent vocabulary of signs.
3. The interpreter should be a good fingerspeller and only use this for when the name of a person, a geographical location and a scientific name is used.
4. A good interpreter does not use a sign for every word.
5. A good interpreter has members of their family who are deaf or who have grown up within the environment of the deaf for several years.

A more complete record of ASL and interpreting dates from 1957, when William C. Stokoe, known as the father of ASL linguistics, began the task of analyzing the language of signs. Stokoe, a faculty member in the English department at Gallaudet University (then Gallaudet College), was intrigued by the constructs of "sign language," which had not been studied in detail. Gannon (1981) recorded that Stokoe started the Linguistics Research Laboratory at Gallaudet University, where he subjected ASL to tests that would verify it as a true language, analyzing all required language components, including phonology, morphology, syntax, and semantics. Lucas (1990) reported that Stokoe found writers had been compiling sign vocabularies from as early as 1776. Stokoe, Casterline, and Croneberg published the *Dictionary of American Sign Language on Linguistic Principles* in 1965, and for the first time, ASL signs were seen as part of a distinct linguistic system.

Prior to Stokoe's research, many U.S. educators did not acknowledge ASL as a legitimate language to be taught alongside foreign languages in colleges and universities; however, over time, higher education programs steadily began accepting ASL for academic credit and in satisfaction of foreign language core requirements within baccalaureate degrees. The availability of ASL classes in colleges (and later, in secondary schools) allowed more students to study the language and develop fluency. Recognition of ASL as a distinct language increased its status in academia, which ultimately impacted the perception of interpreting as a viable profession to be studied in postsecondary education (Ball, 2013).

THE IMPACT OF RESEARCH ON ASL/ENGLISH INTERPRETING

Stokoe's research was a catalyst for the passage of accessibility legislation in the United States that required Deaf people to have qualified interpreters (see Chapter 6, in this volume). Prior to the late 1970s, the vast majority of people who had interpreting skills were either teachers of deaf children or children who had Deaf parents. Interpreting was not yet considered a profession, and these people were not paid; their work was looked upon as a public service. Interpreters usually had jobs in other professional areas, so there were few interpreters available for events and trainings. During these "pre-professional" days, many people without Deaf family members learned to sign as part of a widespread initiative to prepare interpreters for spiritual and religious interpreting within what were called "Deaf ministries." From these religious settings, prospective interpreters were identified to interpret in community settings, such as vocational rehabilitation meetings. It was quite common for those who interpreted religious events for Deaf people to interpret outside events for which parishioners needed communication access with hearing people. For example, a Deaf person may need to communicate with a doctor or an official at the bank, and it was common for someone who went to the same religious congregation to accompany the Deaf person on personal business as a courtesy.

PROFESSIONALIZATION PROCESS OF SIGNED LANGUAGE INTERPRETING

Interpreting began the long road to professionalization when a federal grant was awarded in 1963 to conduct a workshop on interpreting. The workshop was held at Ball State Teachers College in Muncie, Indiana, for the purposes of (1) identifying settings in which Deaf people would need an interpreter, (2) suggesting training curriculum, (3) establishing criteria for admission to training courses for interpreters, and (4) developing a manual or guidelines for interpreters. In November 1963, a planning committee met to prepare the workshop agenda and decide who would be invited to this first national gathering of interpreters. The committee selected June 14–17, 1964, and confirmed the location as Ball State Teachers College (Ball, 2013).

The 1964 workshops at "Ball State" centered on several topics that included interpreter training materials, concepts of interpreting, situations, and recruitment. Participants met in small discussion groups, and each group discussed one of the primary topics. The group that discussed interpreter training included Elizabeth Benson from Gallaudet College, Reverend Roy Cissna of Missouri Baptist Missions to the Deaf, and Lottie Riekehof of Central Bible Institute. This group recommended that the most beneficial workshops for advancing the profession would include (1) curriculum development for interpreter trainers, (2) widespread availability of skills development for new interpreters, and (3) advanced training to upgrade the skills of already-capable interpreters. The group also recommended that federal grants be used to support new training programs in colleges and universities throughout the United States (Ball, 2013).

As a culminating contribution to the profession, the Ball State workshop participants developed a manual, which comprised the beginning of a formal interpreting curriculum and standards for preparing interpreters for the workforce. Material for the manual was drawn from workshop presentations and discussions, and the Foreword illustrated the strong connection between vocational rehabilitation and signed language interpreter training. This selection from Dr. Boyce Williams (as cited in Smith, 1964) emphasized the importance of establishing parameters for interpreter preparation that would serve to promote the profession and organize the process among postsecondary institutions.

> The Vocational Rehabilitation Administration is pleased to make available herewith the report of the first national workshop ever convened to develop guidelines for interpreting for deaf people. This document is another milestone in the Vocational Rehabilitation Administration's mission to promote in all possible ways the occupational adjustment of deaf people. Through the years, we have encouraged and supported similar meetings of experts to pool their thinking in developing better understanding of the deaf and patterns for more effective public services to them. We expect that these guidelines on interpreting will help deaf people share in the thinking and activities of their associates and thus reduce the handicapping aspects of their deafness. Readers will note that this workshop gave birth to a long needed organization, the Registry of Professional Interpreters and Translators for the Deaf (Smith, 1964, p. iii).

As Dr. Williams mentioned, the Ball State workshop marked the formation of what would become the Registry of Interpreters for the Deaf, Inc. (RID). The organization was incorporated in 1972 and serves as the national professional organization for U.S. interpreters. Quigley and Youngs (1965) noted that "at a second meeting of the National Registry of Professional Interpreters and Translators for the Deaf in Washington, DC on January 28–29, 1965, the name of the organization was changed to Registry of Interpreters for the Deaf and became known as RID" (p. 3). Frishberg (1986) described the mission of RID as serving four primary purposes: recruiting interpreters, educating more interpreters, maintaining a list of qualified persons who could interpret, and developing a code of ethics for interpreters. The weight of these four purposes was quite a heavy responsibility for the newly established organization, which "had only 42 interpreters that registered with RID, 22 sustaining members, and only seven qualified themselves as interpreters" (Fant, 1990, p. 5). With the new organization in place and the publication of an interpreter registry of names and qualifications, transitioning the profession away from family-based, pro bono interpreting was not always smooth. In the beginning of this professionalization movement, Deaf people expressed exploitation issues with hearing people earning wages for interpreting, when previously, interpreting services were volunteered. The first Executive Director of RID, Al Pimentel, describes the beginning of the organization as a time of learning to understand what being an interpreter meant. The premise of earning wages as an interpreter appeared to conflict with the traditional model of volunteering for the Deaf community, and perspectives were rapidly changing (A. Pimental, personal communication, July 18, 2015).

The Rehabilitation Services Administration (RSA), a federal agency under the U.S. Department of Education, with input from Dr. Boyce Williams, recognized the increasing need for skilled, trained interpreters, and five-year training grants became available in the 1970s to postsecondary interpreter education programs in an effort to quickly increase the supply. Dr. Williams was instrumental in formalizing U.S. interpreter education, according to Virginia Lee Hughes, a child with Deaf parents and one of the pioneering interpreter educators of the decade (personal communication, July 29, 2012). The National Association of the Deaf (NAD) also contributed to RID's establishment and applied for an RSA grant that provided RID's home office for five years and an executive director from 1967 to 1972 (Fant, 1990). When the grant cycle ended, RID moved to a space at Gallaudet University and relied on a part-time secretary and volunteers to continue its operations. Fant recalls that "if it had not been for the generosity of Gallaudet University providing office space, and some financial assistance from the NAD, we surely would have reverted back to our status in 1964, or even expired altogether" (p. 17).

KEY ORGANIZATIONS THAT PROMOTED THE INTERPRETING PROFESSION

It is important to remember that the NAD and Gallaudet University were a vital part of supporting and sustaining RID. The Professional Rehabilitation Workers with the Adult Deaf (PRWAD) is another example of a Deaf-focused organization that supported the expansion of interpreters and interpreter educators. At a PRWAD Conference in Tucson, Arizona (1974),

Deaf and hearing leaders from several federally funded colleges sat around the hotel swimming pool and expressed their hopes and dreams for Deaf people (Lauritsen, 1997). One of those dreams included having sufficient interpreters for every Deaf person who wished to attend college, and their solution was to establish a national effort to train and recruit interpreters.

Leaders in the field of interpreting and interpreter education met to create the National Interpreter Training Consortium (NITC), which was the first model of federally funded interpreter training programs. Ball (2013) explains "the NITC marked the beginning of formal, standardized interpreter education in the United States" (p. 121), and the first goal was to enhance the skills of those people who were already interpreters (C. Tipton, personal communication, August 22, 2011). The NITC published the first curriculum guide for interpreter educators, marking the beginning of formal interpreter education in the United States (Schein, Sternberg, & Tipton, 1974).

INTERPRETER EDUCATION AND TASK ANALYSIS

The Conference of Interpreter Trainers (CIT) was established in 1979, and its goals included the following:

1. Provide opportunities for the professional development of interpreter educators.
2. Serve as a vehicle for sharing information among interpreter educators.
3. Promote high standards in institutions, faculties, programs, and curricula for the education of interpreter.
4. Advocate for research relevant to the practice and instruction of interpretation.
5. Encourage collegial relationships with professionals in other related disciplines and organizations (CIT, n.d.).

CIT promoted research and evidence-based curriculum development, and one of the most profound influences regarding teaching the process of interpreting occurred at the1984 CIT Biannual Convention in Pacific Grove, California. The conference theme was "New Dimensions in Interpreter Education: Task Analysis—Theory and Application" and highlighted the need for task analysis in interpreter education (Cavallaro & Cook, 1986). Cavallaro and Cook defined task analysis as "breaking a task (interpreting) into subcomponents or subskills and arranging them in a logical order for instruction" (p. 7). Clearly, once the tasks could be identified in a logical order, then students' behaviors (skills) could be evaluated.

In addition to needing a breakdown of the interpreting task into manageable steps, Rust explained, "A major difficulty we have in our profession is the lack of a theory. It is very common for us to document, justify and rationalize to our academic peers what we do, but what is even more of a problem for us is to do this without having a theoretical base as a reference" (1986, p. 21). As a result, during the 1984 CIT Conference, the interpreter educators in attendance developed the task analysis and theory of teaching signed language interpreting. The identification of task components and theoretical foundations of interpreting was instrumental in developing curricula and materials that interpreting programs would need to prepare future interpreters.

CREATION OF INTERPRETING MODELS

The impact of the task analysis project was vital to the education of interpreters and led to the recognition of a need to educate signed language interpreters about the various models that represented the interpreting process. Stewart, Schein, and Cartwright (2004) explain that models can assist our thinking and sharing of ideas, and the creation of models for the interpreting process could help interpreting students analyze the steps needed to become a skilled interpreter. Stewart et al. explain, "There are several models which have been used to provide illustrations of how to advance the teaching of interpreting from theory to practice through the years" (p. 29). Some of the most prevalent models that formed the historical foundation for teaching the interpreting process are included here and also referenced in Chapter 1.

Seleskovitch (1978) believed that the interpreter's task "was not the search for the same words in another language, but that the translator must search for equivalent meaning in two different languages" (p. 84). The Seleskovitch model focuses on message analysis, not on a word-for-word translation. Colonomos (1989) was inspired by the Seleskovitch model and showed the components of the interpreting process that interact to identify the message and its meaning. Colonomos (1989) believed that interpreting was primarily about conveying equivalent meaning (p. 1). Gish (1987) used an information-processing approach in her interpreting model. The processing approach took the source message into a *dynamically equivalent* target message and required efficient organizational and reorganization of data. Cokely (1992) proposed a model that would include not only mediating between two individuals and communities but also cultures. He based his model on an extensive analysis of six interpreters who were working during a CIT conference. He described interpreter errors as *miscues* and categorized what he observed to construct a sociolinguistic model of interpreting. Cokely (1992) defined miscues as a "lack of equivalence between the Source Language message and its interpretation or, more specifically, between the information in an interpretation and the information in the sL message it is supposed to convey" (p. 74). As interpreter educators evolve in their understanding of the interpreting process, new models emerge that supplement the historical models used in interpreter education programs.

LOOKING AHEAD

Historical records of spoken language interpreting and signed language interpreting serve to remind us how professional interpreting has evolved over time. The interpreting and translating profession continues to change in response to global needs for language and cultural mediation (interpreting) in all walks of life, in all areas of the world. Signed language interpreting is considered a young profession, and we have primarily focused on its "coming of age" in the United States. Each country has its own story about its Deaf inhabitants, their language, and the people who provide communication access to education, employment, healthcare, legal, social, and religious services (to name a few). As we move forward, being mindful of the past successes and challenges faced by interpreters, interpreter organizations, and interpreter educators can prevent us from stumbling over the same problems and impeding our growth and professionalism.

References

Ball, C. (2013). *Legacies and legends: History of interpreter education from 1800 to the 21st century.* Edmonton, Alberta, Canada: Interpreting Consolidated.

Cavallaro, C., & Cook, L. (1986). Task analysis: What, why and how. In M. McIntire, (Ed.). *New dimensions in interpreter education: Task analysis—Theory and application.* Proceedings of the 1984 Conference of Interpreter Trainers Convention. Silver Spring, MD: RID Publications.

Cokely, D. (1992). *Interpreting: A sociolinguistic model.* Burtonsville, MD: Linstock Press.

Colonomos, B. (1989). *The interpreting process.* Unpublished manuscript.

Conference of Interpreter Trainers. (n.d.). *CIT by-laws.* Retrieved from http://www.cit-asl.org/new/about-us/by-laws/

de Joinville, J., & de Villehardouin, G. (1963). *Chronicles of the crusades.* Toronto, Ontario, Canada: Penguin Random House.

Delisle, J., & Woodsworth, J. (Eds.). (2012). *Translators through history.* Philadelphia, PA: John Benjamins.

Elmer, L. A. (1948). What is a good interpreter? *American Annals of the Deaf, 93*(5), 545–546.

Fant, L. (1990). *Silver threads: A personal look at the first twenty-five years of the Registry of Interpreters for the Deaf.* Silver Spring, MD: RID Publications.

Frishberg, N. (1986). *Interpreting: An introduction.* Rockville, MD: RID Publications.

Gaiba, F. (1998). *The origins of simultaneous interpretation: The Nuremberg trial.* Ottawa, Ontario, Canada: The University of Ottawa Press.

Gannon, J. R. (1981). *Deaf heritage: A narrative history of deaf America.* Silver Spring, MD: National Association of the Deaf.

Gardiner, A. H. (1969). *Egyptian grammar: Being an introduction to the study of hieroglyphs.* 3rd, revised edition. Oxford, UK: Griffith Institute.

Gish, S. (1987). I understood all the words, but I missed the point: A goal-to-detail/detail-to-goal strategy for text analysis. In M. McIntire (Ed.), *New dimensions in interpreter education—Curriculum and instruction.* Silver Spring, MD: RID Publications.

Lauritsen, R. R. (May 1997). *The early years of PRWAD-ADARA: The 1960's: A different time.* Retrieved from http://www.adara.org/history.html

Lucas, C. (1990). *Sign language research: Theoretical issues.* Washington, DC: Gallaudet University Press.

Morgan, H. W. (Ed.). (1965). *Making peace with Spain: The diary of Whitelaw Reid, September–December 1898.* Austin, TX: University of Texas Press.

Patrie, C. (2005). *The effective interpreting series: Simultaneous interpreting.* San Diego, CA: DawnSignPress.

Quigley, S. P., & Youngs, J. P. (1965). *Interpreting for Deaf people: A report of a workshop on interpreting* (p. 3). Portland, ME: Governor Baxter State School for the Deaf, U.S. Department of Health, Education and Welfare, Office of the Secretary.

Rado, G. (1964). "La traduction et son histoire." *Babel, 10*(1), 15–16.

Roditi, E. (1982). *Interpreting: Its history in a nutshell.* [National Resource Center for Translation and Interpretation Outreach paper]. Washington, DC: Georgetown University.

Rust, K. (1986). Response to Cavallaro and Cook. In M. McIntire (Ed.). *New dimensions in interpreter education: Task analysis—Theory and application.* Proceedings of the 1984 Conference of Interpreter Trainers Convention. Silver Spring, MD: RID Publications.

Schein, J. D., Sternberg, M. A., & Tipton, C. A. (1973). *Curriculum guide for interpreter training.* New York, NY: Deafness Research & Training Center School of Education.

Seleskovitch, D. (1978). *Interpreting for international conferences.* Washington, DC: Pen and Booth.

Smith, J. M. (1964). *Workshop on interpreting for the deaf.* Washington, DC: Vocational Rehabilitation Administration.

Stewart, D., Schein, J., & Cartwright, B. (2004). *Sign language interpreting: Exploring its art and science.* Boston, MA: Allyn and Bacon.

Stokoe, W., Casterline D., & Croneberg, C. (Eds.). (1965). *A dictionary of sign language on linguistic principles.* Washington, DC: Gallaudet College Press.

3

Promoting the Use of Normative Ethics in the Practice Profession of Community Interpreting

ROBYN K. DEAN AND
ROBERT Q POLLARD, JR.

Signed language (SL) interpreting is but one occupation within the broader field of translation and interpreting (T & I). Given that SL interpreters engage in the task of *message transfer*, we share a history as well as a theoretical foundation with all who work between two languages—from a translator of 18th-century French literature to "booth interpreters" working at the United Nations. The field of interpreting includes signed and spoken language interpreters who work in diplomatic, international conferences and community settings. The primary practice environments for SL interpreters are in community settings, including medical, legal, social service, business, and educational settings. SL interpreters share the field of community interpreting with those who work between spoken languages as well. Community interpreting within the broader field of T & I is referred to by several other terms: *liaison, ad hoc, dialogue,* and *public service* interpreting.

When referring to *interpreting* in this chapter, we are referencing the T & I field broadly, including both community and conference interpreting. When we use the term *community interpreting*, we are referring to signed and spoken language interpreters who work in community settings. When we use the term *signed language interpreting*, we are referring to SL interpreters who may be deaf or hearing, who may use a variety of signed languages (e.g., American Sign Language, British Sign Language, French Sign Language, or International Sign).

Although it is important for SL interpreters to understand our shared history and theoretical base within the broader field of T & I, it is equally important for them to recognize what is unique about the practice of community interpreting. Perhaps the most unique aspect of community interpreting versus other forms of T & I activity is that community interpreting is a *practice profession*.

To frame community interpreting as a practice profession is to assert many things. First, it is a commentary on practice realities (e.g., interpreting in a doctor's office is very different than interpreting at an international conference). It also implies that the profession should educate practitioners in community settings differently than would be the case for other T & I professionals. It also means that the profession of community interpreting should *conceive of* and *engage in* ethical practice in ways that may be unique. These ways of thinking and working in community settings are the focus of this chapter.

RECOGNIZING COMMUNITY INTERPRETING AS A PRACTICE PROFESSION

To frame interpreting as a *practice profession* is to set it apart from *technical professions*. Historically, SL interpreting was considered a technical trade in which interpreters were both trained and viewed as *technicians of translation*, whose work would be considered effective if they simply mastered the technique of bilingual message transfer—supplemented, of course, with relevant cultural and ethical knowledge. Breaking from this traditional perception of interpreting as a trade rather than a profession and framing interpreting as a practice profession in particular is to stress that there are other skills interpreters need to be effective that lay outside a traditionally heavy focus on technical (bilingual) skills. The most important of these additional skills are perceptual and judgment abilities regarding interpersonal dynamics, because interpreters are always applying their technical skills in dynamic, socially interactive settings.

Other practice professions require professionals to have a combination of technical skills, interpersonal perception, and judgment skills. Consider the interpersonal skills often referred to as *bedside manner* for medical professionals. These abilities extend beyond their technical knowledge (e.g., anatomy and physiology) and technical skills (e.g., interviewing a patient or suturing a wound). Likewise, teaching, clinical psychology, the law, and community policing may be classified as practice professions, where, as with interpreting, one's technical skills are typically applied in socially interactive settings, requiring keen judgment abilities. Laboratory science, architecture, engineering, accounting, aviation, and many other highly respectable professions also require the acquisition of complex technical skills. However, these technical professionals do not routinely apply their skills in the context of dynamic social realities the way practice professionals do.

Practice professionals need to be directly trained in the interpersonal aspects of their work through extensive periods of closely supervised practice *before* their professional training is deemed complete. Consider the medical intern or resident, student teacher, or rookie police officer who is closely supervised by veterans in their profession before they are ready for independent practice. This instruction on the interpersonal aspect of one's work and a significant period of supervised guidance in the *application* of one's technical skills *in social settings* are essential in the ultimate development of practice professionals.

To prepare highly qualified interpreters, the profession of SL interpreting would have to follow a similar educational and preparatory design. In other words, teaching only technical skills and other academic content is inadequate. Sufficient time and professional oversight need to be invested for a budding practitioner to develop the necessary interpersonal and judgment skills to be successful in their profession.

In other practice professions, practitioners also continually strive for improvement, not only through continuing education (usually mandated), but also through *reflective practice*. Reflective practice, which sometimes goes by other terms, such as *supervision* in the mental health fields, means one-on-one or group conversations where the key elements of the practice situation, practice decisions, and their associated consequences are discussed openly and formally, with a focus on the actions the professional chose, alternative courses of action that might have been considered, and the benefits and drawbacks of these differing choices. Reflective practice is an essential, career-long form of learning and work improvement in the practice professions.

In a recent reflective practice session, an interpreter presented to a small group of colleagues an interpreting assignment, where he knew the situation could have been handled better. He admitted that he had lost his patience with a hearing, patient-care technician who was working with an elderly, deaf woman in a hospital's emergency department. The interpreter first explained the facts of the case and then asked for feedback and help in re-thinking how he could have done better. Here are the key facts he presented.

An elderly deaf woman was brought into the emergency room, because she had fallen and hit her head. Before the medical provider could stitch up her head wound, the patient-care technician needed to get her into a gown. The deaf woman was accompanied by a social worker who also was deaf. Because of the seriousness of her injury, the patient had first been hooked up to a machine that monitored her heart. This made disrobing and then redressing into a gown a challenge. The technician wanted the patient to sit on the side of the bed, because standing could possibly have led to another fall. The technician would then give directions to the woman to help her get disentangled from all the cords. Given that the patient was deaf, she necessarily had several places to divide her visual attention—the interpreter who was signing what the technician said, the clothing and the cords, and the social worker who was standing at her side, helping and giving her positive encouragement in sign language. As a result, the woman's ability to respond to the directions of the technician was necessarily delayed. After several back-and-forth directives and responses, things were not progressing as quickly as the technician had expected. The technician started to get frustrated. His tone of voice became louder and curt. He started audibly sighing and would say, "No, no, not like that!" Finally, the technician started to intervene physically and began to take off the patient's bathrobe. This caused the patient to get very upset. The social worker did not say anything to the technician about his actions while the patient continued to protest his physical help. Finally, the interpreter looked at the technician and putting his hand up to him said, "You're going to need to have more patience in getting her to respond to you!" The interpreter could not believe that the technician was not being more patient in light of the woman's age, her potential disorientation after a head injury, and the several sources of visual data she had to take in at once. He was also surprised that the patient's social worker did not say something to the technician on the patient's behalf. Ultimately, things calmed down, the woman was given the time she needed to get into the gown, and she also did not fall. But, it had come at the expense of several people getting upset, including the patient who was already medically compromised.

The interpreter asked his colleagues what he could have done differently. In the subsequent discussion, several ideas and observations were offered. Commonly, at the beginning of an interpreting assignment, SL interpreters prioritize "staying out of the way" and letting the other professionals in the room handle a situation. This allows the interpreter to focus on communication and the effectiveness of communication. People who have empathy for others pick up on their emotions and begin to feel similarly, so in this instance, it was not unusual for the interpreter to become upset along with the patient. However, one participant pointed out, when such things start to happen, there are ways to think more strategically about what to do next. For example, the group offered, when it started to become obvious that the technician did not fully understand all that was happening (especially the delays created by all of the visual information the woman was trying to take in at once), the interpreter could have taken more action by explaining to the technician what was happening and why the patient was not able to quickly respond to the directions. Second, it was pointed out that the technician, although seemingly upset and impatient, likely had the patient's best interests at heart and was worried about her being in a seated or standing position. If the cause of the original fall was poor heart functioning or low blood pressure, a seated or standing position could lead to another fall. Recognizing that someone might be acting out of concern versus frustration helps us to respond to them more empathetically and respectfully. In turn, this can help deescalate the emotions in the room. Lastly, it was pointed out that helping the technician understand all that would be involved with communication before interaction with the patient began might have better prepared him to expect the longer response times or maybe even led him to come back later when he had more time or even hand off the gowning responsibility to someone else. Although it was too late for this feedback to change that particular situation for the interpreter, this reflective practice discussion is likely to be remembered and benefit this interpreter the next time he is in a similarly tense situation.

Encountering situations that are emotionally tense or dynamically complex is not unique to SL interpreters. All practice professionals face the complexities of the social world in their work. The plots of police, medical, and legal television dramas typically focus on these social aspects rather than the technical skills of these practice professions. As practice professionals interact with their segments of the public (patients, clients, families, or the citizenry in general), they recognize the importance of these relationships as key to effective work. Typically, decisions that are made and actions that are taken between the parties in these relationships are *negotiated* ones; they show an attempt to cooperate and to work collaboratively. This is a significant difference between the effective work of practice professionals and that of technical professionals. How might an interpreter learn to effectively negotiate in decision-making?

Let us continue with the example of the elderly hospital patient and the social worker, both of whom were deaf. Suppose, later during the emergency room visit, the social worker asks the interpreter to stay with the now-sleeping patient while she goes to make a call back to the office to give a status update. The social worker tells the interpreter that if the patient wakes up, she will come right back into the room. The social worker then points out that the patient is on strong pain medication and is not likely to wake up anytime soon.

Some interpreters might see such a request as inappropriate ("It's not my job to watch over the patient.") and therefore, deny the request. Although they would not be wrong per se in making such a decision, it does very little to create the positive rapport with service users that we are proposing is important. Furthermore, denying the request can even serve to impede the care of the patient. What if calling the office meant an aide could bring the patient necessary items from her home, or maybe the call is to arrange transportation from the nursing home to pick up the patient following her impending discharge?

At the same time, the interpreter also does not want to find himself in a position where he is ill equipped to handle a situation where the patient wakes up and starts to get out of bed. The interpreter should seek to find ways to agree to the request, maximizing the value of collaboration while minimizing the potential harm. In this case, the interpreter could ask some questions. Are the bed rails up, to ensure the patient cannot easily get out of bed? How far away is the videophone the social worker plans to use? Where is the emergency room technician, and is he able to be present or at least close by in case of an emergency? If such information and protections are satisfactory, the interpreter should feel comfortable granting the social worker's request.

TYPES OF ETHICAL DECISIONS

In the above example, the interpreter negotiates decision-making by trying to determine what is best for all persons involved. This requires thinking through the *consequences* of the decision. Consider the interpreter's following thoughts:

> *If I comply with the request to stay with the patient and ensure that she does not try to get up, the social worker can arrange for the patient to get home sooner. If I stay with the patient, I need to make sure that the patient is with someone who can keep her safe if she were to wake up. How is it possible to reasonably maximize the value of cooperating with the social worker while minimizing any potential harm?*

Note how the above consequences are determined by *values*, in particular, the values inherent in the service setting where the interpreter is working (in this case, the medical setting). The importance of recognizing the values of the work setting when determining the most desirable consequences of a decision is addressed further in this chapter.

Of course, the interpreter could have made a very different decision. He could have said, "No, my ethical code does not allow me to participate in situations in that way; I can only interpret." Such a decision, formulated differently than the decision made above, would yield a different outcome (in this case, not collaborating with the social worker). This decision would be based on the interpreter prioritizing a rule (i.e., it stems from thinking, "What is the proper rule to follow in this situation?"), whereas the former, collaborative decision was based on consideration of the consequences or the most desirable outcomes of the situation.

To make decisions based on rules is what ethicists refer to as reasoning in a *deontological* fashion. To make decisions based on consequences or desirable outcomes is referred to as reasoning in a *teleological* fashion. Because the work of practice professionals is embedded in a dynamic, social context, the outcome of which is dependent on the quality of the rapport and relationship with the individuals they serve, practice professionals usually make ethical decisions from a *teleological* or consequences-based perspective. Teleology requires decision-makers to consider the unique context in which the decision is being made. Decision-making from a deontological or rules-based perspective means upholding what is predetermined to be the right action, irrespective of the situational context.

Different Types of Ethics Relevant to Community Interpreting

Ethicists differentiate *normative* ethics from *descriptive* ethics. Normative ethics concern those behaviors that are deemed as *right action*. They are understood as addressing what one *ought* to do or what one ought *not* to do. The terms *deontology* and *teleology* are both derived from the normative ethics field, because both forms of reasoning are intended to lead to decisions about right action. As noted earlier, practice professionals usually make ethical decisions via teleological reasoning, focusing on the consequences or outcomes of potential decisions. Sometimes, although less frequently, practice professionals do make deontological or rule-based decisions. Examples include the rules associated with the sharing of private healthcare information. Healthcare professionals must obtain a patient's written permission before releasing medical records. Usually though, the nature of practice professionals' work is not so straightforward, hence their more frequent reliance on teleological ethical reasoning.

Descriptive ethics differ from normative ethics in that instead of identifying what should be done, the focus is based on an analysis of what individuals *actually do*. Although normative ethics seeks to determine what is (or is not) right action, descriptive ethics is focused on determining simply *what is*. Descriptive ethics do not focus on judging a behavior but instead focus on describing it. As a result, it is possible for what one thinks is right action (their normative ethics) to be in direct conflict with what one actually does (descriptive ethics). Take for example, a person who believes that it is right to reduce the use of plastics in the environment but does not recycle or re-use plastic products. This mismatch between what one believes is right action versus the behavior one exhibits can be true for anyone, practice professionals included.

There are many ways in which a profession expresses its normative ethics, or what the profession proposes to be right and wrong action. The most common way is through a profession's code of ethics. However, even when a profession has such a code, there is usually a collection of other publications, informal documents, and commonly shared beliefs regarding ethical behavior that the profession draws upon. For example, some professions have *standards of practice* documents that express ethical ideas. The Registry of Interpreters for the Deaf, Inc. (RID) has a series of standard practice papers (SPPs) on a variety of topics—from content-specific work settings (e.g., mental health and legal settings) to topics such as team interpreting. Normative ethical material also can be found in professional literature that describes best practices within a field.

Despite the wide range of ethical material available within a profession, people tend to look to ethical codes as the most important form of guidance. Ethical codes are generally regarded as authoritative and, therefore, hold a prominent place amidst other types of ethical material that may exist within a profession.

How Ethical Codes Can Be Problematic

Ethical codes in the T & I field have frequently been criticized as restrictive and overly prescriptive (i.e., as rigid "do this and don't do that" rules that are "carved in stone"). In part, this is because many ethical codes constructed for the T & I field have been written in the rule-based or deontological manner noted earlier. The current National Association of the Deaf-Registry of Interpreters for the Deaf Code of Professional Conduct (CPC) is no exception. (See https://www.rid.org/ethics/code-of-professional-conduct/.) Although ethical codes certainly need to include some definitive guidelines or distinctions between acceptable and unacceptable behavior (in order to protect service-users), they also should ideally be derived from and specifically describe the values upon which they are based—the central values that the profession seeks to uphold and put into practice.

Within the community interpreting field, ethical codes have tended to focus on a few common topics: message transfer (e.g., accuracy and fidelity to the message), business practices, professional discretion (including confidentiality), and continued professional development. Ethical codes also often provide behavioral guidance, such as maintaining neutrality or impartiality. Two additional ethical ideals also are often conveyed—professionalism and respect for colleagues and consumers. Although many codes illustrate behaviors associated with professionalism and respect, they tend to be broad and quite open to interpretation, given the unique circumstances of a given work situation.

Some have argued that general (profession-wide) ethical codes do not provide sufficient guidance for community interpreters and have proposed that the field is in need of developing setting-specific ethical codes (Angelelli, 2004; Leneham & Napier, 2003). Examples of setting-specific codes include those of the National Council on Interpreting in Healthcare (NCIHC) in the United States and the Association of Sign Language Interpreters in the United Kingdom, which has an ethical code for working in mental health settings. Rather than developing setting-specific codes, RID instead offers SPPs, which include ethical guidance for working in medical, mental health, legal, educational, and religious settings.

In contrast, some have disagreed that ethical codes are too rigid and prescriptive and, instead, have proposed that ethical codes are not intended to be all-encompassing and should not be seen as a substitute for individual critical thinking and judgment skills (Fristch-Rudser, 1986; Pope & Vasquez, 2010). Indeed, in the preamble of RID's CPC, it is stated that interpreters must "exercise judgment, employ critical thinking, apply the benefits of practical experience, and reflect on past actions in the practice of their profession" (Registry of Interpreters for the Deaf, 2005). These differing viewpoints have led to debate within the profession, not only as to which viewpoint is more valid, but also how to reduce the indecision interpreter practitioners may face as they consider these differing views on ethical codes.

THE POWER OF ROLE METAPHORS IN COMMUNITY INTERPRETING

Since the profession of SL interpreting was formalized in the mid-1960s, different *role metaphors* have been proposed, in part, as a means for providing another form of behavioral guidance for interpreters in light of inconsistencies in how codes of ethics have been viewed, written about, and taught. Role metaphors not only remain influential in interpreting education and practice, but also have proliferated and evolved over time as the profession (and the Deaf community) also have evolved. A role metaphor is a shorthand way of describing a pattern of behaviors one performs on the job: "I will act as if I am a ___." *Conduit, bilingual/bicultural (bi/bi) mediator*, and *member of the team* are just a few role metaphors used widely in the interpreting field.

Recognizing the powerful influence that role metaphors have had in the way the interpreting profession thinks about ethical behavior is a vital aspect of understanding the broader development of ethical thought in community interpreting. In SL interpreting, role metaphors have been developed and promoted as a concise way of applying or operationalizing the ethical code to practice.

At the time of the adoption of the 1979 code (RID's longest-standing code to date), the conduit metaphor was most popular. A conduit is like a pipe or a tube conveying (or moving) something from one place to another. In this case, it is the movement of language between two people—the source language enters one end of the tube, and the target language exits the tube. As a result, many of the code's ethical tenets were framed, or at least interpreted, as behavioral choices interpreters should make from the perspective that their job was to merely serve as a bridge between two languages. Accordingly, this view further suggested that interpreters should have no other impact, purpose, or involvement in the situation, apart from message transfer alone.

It has been argued that this restrictive conduit view is still the default role metaphor influencing community interpreting today (as cited in Hsieh, 2006) and that the conduit metaphor (which is also a conceptualization of ethical behavior) emerged out of our shared history with international conference interpreting (Angelelli, 2004). Attempts to unseat the conduit metaphor as the predominant, normative role metaphor in community interpreting have failed (Clifford, 2004; Roy, 1993).

The development and progression of role metaphors is a lens through which our profession documents its history (Janzen & Korpinski, 2005; Roy 1993). Most scholars frame the development of the SL interpreting profession through a progression of four role metaphors: 1) interpreters as helpers, 2) interpreters as conduits, 3) interpreters as communication facilitators, and 4) interpreters as bi-bi mediators (Roy, 1993). By the time the RID CPC was adopted in 2005, two more metaphors were gaining popularity: interpreters as allies and interpreters as members of the team.

Interpreters as helpers was not an intentional metaphor to educate the public or guide professional practice. It was merely used to highlight the contrast between the pre-professionalization of SL interpreting and later ethical thinking. At the outset of the profession, interpreting for deaf people was almost exclusively a voluntary activity, provided mostly by family members, teachers, counselors, or clergy (Cokely, 2000). Frishberg (1986) further noted that many of these ad hoc interpreters were compelled to help out in settings, such as churches and doctor's offices, for good-intentioned reasons. As a result, these helpers were free to, "offer advice . . . and make decisions for one or both sides" (Roy, 1993, p. 139). Consequently, deaf people were frequently impeded from functioning as autonomous decision-makers, calling into question issues of oppression. It was against this backdrop of interpreters as helpers that leaders in the field, and more specifically the RID, began to formalize and define what constituted ethical practice.

Interpreters as conduits was the first intentional practice metaphor to emerge. It was intended to convey the ethical ideal that interpreters merely relay messages back and forth but should otherwise remain detached from the social aspects of the situation, the meaning of the messages conveyed, and the outcome of the communication event, beyond effective message transfer (i.e., the interpreter should be otherwise invisible). This same idea often has been expressed by interpreters who pose the question, "What would have happened if I had not been there?" and basing ethical decisions on that illogical proposition. Many have suggested that the conduit framework for ethics emerged from the field of conference interpreting. Community interpreters were encouraged to emulate the conference interpreters' *booth experience*, being removed from the social interaction taking place and required only to supply the interpretation via a microphone and headphones.

The metaphor of an interpreter being a *communication facilitator* came into popularity in the early 1980s as the field began to consider theoretical ideas being discussed in related disciplines, such as communication theory. This perspective emphasized that the communication event included a sender, a message, and a receiver. Therefore, instead of being mere conduits of communication, interpreters were "language and communication-mode experts" (Roy, 1993). Now, interpreters were expected to meet the more specific linguistic needs of the communicating parties, in particular the deaf individual, by adapting to that consumer's communication mode.

Not long after this shift in thinking began, the proposition emerged that a language cannot be separated from its cultural context. Interpreting now began to be perceived as a bi/bi task. Accordingly, the corresponding ethical reasoning was that interpreters should not only be responsible for message transfer, but also for cultural adaptations in their translation decisions as well. In SL interpreting, we refer to this role metaphor as the *bi-bi model*. In the field of spoken language interpreting, a similar metaphor is referred to as the *cultural broker*.

Arguably, each new role metaphor that came into popular use, and the ensuing ethical discourse stimulated by it, was an attempt to correct overly literal interpretations of the 1979 RID Code of Ethics. As the predominant metaphors shifted, practitioners were encouraged to conceive of the consequences of their decisions and engage more flexibly in their practice decisions. However, Roy (1993) concludes that attempts to utilize newer metaphors have proven unsuccessful, because these metaphors still could be distilled down to promoting conduit-like behaviors.

Being a member of the "team" refers to the professional team with whom the interpreter is working—whether in health care, law, social service, or educational settings. Each SPP that addresses content-specific work settings endorses the team member metaphor. That is, interpreters are expected to work in concert with (or at least not against) the goals and values of the professionals in that setting.

The team member metaphor seems contradictory to the *interpreter as ally* metaphor. Being an ally emphasizes the unique relationship of solidarity between SL interpreters and the Deaf community. Although it makes sense to support those who have been historically marginalized or even oppressed, how does an interpreter balance alliances between the team (usually hearing) and the deaf consumers with whom they are interacting? If the institutions employing these (hearing) team members are perceived as inherently oppressive to deaf people (Baker-Shenk, 1991), then to work in collaboration with the purveyors of this oppression would result in working against deaf people, not in alliance with them.

How can practicing interpreters understand these metaphors as a source of guidance for their ethical decisions, if they seemingly contradict one another? The answer lies in distinguishing the devices used in normative ethics versus descriptive ethics.

Metaphors are a device used properly only in regard to descriptive ethics; they are intended to convey, in a broad sense, the behavior of individuals, *without* evaluating that behavior as desirable or undesirable. However, when metaphors are perceived as behavioral guidance, they are being regarded as a normative ethics device—directing what people *should* do. Ethicists would regard this use of metaphor as inappropriate.

Furthermore, metaphors, when viewed as behavioral guidance, do not provide sufficient guidance regarding the specific situations interpreters face on a day-to-day basis. Because they are a tool of descriptive, not normative, ethics, it is a misuse (or misappropriation) of metaphors to serve as tools of guidance or evaluation. In other words, you cannot use a metaphor to measure the effectiveness of a decision.

THE PROFESSION'S MOVE AWAY FROM NORMATIVE ETHICS AND TOWARD DESCRIPTIVE ETHICS

The problem of mixing the terms and devices of descriptive and normative ethics through the use of metaphors is not unique to community interpreting. Pym (2001) explained how descriptive ethics also came into prominence in translation studies in the early 1990s. Pym suggested that it was the perception that ethical codes (normative ethics) were restrictive that led the broader translation studies field to embrace a descriptive ethics approach. In other words, T & I theoreticians and researchers became less focused on dictating what practitioners *should* do and instead wanted to learn what these practitioners *actually* did.

Community interpreting scholars followed suit. Researchers from the fields of sociology and sociolinguistics began turning their attention to community interpreting. Their scholarship aimed to report without judgment on the actual practices of community interpreters (e.g., Cokely, 1992; Roy, 2000; Wadensjö, 1998).

The seminal study that has been credited with initiating what is referred to as *the social turn* in interpreting scholarship was conducted by Cecelia Wadensjö (1998). The social turn was an influential shift away from the prevailing research focus on linguistics or message transfer toward the inclusion of social and cultural factors relevant to interpreted interactions.

When interpreters started working in community settings (the result of increasing immigration and emerging American law regarding language access for non-English speakers and deaf people), it was no longer fitting to study message equivalence solely through the lens of linguistics. Interpreters were no longer working in booths with headphones on, physically removed from the interaction between their consumers, but were now directly present in doctor's offices, elementary school classrooms, etc., and were obvious participants in the communication event. The interpreter's presence, along with the recognition of social and cultural factors associated with interpreting service users and their communication goals, fundamentally changed the standards for studying and defining effective and ethical practice. This was the "social turn" in the T & I field.

Because the conduit metaphor was predominant in the late 1980s, it follows that scholars interested in descriptive ethics would want to find out if interpreters did indeed act in these ways. More often than not, researchers found that interpreters did *not* act like invisible nonparticipants, as the conduit metaphor predicted. Rather, they observed that interpreters often were quite active participants in these interpersonal work situations.

Wadensjö's influential research was strongly influenced by sociologist Erving Goffman (1959) and his *participation framework*—an approach for examining the roles different parties play when interacting in a particular setting. His framework was embraced by scholars studying community interpreting and, in part, it fostered the social turn in the T & I field. The participation framework became so influential in T & I scholarship that Mason (2000) claimed, "no serious study of [community] interpreting can afford to overlook the participation framework" (p. 219). Even publications decades later have found Goffman's work applicable to community interpreting.

Goffman used two sociological tools in presenting his participation framework: the construct of *role-taking* and the use of metaphors in describing how humans behave during their interactions. Goffman and Wadensjö's influence not only led the profession of community interpreting to embrace the use of metaphors as a tool for describing interpreters' behaviors, it also led to the profession's widespread, vigorous adoption of the term *role* in the way it was being used in the field of sociology.

In a sociological sense, the term *role* is meant to convey an expected set of behaviors that are commonly performed by someone defined by a particular social framework (such as the role of mother, doctor, teacher, citizen, etc.). However, outside of sociology, the term *role* simply conveys what one does—one's function—usually the term is used in an occupational context. In this regard, one could propose that an interpreter's role is simply to tell individuals using one language what others are saying in another language, and vice versa (regardless of the spoken or signed languages involved). However, the term *role* in the community interpreting literature is commonly used to convey much more than an interpreter's function; it is typically used as an ethical device to convey desirable and undesirable behavioral and other ethical decisions (Dean, 2015). Although other professions are using the term *role* as a synonym for function, the interpreting field has adopted the sociological definition.

Deliberating over the role of the interpreter in this or that situation, often by employing role metaphors, is to misuse the term *role* by treating it as an ethical device. One's function does not direct or evaluate the appropriateness of specific behaviors. Other practice professions tend to use the concept of responsibility to compel or constrain a practitioner's behavior. Identifying what a professional is responsible for is a clearer method for determining when or when not to take action, which actions to take and, most importantly, which outcomes one is attempting to achieve. Other practice professions do not discuss role (function) in isolation; role is always coupled with the term *responsibility*.

As noted above, in addition to the descriptive term *role*, sociologists have employed the device of metaphors to convey complex or abstract ideas by connecting them to something concrete and more easily understandable (e.g., an interpreter is like a bridge). They are useful shortcuts that help people understand something quickly, without greater explanation.

We have already outlined several (but not all) metaphors used in SL interpreting. Additional metaphors offered in recent publications about community interpreting include *institutional gatekeeper* (Davidson, 2000), *co-diagnostician* (Hsieh, 2007), *family supporter* (Leanza, 2005), *counselor* (Angelelli, 2006), *patient advocate* (Dysart-Gale, 2005), and *conciliator* (Hale, 2007). Roy (1993) concluded that the use of metaphorical language has "limited the profession's own ability to understand the interpreting event. . . ." (p. 127). Roy further suggested that the profession needs to adopt a different paradigm or way of looking at the interpreter's work. Pym (2001) suggested that the T & I profession is in need of a return to ethics and that a sole reliance on descriptive ethics, such as conveyed by role metaphors, does not provide the traction necessary for defining sound, ethical standards.

USING THE COLOR BLUE TO MEASURE A ROOM: THE MISUSE OF METAPHORS

The chapter authors propose something of a paradigm shift by suggesting that community interpreting is a practice profession. As we have noted, this shift requires a different view of what constitutes ethical and effective practice and how to determine these desired outcomes. Like Pym, Roy, and others, our demand control schema (DC-S) proposes a return to ethics, in particular, ethical constructs, such as teleological or values-based decision-making, the significance and nature of values conflict, explorations of decision consequences through engagement in reflective practice, and the predominance of professional responsibility over the limited concept of role (Dean & Pollard, 2013). All of these ethical devices are from normative ethics.

Whereas community interpreting has historically borrowed the devices of descriptive ethics, such as the use of role metaphors, to convey or propose normative ethical ideals, this is a significant departure from the ways in which other practice professions conceive of and talk about ethics. If interpreters are expected to collaborate with fellow practice professionals in the settings in which they work, they would need to think and talk about ethics in ways that their colleagues understand and find acceptable. Imagine explaining to another professional why you made a decision by saying, "It is like I am not really here." Although your interpreter colleagues might understand what you mean (i.e., the conduit metaphor), this explanation would likely not be understood by other professionals. You cannot use metaphorical language to justify a decision, just like you cannot measure a room with the color blue. Color is a description just like metaphors.

Figure 1 is another illustration of how the interpreting profession has adopted descriptive ethics devices in its attempt to express normative ethics.

As this figure shows, the *should be* reflects normative ethics (what a practitioner ought to do); whereas, *member of the team* reflects descriptive ethics (a characterization of a pattern of behavior). Remember, descriptive ethics and the devices used in descriptive ethics simply describe; they are not intended to direct behavior nor evaluate it. If we wanted to describe what an interpreter did, then it would be accurate to report on their behavior: The interpreter behaved as if she were a member of the educational team serving the deaf child. However, if we wanted to assert an evaluation about what the interpreter should do, we would have to do so in a manner employing normative ethics in looking at the actual behavior. In Figure 1, how the interpreter actually behaved is hidden by the use of the team member metaphor.

Examples of evaluating an interpreter's actions using normative ethics might include using a rule (e.g., interpreters should not omit information), the application of values (e.g., interpreters should respect the autonomy of service users to make their own decisions), or considerations of practice consequences (e.g., interpreters should ensure that decisions advance the values of the service setting). In the practice professions, it is the consideration

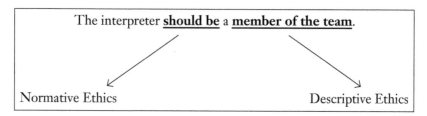

Figure 1. Misuse of Ethical Types.

of values that predominates normative ethics, whether they are expressed in deontological (rule-based) or teleological (consequences-based) ways.

Consider the following example from a values-based, normative ethics view. An interpreter asked a surgeon to clarify, during an informed consent discussion with a patient, what he meant by, "the normal risks associated with general anesthesia." She did so, because she questioned whether the deaf patient would have readily understood that the normal risks of anesthesia include many things, including the extremely rare but actual risk of death. Instead of saying, "the interpreter acted as a member of the team" by requesting that the surgeon elaborate on this phrase (which does not evaluate whether or not the behavior was a good one), evaluating the interpreter's decision would be better stated via recognizing her application of a value. The interpreter understood that the surgeon was pursuing the value of informed consent but used only a vague reference to anesthesia risks, assuming that the patient had more familiarity with the implications of normal risks than the interpreter was confident of. Thus, the interpreter's request to clarify was in keeping with the value of informed consent that both these practice professionals shared.

COMMUNITY INTERPRETING'S VALUES-BASED NORMATIVE ETHICS

The normative ethics of a profession convey its rules, values, and professional responsibilities. In this way, practitioners can apply these values in their unique practice contexts to determine the most desirable practice consequences. Although some rules are required to protect service users from poor practices, more often than not, outlining broader values allows practitioners necessary, situation-dependent behavioral flexibility. Yet, as noted earlier, many of interpreting's ethical codes are written as a series of rules.

Although rules fall within the category of normative ethics, the term *normative* should not be equated with prescriptive or inflexible directives (i.e., a list of dos and don'ts). Keep in mind that other practice professions employ normative ethics and still allow for behavioral flexibility. As explained earlier, practice professionals are continually faced with ever-changing situations in their work, so how practitioners choose to act in a given situation requires them to uniquely apply the values of that profession. The adherence to values as opposed to restrictive rules allows for needed flexibility within professional practice.

That values can be derived from rules, to allow for a less rigid understanding of the RID ethical code, was illustrated by Fritsch-Rudser (1986). He proposed that the tenet taken from the 1979 version of RID's Code of Ethics, which stated that interpreters shall not "counsel, advise, or offer personal opinions," was not to be taken as an absolute. He proposed that the tenet reflected the broader value of respecting service users' self-determinacy—the ability to make decisions for themselves. This value is readily understood in many practice professions as a derivative of respecting service users' autonomy.

The field of community interpreting is at a crossroads as we seek to revise ethical content material to emphasize values rather than rules. In some instances, rules could be reinforced by linking them to their underlying values. For example, "do not counsel" can shift from a directive to a values-based statement affirming consumer self-determinacy. Similarly, role metaphors can be investigated to reveal the underlying values upon which the metaphor is based. The profession could pursue this by asking, "What values are implied by suggesting an interpreter should be an ally, a member of the team, or a conduit?" Strong (2000) noted that professional ideals expressed through other means, such as metaphors, can always be distilled to a foundation reflecting a profession's values.

Some organizations already have begun to transform ethical material into values-based language. The ethical code of the Association of Visual Language Interpreters of Canada (AVLIC) is an outline of professional values that are not conveyed in a prescriptive, rule-based manner. (See www.avlica.ca/ethics-and-guidelines.) The list of values, followed by illustrative behaviors, conveys a sense of behavioral flexibility and professional discretion.

In addition to ethical codes, other literature within the SL interpreting field has offered decision-making models using normative ethical constructs. The values of SL interpreting, along with several examples of decision-making models from interpreting and other fields, were offered in Humphrey's *Decisions? Decisions!* (1999). Hoza (2003) also proposed a decision-making model, which he identified as being an outgrowth of the bi/bi mediator model of interpreting. More recently, the decision-making model used in DC-S expands our thinking about how interpreters make ethical decisions.

Each of these decision-making models can be distilled into a common series of steps: (1) identify or define the problem or issue, (2) consider the options of action, (3) imagine the consequences of each decision (teleological reasoning), (4) minimize negative outcomes, and (5) choose accordingly. Note that the concepts of consequences and responsibility are continually emphasized in these decision-making models. Decision-making models that are directly linked to a stated list of professional values are examples of the types of normative ethical material available to other practice professions. It is logical that community interpreting should follow suit.

ADDRESSING VALUES AND VALUE CONFLICT IN COMMUNITY INTERPRETING

How should the field of community interpreting build normative ethical material that is current, in alignment with the broader field of professional ethics, and more effective in guiding the decisions of community interpreters? The first ingredient needed is a list of the profession's values. It is not our intention to propose a new or different set of values; much of what is needed can be found in ethical material currently in the field. However, some of this material is conveyed in the form of rules. Other material is conveyed through a series of metaphors. It is our goal to transform some of this ethical material from rules and metaphors to values. For example, the following values are often articulated in T & I ethical codes:

- Accuracy
- Confidentiality
- Neutrality
- Fidelity (truthfulness)
- Professionalism
- Respect for colleagues/service users

However, the field has also expressed values through other means than the publication of ethical codes. The conduit metaphor conveys values that are still important to the practice of interpreting, even if the metaphor itself is limited—values such as respect for autonomy, agency, and self-determinacy. Another value underpinning the conduit metaphor is noninterference— allowing people to behave as they naturally would without interference from the interpreter. Given the long-standing and arguably important function of the conduit metaphor, its intent could also be distilled to underlying values. Therefore, to the above list we would add the following:

- Respect for autonomy (self-determinancy)
- Noninterference

This is the beginning of our proposed list of professional values that is necessary, we argue, for effective community interpreting work. However, these are the same values that compel the work of conference interpreters. That is, there is nothing in this list that accounts for the unique social and other elements and challenges of community interpreting. A further complication is that the work of community interpreters is situated within systems and institutions that have their own unique values. If community interpreters merely focus on values pertaining to message transfer alone, it is possible that other values, specifically relevant to community interpreting settings, could be compromised.

Consider the following example: An interpreter is called in to substitute for a regular interpreter in a fourth-grade classroom. The teacher is giving a spelling test. One of the words on the test does not have a corresponding sign, so the interpreter considers fingerspelling the word. Although this might respond to a value regarding accuracy or clarity of the message, doing so would compromise a value specific to this setting. In this case, that value would be accurate assessment of student learning. By fingerspelling the word, the interpreter would give away the answer to the deaf student, countering that value of the setting. Therefore, consideration of values of interpreting alone are not enough to be an effective community interpreter. Community interpreters need to consider the values of the setting as well (as in *accurate assessment of student learning*, which is derived from education).

Choosing between accuracy and assessing student learning is an example of *value conflict* or what Aristotle referred to as *incommensurable values*. Decisions between right and wrong are fairly straight forward, but what about decisions between right and right? The substitute interpreter in this example is faced with a decision between two rights: It would be sound reasoning to want to convey the utterances of the teacher accurately and clearly, but it is also right that the interpreter not interfere with the situational (educational) values of the work setting. When values conflict, as they sometimes do, a weighing of the consequences (teleological reasoning) is necessary. Whatever behavioral choice ultimately is made, one of the conflicting values necessarily will have to be forfeited. This weighing, choosing, upholding, and forfeiting of values is the very essence of maintaining responsibility in professional practice. It is what ethical processes are intended to elucidate—especially within practice professions.

As practice professionals, community interpreters are service-based professionals. The service-based professions tend to rely on four core *principles* (a term often used interchangeably with *values*) in their practice (Beauchamp & Childress, 2012). They are autonomy, nonmaleficence (do not harm), beneficence (to do good), and justice. Most codes of ethics in service-based professions derive their more specific practice values from these four core principles. Consider the value of informed consent in the field of medicine. Informed consent is an ethical construct derived from the broader value of the nonmaleficence or the *do no harm* tenet. Autonomy, another of the four core principles, already has been noted as inherent in the conduit metaphor. Additionally, do no harm (nonmaleficence) is included in the preamble of RID's current ethical code. Arguably, justice is the value inherent in the ally metaphor. This would leave the remaining principle of beneficence to be considered as a potential core value of community interpreters. There already is precedence for this value being asserted in NCIHC's standard of practice document for healthcare interpreters.

Finally, consider the normative ethical material inherent in the metaphor of team member. If an interpreter is acting as a member of the (healthcare, educational, or legal) team, what is she considering and doing at an ethical level, in light of the particular setting in which she is working? We would suggest it should be the same thing we described in the spelling test example above—recognizing the potential values conflicts at play and making a thoughtful decision about which values to uphold and which values to forfeit. Arguably, many interpreters already make these types of decisions. What is lacking in our profession is the ability to explain or reason through those decisions by using normative ethics constructs.

We propose, therefore, that the way in which community interpreters should consider and reason through their decisions is to articulate the values inherent in the settings where they work. This means that interpreters must consider how the values of the work setting may, at times, conflict with traditional interpreting values and make wise choices while being open with all relevant parties about the reasons behind their decision-making. Further, interpreters must recognize their responsibility to respond to the

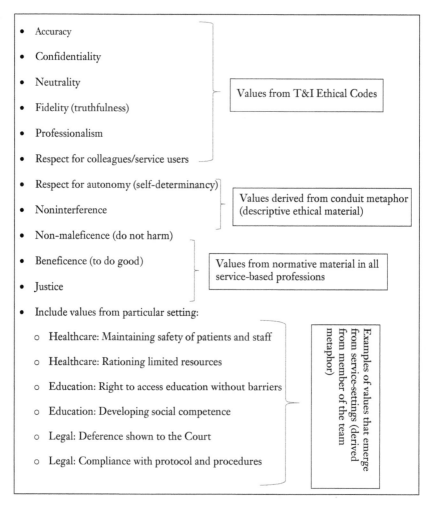

- Accuracy
- Confidentiality
- Neutrality
- Fidelity (truthfulness)
- Professionalism
- Respect for colleagues/service users

    Values from T&I Ethical Codes

- Respect for autonomy (self-determinancy)
- Noninterference

    Values derived from conduit metaphor (descriptive ethical material)

- Non-maleficence (do not harm)
- Beneficence (to do good)
- Justice

    Values from normative material in all service-based professions

- Include values from particular setting:
  - Healthcare: Maintaining safety of patients and staff
  - Healthcare: Rationing limited resources
  - Education: Right to access education without barriers
  - Education: Developing social competence
  - Legal: Deference shown to the Court
  - Legal: Compliance with protocol and procedures

    Examples of values that emerge from service-settings (derived from member of the team metaphor)

Figure 2. Proposed values for community interpreters (combining normative and descriptive ethical material already existing in the field).

consequences of any forfeited values and to be open and responsive to consumer feedback regarding their decision-making.

Finally, piecing together the sources of values that converge when an interpreter is working in a specific setting, the ensuing list of values are illustrated in Figure 2.

CONCLUSION

As we have suggested in the examples earlier in the chapter, it is important for interpreters working in community settings to find ways to collaborate with the professionals and the clients in the service settings in which they work. We have also argued that this is what is meant by the use of the team member metaphor. James Rest and his colleagues (1999), as well as other ethicists in the field of justice reasoning would also agree. They have proposed that the most sophisticated and ethically defensible approach to professional practice is to find ways in which individuals can cooperate with service users in a given setting. (For SL interpreters, this would mean both deaf and hearing people.) Finding ways in which the values of our profession (potentially discernable in our ethical codes and metaphors, as described above) can be adhered to in ways that uphold, or at least do not thwart, the values of other practice professionals and those of our shared clientele is the most effective way to negotiate pathways toward effective practice. Illumination and open discussion regarding values conflict is consistent with this view. Pym (2000, p. 182) stated, "Translating is by nature a cooperative act" and therefore, "defection [from the professional aim of cooperation] is definitely not a professionally correct move." This definition of ethical practice is consistent within the T & I field, the field of professional ethics, and the field of moral philosophy.

The challenge lying ahead for community interpreters, their educators, and the field's scholars is to focus on the process of elucidating the field's values and how they are optimally applied in specific practice situations. The process of applying or specifying a broader principle to the circumstances of a practice situation is referred to in the field of normative ethics as *specified principlism*. Learning to take a principle or a value and make it operable, or applying it specifically to a given situation, is a necessary type of ethics education that other practice professions build into their training programs (in particular, through a period of supervised practice, such as internship or residency). Applying professional values in situated, dynamic, interpersonal practice situations is neither a natural nor intuitive process but a learned skill that takes time to develop. This development necessitates increasing exposure to practice situations coupled with reflective practice discussions with educators and peers. This trend must be pursued with vigor in the 21st century, making its way from the literature to the classroom to the practice setting.

REFERENCES

Angelelli, C. V. (2004). *Revisiting the interpreter's role: A study of conference, court, and medical interpreters in Canada, Mexico, and the United States* (Vol. 55). Amsterdam: John Benjamins Publishing.

Angelelli, C. V. (2006). Validating professional standards and codes: Challenges and opportunities. *Interpreting*, 8, 175–193.

Baker-Shenk, C. (1991). *The interpreter: Machine, advocate, or ally*. Paper presented at the Expanding horizons: Proceedings of the 1991 RID convention, Silver Spring, MD.

Beauchamp, T. L., & Childress, J. F. (2012). *Principles of biomedical ethics* (Vol. 7th). New York: Oxford University Press.

Cokely, D. (1992). *Interpretation: A sociolinguistic model*. Burtonsville, MD: Linstok Press.

Cokely, D. (2000). Exploring ethics: A case for revising the Code of Ethics. *Journal of Interpretation*, 25–60.

Clifford, A. (2004). Is fidelity ethical? The social role of the healthcare interpreter. *TTR: Traduction, Terminologie, Rédaction, 17*(2), 89–114.

Davidson, B. (2000). The interpreter as institutional gatekeeper: The social-linguistic role of interpreters in Spanish-English medical discourse. *Journal of Sociolinguistics, 4*(3), 379–405.

Dean, R. K. (2015). *Sign language interpreters' ethical discourse and moral reasoning patterns*. (Doctoral thesis, Heriot-Watt University, Edinburgh, Scotland).

Dean, R. K., & Pollard, R. Q (2013). *The demand control schema: Interpreting as a practice profession*. North Charleston, SC: CreateSpace Independent Publishing Platform.

Dysart-Gale, D. (2005). Communication models, professionalization, and the work of medical interpreters. *Health Communication, 17*(1), 91–103.

Frishberg, N. (1986). *Interpreting: An introduction*. Silver Spring, MD: RID Press.

Fritsch-Rudser, S. (1986). The RID Code of Ethics, Confidentiality, and Supervision. *Journal of Interpretation, 3*, 47–51.

Goffman, E. (1959). *The presentation of self in everyday life.* New York, NY: Anchor Books/Doubleday.

Hale, S. (2007). *Community interpreting.* Hampshire/New York: Palgrave Macmillan.

Hoza, J. (2003). Toward an interpreter sensibility: Three levels of ethical analysis and a comprehensive model of ethical decision-making for interpreters. *Journal of Interpretation, 48,* 1–43.

Hsieh, E. (2006). Conflicts in how interpreters manage their roles in provider–patient interactions. *Social Science & Medicine, 62*(3), 721–730.

Hsieh, E. (2007). Interpreters as co-diagnosticians: Overlapping roles and services between providers and interpreters. *Social Science & Medicine, 64*(4), 924–937.

Humphrey, J. (1999). *Decisions? Decisions!: A practical guide for sign language professionals.* Amarillo, TX: H & H Publishers.

Janzen, T., & Korpinski, D. (2005). Ethics and professionalism in interpreting. In T. Janzen (Ed.), *Topics in signed language interpreting* (pp. 165–202). Amsterdam/Philadelphia: John Benjamins Publishing.

Leanza, Y. (2005). Roles of community interpreters in pediatrics as seen by interpreters, physicians and researchers. *Interpreting, 7*(2), 167–192.

Leneham, M., & Napier, J. (2003). Sign language interpreters' codes of ethics: Should we maintain the status quo? *Deaf Worlds, 19*(2), 78–98.

Mason, I. (2000). Models and methods in dialogue interpreting research. In M. Olohan (Ed.), *Intercultural faultlines: Research models in translation studies I: Textual and cognitive aspects* (pp. 215–231). Manchester, U.K.: St. Jerome Publishing.

Pope, K. S., & Vasquez, M. J. (2010). *Ethics in psychotherapy and counseling: A practical guide.* Hoboken, NJ: John Wiley & Sons.

Pym, A. (2001). Introduction: The return to ethics in translation studies. *The Translator, 7*(2), 129–138.

Registry of Interpreters for the Deaf (2005). Code of Professional Conduct. Retrieved from https://www.rid.org/ethics/code-of-professional-conduct/

Rest, J. R., Narvaez, D., Bebeau, M. J., & Thoma, S. J. (1999). *Postconventional moral thinking: A neo-Kohlbergian approach.* Mahwah, NJ: Lawrence Erlbaum Associates.

Roy, C. B. (1993). The problem with definitions, descriptions, and the role metaphors of interpreters. *Journal of Interpretation, 6*(1), 127–154.

Roy, C. B. (2000). *Interpreting as a discourse process.* New York: Oxford University Press.

Strong, C. (2000). Specified principlism: What is it, and does it really resolve cases better than casuistry? *Journal of Medicine and Philosophy, 25*(3), 323–341.

Wadensjö, C. (1998). *Interpreting as interaction.* New York: Routledge.

Appendix

Dean and Pollard Publications Relevant to this Chapter

Dean, R. K., & Pollard, R. Q (2001). Application of demand-control theory to sign language interpreting: Implications for stress and interpreter training. *Journal of Deaf Studies and Deaf Education, 6*(1), 1–14.

Dean, R. K., & Pollard, R. Q (2005). Consumers and service effectiveness in interpreting work: A practice profession perspective. In M. Marschark, R. Peterson, & E. Winston (Eds.), *Interpreting and interpreter education: Directions for research and practice* (pp. 259–282). New York: Oxford University Press.

Dean, R. K., & Pollard, R. Q (2009). Challenges in interpreting addressed by demand-control schema analysis. In B. E. Cartwright (Ed.), *Encounters with reality: 1,001 interpreter scenarios* (pp. 307–316). Alexandria, VA: RID Press.

Dean, R. K., & Pollard, R. Q (2009). Effectiveness of observation-supervision training in community mental health interpreting settings. *REDIT E-journal on the Didactics of Translation and Interpreting, 3*, 1–17.

Dean, R. K., & Pollard, R. Q (2011). Context-based ethical reasoning in interpreting: A demand control schema perspective. *Interpreter and Translator Trainer, 5*(1), 155–182.

Dean, R. K., & Pollard, R. Q (2012). Beyond "interesting": Using demand control schema to structure experiential learning. In K. Malcolm and L. Swabey (Eds.). *In our hands: Educating healthcare interpreters* (pp. 77–104). Washington, DC: Gallaudet University Press.

Dean, R. K., & Pollard, R. Q (2013). *The demand control schema: Interpreting as a practice profession.* North Charleston, SC: CreateSpace Independent Publishing Platform.

4

Aptitude and Disposition: Learned vs. Nurtured Characteristics of Student Interpreters

SHERRY SHAW

Aptitude refers to the cognitive capacity that contributes to learning a specific skill, usually for work purposes. For example, mastering the art of crane operation requires the person to have an eye for precision, excellent depth perception, manual dexterity, decision-making abilities, analytical skills, personal integrity, interpersonal collaboration skills, and many other traits that are brought to the learning process. These attributes suggest, if not predict, a successful career operating cranes in what are often stressful situations. Distinguishing those skills that can be trained from those that cannot is at the center of aptitude research. People usually take aptitude tests to identify a profession that suits them and guarantees them success, based on their personal characteristics. They may assume that the test results will point them in the right direction and possibly even narrow their choices when it is time to declare a course of study at a higher learning institution.

Sometimes, people allow aptitude tests to make their decisions for them, assuming the tests reliably predict professional success in a given field. Unfortunately, aptitude is difficult to study, and test results do not always predict a definite "fit" for everyone's personal attributes. At this time, there is no aptitude test for becoming a signed language interpreter, so in this chapter, you will learn about the current research regarding interpreting aptitude and admission testing from the spoken and signed language interpreter education context.

INNATE AND TRAINED ABILITIES: THE IMPORTANCE OF RESEARCH

Aptitude is generally understood as a characteristic that is innate, as opposed to something that can be acquired over time, or learned. *Innate* versus *acquired* is an important distinction for determining if a student has what it takes to learn how to interpret and become a successful interpreter. Researchers are working diligently to identify, with a reasonable amount of certainty, the attributes aspiring interpreters must bring to the learning process and the skills that can be developed through training. Research that clearly shows what students need to enter a program and what students could enhance and develop during a program can guide interpreter education programs when they screen applicants for those who fit the aptitude profile for admission. After all, if a person does not have the aptitude, or innate ability, for learning a certain skill, it is likely a waste of time and resources to try to teach the skill, no matter the motivation for wanting to learn it.

Seeking to identify one or more predictors of student success, researchers have collaborated across the modalities of spoken and signed languages to study similarities and differences in these two groups of interpreting students (Shaw, 2011). Thus far, the results can only suggest, not predict, the ease with which a student can learn the complex tasks involved in the interpreting process. Most likely, predictors of interpreting student success are a combination of many factors that are present at birth but can be enhanced through training, including disposition, motivation, gross and fine motor skills, reaction time, and visual-auditory discrimination.

SELF-ASSESSMENT AND ADMISSION TESTING

Studying literature generated from research can help prospective students identify traits within themselves that might promote or deter their learning process in an interpreting program. Motivated, and often enamored by signed language and its cultural context, students may have an instinctive sense that using two languages for the purpose of promoting communication between people who do not share a language (the general definition of an interpreter) suits their personal ambition to become interpreters.

However, because there is not a test for confirming that, indeed, instinct reflects aptitude, prospective students can investigate self-assessment tools that will clarify personal strengths (e.g., growth mindset) and challenges (motivation or lack thereof). An objective self-assessment can help an aspiring interpreter confirm the feasibility of pursuing an interpreting career. The payback for a diligent self-assessment is highlighted in the research of Timarová and Salaets (2011), who documented that students who self-selected for the profession were less affected by anxiety during the learning process, a benefit that will prove beneficial as program expectations become more difficult and complex.

Once a student makes an informed decision to enter an interpreter education program, he or she should begin to prepare for an admission test that might be administered by the program to determine readiness for learning the interpreting process. In the United States, accredited interpreting programs are required to screen for bilingual skills prior to admission to interpreting skills courses (Commission on Collegiate Interpreter Education Accreditation Standards, 2014). Entrance examinations for prospective interpreting programs continue to be deliberated by interpreter educators, as programs are not yet able to screen prospective students based on the predictive validity of discrete traits. Without evidence upon which to build screenings, it is still quite possible for an interpreting program to accept students who can pass an entrance examination but who cannot pass interpreting performance exams, once they are in the program. Likewise, it is possible for programs to deny admission to prospective students who could have performed well in the program. Aside from language mastery and basic cognitive processing abilities as foundations for learning to interpret, there is no profile that applies to all students who think they want to be interpreters. For now, educators use research results to facilitate screening; however, they must cautiously apply anecdotal evidence, which means the collective wisdom and experience of teachers and Deaf community members, until we learn more about early predictors for student success. In addition to facilitating the screening of prospective students, ongoing research has the potential to help programs advise students who are already admitted to a program about continuing in the profession or seeking a comparably satisfying option in another field. Decisions that affect student admission and retention will continue to be based on a combination of empirical (scientific and experimental) and anecdotal (personal) evidence until additional data are available to make reliable predictions.

Everyone has personal strengths, and determining if those strengths must be innate or they can be developed and nurtured within an interpreting program is the heart of aptitude research. Most professions are interested in aptitude research, because preparation programs, and universities themselves, desire to allocate resources to the students who have the greatest likelihood to meet program outcomes and complete their training courses. Many of us have wanted to become or do something that seems appealing (like dancing, in my case) but are not equipped to achieve it, whether for physical reasons or the cognitive processing differences we all have. Research contributes to our understanding of the interpreting process and specifically what it takes for us to learn all the complexities of that process. Our dreams and passion for a given profession sometimes intersect favorably with our abilities, and other times, our dreams need to shift to a related (or totally new) profession that matches our capabilities. Most definitely, the field of interpreter education is one profession that is extremely keen on continuing the research and identifying predictors of student performance that will enhance the learning process and eventually lead to more qualified interpreters in the community.

THE BALANCE BETWEEN SOFT SKILLS AND HARD SKILLS

Once students identify interpreting as a possible career track, they tend to ask several questions; for example, Is interpreting the right career choice for me? Do I have all the necessary skills I need? and Am I able to do this? Learning the interpreting process and becoming a qualified interpreter depend on the interaction of soft skills and hard skills so that the learning process is manageable and rewarding. With this in mind, let's discuss the characteristics a student can bring to the learning process and those that must be developed.

Everyone has soft skills and hard skills that contribute to how they work and live. The term *soft skills* refers to affective (emotional) traits that are not tangible or easily measured, like a growth (versus fixed) mindset and receptivity to feedback. *Hard skills* are recognizable and measurable abilities, like visual-motor response time and auditory or visual discrimination between key points and the context of a message. The interpreter's combination of soft and hard skills applies to a wide variety of demands within *simultaneous* interpreting (slight delay between receiving a message in the *source language* and delivering it in the *target language*) and *consecutive* interpreting (interpretation occurs after a person stops speaking or signing). The rapid message transfer between two languages in simultaneous interpreting (a hard skill) requires the complementary use of soft skills, such as managing performance anxiety, to create a combination of skill types that results in effective interpreting.

Several soft skills that are recognized as important for learning to be an interpreter are personality, learning style, motivation, cognitive flexibility, and emotional stability (Bontempo & Napier, 2011). One soft skill that is particularly applicable to maintaining stamina during an interpreting program is a person's *disposition* (attitude about learning). Disposition is comprised of other soft skills, such as learning styles (preferably more than one style), self-directed learning, and constructive thinking. Attitude and motivation are also key players in determining whether or not a person has the tools necessary for achieving the goal of completing a preparation program and becoming an interpreter.

Personality type has been hypothesized to influence successful skill acquisition and interpreting and continues to intrigue researchers. Research into this area in the United States started in the 1970s with a focus on interpreter personality types (Schein, 1974); however, Schein's study and subsequent studies have not been able to confirm that certain personality types are more likely than others to result in successful interpreters (or students) (Stauffer & Shaw, 2006). Researchers are hesitant to say one personality type over another can predict a student's successful skill acquisition; in reality, researchers fall back on the *combination theory*; that is, interpreting skill acquisition happens as an interaction between soft and hard skills, and no single variable associated with either kind of skill can serve as a predictor to be used in admission evaluation. In other words, the interpreting profession attracts diverse personalities, and there is not a specific personality type that enhances the ability to learn the interpreting process or gives one person an advantage over another. However, there are manifestations of personality that can be trained (Dweck, 2016), and that truth leads to research on the characteristics that students must have when they enter interpreter education programs and the characteristics that can be learned during the course of one's professional study. To be more precise, sustaining a high level of motivation (whether intrinsic or extrinsic in nature) during the learning process also requires a student to demonstrate positivity, accept challenges, focus on solutions rather than problems, cope with stress, take risks, communicate, be assertive, demonstrate empathy, and tolerate ambiguity during each day of the learning process. If all of these skills are mandatory for learning the interpreting process, the best way to fail would involve allowing oneself to succumb to negative thinking, resisting feedback, dwelling on problems, poorly managing stress, and isolating or surrounding oneself with people who drain energy and provide no support.

The hard skills that must be present before a person can learn to interpret include mastery of two languages. One mistake that is common to beginning signed language students is the notion that excelling in signed language acquisition (and its accompanying culture) is a sufficient predictor of being able to use the language to interpret. The mistake is that being able to sign accurately and fluently does not necessarily mean the person can manipulate two languages in the interpreting process. Interpreting involves a complex series of tasks, and although a sufficient language base (in both languages) is obviously important, other hard skills, such as active listening and analyzing linguistic messages for meaning and speaker intent, are equally as important to the overall process. Additional hard skills include the ability to match the *register* (level of formality) of the *interlocutors* (people who are communicating) by selecting the appropriate vocabulary (signed or spoken) for that scenario. If an interpreter uses the wrong register, perhaps due to his or her own weak vocabulary or lack of personal schema, there is an inherent danger of misrepresenting clients and giving false impressions that could change the course of events. To demonstrate, when an interpreter is working with a Deaf professional (perhaps a physician or scientist) in a conference setting, the interpreter must rely on a vast storage bank of vocabulary options that accurately represents the presenter and audience. If an informal register is used in a conference presentation, the result is a loss of respect or devaluation of one's professional work being presented because the interpreter gave a false impression due to inadequate hard skills or used the wrong techniques needed for that particular setting. Listening, analyzing, filtering, paraphrasing, rapid processing, and reformulating messages are some of the core "hard skill" sets needed to perform an interpretation. Interpreter educators tend to build programs around hard skills like these, and more recently, educators are recognizing that a combination of hard and soft skill training, as directed in the Commission on Collegiate Interpreter Education accreditation standards, results in a more adequately prepared interpreter (Commission on Collegiate Interpreter Education, 2014).

Interactions between skill types (soft and hard) can occur between a multitude of skill sets, and any of those combinations could result in an effective interpretation. One example of a balanced combination of soft and hard skills involves recalling information from the source language long enough to simultaneously interpret it into the target language while continuing to absorb more source language stimulation (known as *working memory*) *and* demonstrating the professionalism to ask for clarification and correct any errors. In this case, personal monitoring supplements cognitive processing, and the end result is an accurate message transfer. Another example would be organizing a source's key concepts into a mental map for easier retrieval during consecutive interpreting while not allowing your disagreement with the content to affect your impartiality. Filtering personal feelings and interpreting without bias or interference requires a definite combination of cognitive and dispositional attributes.

REFERENCES

Bontempo, K., & Napier, J. (2011). Evaluating emotional stability as a predictor of interpreter competence and aptitude for interpreting. *Interpreting, 13*, 85–105.

Commission on Collegiate Interpreter Education. (2014). *CCIE Accreditation Standards 2014*. Retrieved from www.ccie-accreditation.org/standard

Dweck, C. S. (2016). *Mindset: The new psychology of success*. New York, NY: Ballantine Books.

Schein, J. (1974). Personality characteristics associated with interpreter proficiency. *Journal of Rehabilitation of the Deaf, 7*, 33–43.

Shaw, S. (2011). Cognitive and motivational contributors to aptitude: A study of spoken and signed language interpreting students. *Interpreting, 13*, 70–84.

Stauffer, L., & Shaw, S. (2006). Personality characteristics for success in interpreting courses: Perceptions of spoken and sign language interpretation students. *Journal of Interpretation*, 11–24.

Timarová, S., & Salaets, H. (2011). Learning styles, motivation and cognitive flexibility in interpreter training: Self-selection and aptitude. *Interpreting, 13*, 31–52.

RECOMMENDED READINGS

Bontempo, K., Napier, J., Hayes, L., & Brashear, V. (2014). Does personality matter? An international study of sign language interpreter disposition. *Translation and Interpreting, 6*(1), 23–46.

Gerver, D., Longley, P. E., Long, J., & Lambert, S. (1980). Selection tests for trainee conference interpreters. *Meta, 34*(4), 724–735.

Rudser, S. F., & Strong, M. (1987). An examination of some personal characteristics and abilities of sign language interpreters. *Sign Language Studies, 53*, 315–331.

Russo, M. (1993). Testing aptitude for simultaneous interpretation: Evaluation of the first trial and preliminary results. *The Interpreters' Newsletter, 5*, 68–71.

Shaw, S., & Hughes, G. (2006) Essential characteristics of sign language interpreting students: Perspectives of students and faculty. *Interpreting, 8*(2), 195–221.

Timarová, S., & Ungoed-Thomas, H. (2008). Admission testing for interpreting courses. *The Interpreter and Translator Trainer, 2*, 29–46.

5

Interpreting in Healthcare Settings: More than Needles, Blood, and Terminology

LAURIE SWABEY

MEDICAL INTERPRETING OR HEALTHCARE INTERPRETING?

Although the terms *medical interpreting* and *mental health interpreting* have been used for many years, it is now more common for interpreters to use the term *healthcare interpreting*. This broader term has been adopted for several reasons It includes both physical and mental health (including addiction and recovery) as well as a variety of approaches that might be better classified as health care or therapeutic than medical (e.g., massage, aromatherapy, acupuncture). Perhaps most importantly, distinguishing between medical and mental health care can be difficult. For example, an interpreter might be called to the emergency room for a "medical" interpreting situation, such as a gunshot wound, only to arrive and find out that the gun wound was self-inflicted by a young man who wanted to kill himself. In a family practice clinic, practitioners commonly ask patients if they "feel safe at home." If a patient answers "no," you may find yourself interpreting for a more complex situation than the nagging cough that was the stated reason for the visit. A qualified healthcare interpreter may specialize in one particular area (e.g., pediatrics, oncology, psychiatry), but all interpreters working in the healthcare setting need to have had some education in both the medical and mental health fields, because they frequently overlap.

73

How Is the Healthcare Setting Different from Other Settings?

Interpreting in healthcare settings is different from interpreting in other settings, and these differences may affect what you do before, during, and after interpreting.

Observing Physical or Emotional Pain

In the healthcare setting, patients you will see are often not at their best. They may be in physical or emotional pain, or both. They may have just received bad news about their own health or the health of a child, parent, or other family member. If a Deaf patient has an acute injury or chronic condition in her arms or hands, it will affect the way she uses signed language. If Deaf patients are on medication or in the recovery room, their language may be altered, and they may not be able to keep their eyes open to focus on the interpretation.

Managing Intimacy and Respect

Healthcare encounters can be routine (e.g., allergy shots, a well-baby checkup, a culture for strep throat), or they may be more complex or even life threatening. Regardless of the level of complexity, most healthcare interpreting assignments, by definition, are foregrounded in intimacy. By *intimacy*, we mean that you will see what is normally physically or emotionally private or personal. Patients may be wearing hospital gowns instead of regular clothing. They may discuss topics that you may not normally talk about with someone that you do not know well, such as bathroom habits, infertility, erectile dysfunction, and sexually transmitted diseases, just to name a few. You may also hear patients sharing very personal stories with the healthcare provider or another family member. You may be present for births and deaths, as well as other important life milestones that are generally private. Healthcare interpreting requires a level of intimacy and involvement that does not routinely occur in other settings.

You may be present for pelvic exams, prostate exams, breast exams, or other intensely personal medical situations. In these and many situations in the healthcare context, you can demonstrate respect by positioning your-self to give the patient the most privacy. For example, during a pelvic exam, you might stand near the patient's shoulder, where you can see each other but not the actual exam.

The gender of the interpreter is also a concern for many patients, due to the intimacy of the medical setting. Spoken language interpreters can stand behind a screen and thus are able to hear and speak for patients and pro-viders without being able to see the patient. However, this is not possible for signed language interpreters. Depending on the reason for the appoint-ment, the patient's preference for the gender of the interpreter should be respected. Respect is also demonstrated by maintaining the highest levels of confidentiality about the people and events you encounter in healthcare interpreting.

Taking Precautions: Infection Control and Industrial Safety

In healthcare settings, you will need to follow certain precautions to pro-tect yourself and the people around you. These may include a tuberculosis skin test and vaccines for Hepatitis B, measles, mumps, rubella, influenza, and pneumococcal disease.

You will need to learn and carefully follow safety precautions to avoid potential risks from bodily fluids or sharp objects. If the patient is in a burn unit, ICU, or other type of isolation, the healthcare team wears protective clothing, and you will do the same. In addition, when you interpret for procedures, such as taking X-rays, you will need to position yourself for communication and your own safety. Depending on the setting, there may be rules regarding such things as the type of shoes you should wear, how and when hand washing is required, and what surfaces and objects you may touch. Again, keep in mind that these policies are in place to protect you, patients, staff, and others in the environment.

Self-Care and Vicarious Trauma

As a healthcare interpreter, you may see blood, smell excrement or vomit, or hear someone wailing in pain. If the sights and sounds of a healthcare environment are difficult for you, this may not be the specialty you want to pursue. However, even those who are used to these experiences will still need to know when and how to get a breath of fresh air, a drink of water, or a few minutes to breathe deeply and refocus.

Although for many years, it was said that interpreters should be "neutral," we now have sufficient evidence to show that interpreters are not neutral, but, in fact, participants in the situation (Metzger, 1999). We are affected by the situations we see and experience. Because of this, interpreters need to be aware of their "trigger" points and have strategies for taking care of themselves before, during, and after interpreting. If you have recently lost a family member or close friend to cancer, you might find it difficult to interpret oncology appointments. Some healthcare interpreters say that severed hands or fingers are unnerving for them to see, whereas others might have a difficult time interpreting for a tooth extraction. You might be interpreting a routine ultrasound for a pregnant woman and then need to convey the news that a heartbeat cannot be detected. On another level, if you interpret for difficult situations (e.g., for survivors of domestic assault), you might experience vicarious trauma. This happens to service providers who see or hear about intense pain, violence, or loss and start to absorb the trauma themselves. As you continue your education, you will learn ways to identify and handle these difficult and intensive parts of healthcare interpreting.

WHO DO INTERPRETERS WORK WITH IN THE HEALTHCARE SETTING?

As an interpreter, you will be working with people who do not share a common language. When you think about interpreting in the healthcare setting, whom do you picture yourself working with? In the healthcare setting, you will work with a variety of people who may be Deaf or who can hear, including providers, patients, and family members. You may also work with other interpreters. Remember that you are interpreting *between* people who use a different language, not *for* the deaf person or *for* the hearing person in the situation. Frame your work as interactive, not for one particular person or the other.

Consider how the interpreting requirements would be different in each of the following situations:

A couple is going for an obstetrician visit. The woman is hearing, and the man is Deaf; both are fluent ASL users. The midwife and healthcare team are hearing and do not know ASL.

A Deaf parent of an 11-year-old hearing child with a concussion arrives at the ER, and the triage nurse needs to get information about the accident.

A Deaf physician, who is also a professor at a university medical school, is conducting rounds with hearing medical students and patients who do not sign.

A Deaf researcher is interviewing elderly hearing patients with Type II diabetes for a research study.

A Deaf (adult) daughter is caring for her terminally ill hearing father in her home. The father is now in hospice care, and the Deaf daughter interacts with the hearing hospice care worker during home visits.

The patient is a Deaf teenager who uses ASL. The patient's hearing mother is with him. She speaks Spanish fluently but is not fluent in ASL or English. The doctor is hearing and speaks only English.

Patients

Almost every person, deaf or hearing, will interact with the healthcare system at various points during their lifetime. As such, you will work with patients from a variety of backgrounds. Remember, as illustrated in the examples above, you will interpret for a variety of Deaf and hearing people—patients, family members, and providers. Some have been born and raised in the United States; others are immigrants or refugees. Some will have completed advanced degrees; others will not have graduated from high school. Some may be fluent in several languages; others may be alingual (i.e., not fluent in any language). Patients may have knowledge about their own health and the healthcare system; others may not. The patients you see may be young, old, or middle aged. Some will be wealthy; others may be living in poverty. Patients may identify as lesbian, gay, bisexual, transgender, intersex, or asexual. Patients may use the healthcare system regularly, or they may have only been to a doctor only occasionally. Some Deaf patients have a preferred list of interpreters they request through a referral agency to obtain interpreters they know and trust. Other Deaf patients prefer not to have the same interpreters each time, as a way of maintaining more privacy about their healthcare. If you are doing on-call, emergency healthcare interpreting, are a full-time staff interpreter, and/or interpret video-relay service (VRS) or video-relay interpreting (VRI) calls, you will see patients from all walks of life.

Family Members

Like patients, family members come from a variety of backgrounds and may be deaf or hearing. Healthcare interpreting is often called *triadic*, meaning the interaction is between the provider, patient, and interpreter. However, you may find in some situations, that family members or friends are often present. For example, a patient might be accompanied by small children, or extended family might be present. Family members may or may not use ASL. Some may be fluent; others may use signs that are idiosyncratic to that particular relationship. Some family members may want to interpret for their own sibling or relative. Other times, you might find yourself interpreting between family members that you might assume could communicate with each other (e.g., a Deaf adult who is fluent in ASL and is communicating with a parent who never learned more than a few basic signs). Family members may be supportive or oppositional. As you move forward in your education, you will learn more about interpreting interactions between family members in potentially stressful and intimate situations.

Interpreters

Because of the complexity of the healthcare setting and the high stakes that are involved, it is imperative that healthcare interpreters are highly competent. In the healthcare setting, if doctors feel they do not have the needed expertise to best treat a patient, it is common practice to refer the patient to a respected colleague, or there is often a healthcare team in place. One marker of a highly competent interpreter is to know when an interpreting specialist is needed. One type of interpreting specialist is a Certified Deaf Interpreter (CDI) or Deaf Interpreter (DI) with a specialization in healthcare. DIs or CDIs are qualified interpreters who are themselves Deaf and fluent in ASL and written English. DIs or CDIs often are crucial to ensuring the best communication for Deaf patients in the healthcare system. DIs or CDIs are particularly needed in situations in which the Deaf patient is facing an array of complicated decisions; has limited mobility to sign or understand signed language (possibly due to their illness); is from another country and is not fluent in the form of ASL known by the hearing interpreter; has one or more disabilities (e.g., cerebral palsy, vision loss or blindness, autism), and, possibly due to mental health issues, is signing disfluently. DIs or CDIs often are better able to understand and convey nuanced communication across a range of signing styles that may be influenced by region, culture, age, literacy, education, class, and physical, cognitive, and mental health (Boudreault, 2005). CDIs or DIs also work as translators and provide translations of consent forms, healthcare directives, and medication directions.

Besides the need and benefit for a deaf–hearing interpreting team in the healthcare setting, you may also find yourself working in situations where an interpreter who works between two spoken languages (e.g., Spanish-English, Russian-English, Somali-English) is needed. This might occur as in the situation above, when the parent speaks only Spanish and her son, the patient, is Deaf and uses ASL. Some large hospitals and clinics may have full-time staff interpreters who work between the most common spoken languages used in the area. Other healthcare facilities may connect with spoken language interpreters via phone or video remote technology.

Healthcare Providers

As with the other people you will work with in the healthcare setting, providers come from a variety of backgrounds. Often healthcare providers have not had training in how to work with interpreters or with patients who do not speak English. However, medical schools are now beginning to recognize the importance of effective communication in the diagnosis and treatment of patients, including the fact that some patients may require interpreting services.

The number of Deaf healthcare providers and Deaf students in health-care programs and medical schools continues to grow (Moreland, Latimore, Sen, Arato, & Zazove, 2013). There is a national organization (Association for Medical Professionals with Hearing Loss) made up of healthcare professionals and students in healthcare professions who are Deaf or hard of hearing. Gallaudet University and the National Technical Institute for the Deaf, a college of the Rochester Institute of Technology, are encouraging students to pursue STEM (science, technology, engineering, medicine) programs. Highly skilled, knowledgeable, and flexible interpreters are needed for these students and professionals.

Oftentimes, Deaf healthcare professionals or graduate students work with *designated interpreters*. A designated interpreter works regularly (over a period of time) with the same healthcare professional or medical student. A designated interpreter uses knowledge gained in a particular setting to contribute to the effectiveness of the interpretation; is familiar with the goals of the Deaf healthcare professional, as well their communication style and preferences; and develops a level of rapport and trust over time that enhances the overall interpretation (Swabey, Agan, Moreland, & Olson, 2016). This is a specialized and unique role that is often negotiated between the interpreter and Deaf professional.

What Knowledge and Skills Are Required for Interpreting in Healthcare Settings?

Take a few moments to write down some of the knowledge and skills you think you might need before working in a healthcare setting. As you read, see how well your list compares with what is in this section.

For many years, it was assumed that once certified, interpreters were competent to work in any setting: legal, medical, mental health, or educational. However, as the field has progressed, specialized national certificates have become available for legal interpreting and educational interpreting, but not healthcare interpreting. Given the potentially high risks and complexity in the healthcare setting, a national credential is needed. The RID membership voted in 2013 that the establishment of such a credential must be investigated. Our colleagues in spoken language interpreting have already established both written and performance exams for healthcare interpreters. To date, because a national certification for ASL healthcare interpreters does not exist, other measures must be considered, such as self-management of one's own entry to, and progression within the field of healthcare interpreting. Each interpreter is called upon to achieve high levels of proficiency and accountability and to document their own progress at this time.

In addition to having the competencies of a nationally certified interpreter, those who work in healthcare settings should possess the following:

- Understanding of linguistic, social, and cultural influences that impact healthcare interactions
- Ability to balance the need for maintaining professional distance with empathy and flexibility
- Knowledge of the laws/policies related to healthcare settings
- Understanding of general physiological and psychological implications of healthcare
- Familiarity with the underlying practices of various healthcare delivery systems.

The five bullet points above may seem more relevant to you as you consider them in relation to situations you will encounter in the healthcare setting. Which of the competencies listed above would you need to function effectively in each of the following situations?

> You are interpreting for a routine eye exam. To test the patient's vision, the ophthalmologist turns out the lights, has the patient look into a machine, and then continues to ask the patient questions.

> An elderly lady is waiting in the exam room for the doctor to see her. She usually comes with a friend or relative but is alone today. She would like you to wait in the exam room with her until the doctor arrives, as she is scared and nervous.

> The nurse says she doesn't need an interpreter to take the Deaf patient's health history, as she took several ASL classes in college.

> The Deaf patient is an immigrant from Somalia and is being seen by a gynecologist for the first time. She has never had a pelvic exam before now.

> The psychologist asks the Deaf patient if she is hearing voices.

During a C-section, the doctor tells the Deaf couple there is only space in the operating room for one extra person—either the husband or the interpreter must leave.

As you continue to read this chapter, keep these situations in mind and keep the list you made. You will review your list in a later section.

Knowledge of Healthcare Systems and Settings

Before you work in a healthcare setting, you will need to become familiar with the healthcare system. Just like the educational setting or legal setting, the healthcare setting has systems, procedures, and hierarchies you need to be aware of and able to navigate effectively. You should generally understand the differences between public and private healthcare systems and the differences among the healthcare facilities in your community. Knowledge about the rights of patients and general laws pertaining to healthcare access is also needed.

You will need to become familiar with a variety of medical specialties and body systems, including neurology, cardiology, urology, hematology, orthopedics, the muscular system, the sensory system, the immune system, the endocrine system, the digestive system, the respiratory system, and the reproductive system. Further, you will need to know about the wide range of people who work within the healthcare system, including various types of nurses, physician assistants, doctors, residents, and many types of technicians. You will notice that all medical personnel wear name badges, and many wear lab coats that distinguish their roles. Increasingly, interpreters are required to use a name badge to work in healthcare settings. It is important for healthcare staff and patients to be able to identify the people with whom they are working.

Health literacy is defined as the ability to get information a person needs about one's health, understand that information, and use that information to make informed decisions about one's health and the care one receives from doctors. According to the National Library of Medicine, about 9 out of 10 American adults have some challenges with health literacy and may not have the background needed to do things, such as fill out complicated forms or manage a chronic disease (U.S. Department of Health and Human Services). If you are thinking about becoming a healthcare interpreter, consider your own level of health literacy. Before you take interpreting work in the healthcare setting, you will need to have a high level of health literacy. You will need to understand the healthcare system, the structure/hierarchy within the system, and the rights of patients. For example, you have probably been asked to sign a HIPAA (Health Insurance Portability and Accountability Act) consent form when you visit the doctor. Do you know what that means related to confidentiality?

Healthcare interpreting takes place in a variety of settings. You may interpret in a dental clinic, mental health clinic, or pediatric clinic. Interpreters are needed in urgent care facilities and at trauma centers. You may interpret for patients at one-day surgical centers and on surgical units in small and large hospitals. You may interpret for a surgical prep as well as a recovery and follow-up phase. At a hospital, you might interpret for the admissions process and discharge process. Again, these settings may require simultaneous interpreting, consecutive interpreting, sight translation, or translation, and all may be required during one appointment.

Adaptability

Adaptive performance is a term used in the field of organizational psychology to describe how a person adjusts to changes and stress in the workplace. Generally, employees who are highly adaptable are sought by employers, because they tend to perform well, have positive attitudes, and deal well with stress. Healthcare interpreters report that their jobs require a high degree of adaptability (Olson & Swabey, 2016), specifically related to the following:

- Working in a variety of different settings and locations
- Working with a variety of providers and patients
- Dealing with uncertain and unpredictable work situations
- Adapting to different cultural backgrounds
- Solving problems creatively
- Handling crisis situations.

As you consider your interest and suitability for the healthcare setting, think about how this type of work environment fits with your personality and work style.

Understanding Doctor–Patient Communication

It is crucial for healthcare interpreters to understand how professionals talk with each other and with patients in the healthcare setting. You may be surprised to learn that language is one of the most powerful tools healthcare providers have in diagnosing illnesses. The healthcare provider often depends on the patient's description of their pain to diagnosis the condition that brought them to the office. Think about what happens when you go to see a doctor. The appointment generally starts with a series of questions. The healthcare provider uses the information gained to determine what, if any, tests or procedures will be needed. The appointment ends with a diagnosis and treatment plan. Further, in mental health settings, many therapies are talk-based and rely heavily upon the interaction between provider and patient. Several research studies have shown that patients who trust their healthcare provider and have effective communication are much more likely to follow through with treatment, resulting in better health outcomes (McKee et al., 2011). As you develop your knowledge, you will want to study interaction in the healthcare setting, including the structure and goals of the healthcare interview and how healthcare providers establish rapport with patients.

Mastering Medical Terminology in English and ASL

When students think about the knowledge a healthcare interpreter needs, medical terminology in ASL and in English is often one of the first things that comes to mind. You need to learn terms for medical conditions and diseases, anatomy and body systems, common drugs, as well as tests and procedures. Further, you will need to be familiar with commonly asked questions in healthcare interviews and how to convey degrees of pain. In English, you will need to become familiar with Greek and Latin roots for words, as well as suffixes and prefixes. In ASL, you will need to study how to use depiction, space, and other linguistic features to convey medical terms.

As with many language pairs, there is an absence of standard lexical correspondents between English and ASL for many medical terms. This means that, although there are some standard ASL signs for terms like *diabetes* and *blood pressure*, there are not standard ASL signs for *glaucoma* and *osteoporosis*. This absence of lexical correspondents in any language pairing may be due to a number of reasons—young vs. old languages, different syntactic structures, languages that are very far apart historically, and different language modalities. However, ASL has a rich array of linguistic features that allow for the expression of these concepts, including use of depiction, nonmanual markers, and space around the signer. It is imperative you learn how to express and comprehend medical concepts in ASL and in English in a variety of registers, from intimate (e.g., mental health counseling for couples) to formal (medical conference). Again, often a deaf-hearing team (Forestal & Clark, 2014) is crucial due to the linguistic and cultural complexities of interpreting between ASL and English in healthcare settings.

When communicating information about health conditions or treatments, healthcare providers and patients often find the use of visual aids to be extremely helpful. These may include a three-dimensional model of the eye, a diagram of the skeletal system, or a plastic representation of the layers of the skin. Many interpreters bring an iPad with them and use online visual medical dictionaries both for their own knowledge and to have available for doctors and patients to use during an interpreted explanation. If you see models or diagrams in the consultation room, it may be appropriate to ask the healthcare provider to use those in their description, as it will aid in your interpretation. Many patients, deaf or hearing, find this useful.

Demonstrating Professional Practices in Healthcare Settings

In Chapters 2 and 4, you learned about interpreting as a practice profession, the National Association of the Deaf-Registry for Interpreters for the Deaf (NAD-RID) Code of Professional Conduct (CPC), ethics, decision-making, and boundaries. As in other settings, you will follow the CPC in your work as a healthcare interpreter. In addition, you will find it instructive to look at the codes of conduct and standards of practice for healthcare interpreters who work with spoken languages in healthcare settings. The National Council on Interpreting in Healthcare (www.ncihc.org), the International Medical Interpreters Association (www.imiaweb.org), and the California

Healthcare Interpreters Association (chiaonline.org) all have websites with links for CPCs and standards of practice. The principles are similar to that of the NAD-RID CPC but have specific references to the healthcare setting and the "do no harm" ethos for the medical field. In the healthcare setting, the patient's health and well-being is the ultimate goal.

As you have read, interpreters for many years were taught they were, or should be, invisible and neutral. We now have much research to show this is neither possible nor desirable. You should always be aware of how your presence in the environment influences the healthcare encounter. The interpreter in healthcare settings, like the other professionals in healthcare, must carefully manage empathy and caring with clear professional boundaries. Healthcare interpreters need to be ethical and accurate, professional yet responsive, as well as communicative and collaborative in nature. Interpreting involves people, and the relationships between the people involved are a very important part of the communication. Effective communication, trust, and respect are crucial for the health and well-being of patients.

As you have learned in previous chapters, interpreting is a practice profession. Just as with other types of interpreting, you will need to observe the healthcare setting and discuss what you see with a supervising instructor. You will also need to have a fellowship or practicum experience where your work as a novice healthcare interpreter is observed and supervised by an expert healthcare interpreter. You will engage in reflective practice, analyzing and reflecting upon your decisions and actions as an interpreter with your supervisor and classmates. Even if you have had supervision and/ or mentoring in other settings, you still need to experience this type of learning in the healthcare setting before accepting work in this specialty. The interactions you will encounter and the decisions you will have to make in order to convey an accurate, understandable, and culturally appropriate message cannot be fully learned without supervised experience in the healthcare setting.

Knowing the Uses of VRI and VRS in Healthcare Settings

As a VRS interpreter, you may handle a variety of calls related to healthcare. These might include describing symptoms in order to schedule an appointment, consultation with a nurse regarding questions about a treatment plan, or hearing the results of medical tests. These calls may be routine (e.g., scheduling appointments, getting general questions answered), or these calls may be emotionally intense, for example, if a patient is in distress or receiving bad news. As a video-relay interpreter, you might also get a 911 call about a medical emergency. This is an area where it is important to have specialized training both to handle the call effectively and any trauma you may feel after having relayed a distressing emergency situation.

The use of VRI is quickly growing in healthcare settings, and it may occur in one of two ways. The interpreter may be with a patient at a clinic and then connecting with a physician, perhaps a specialist, at another location. More commonly, the patient and healthcare provider are in a clinic or emergency room, and the interpreter is in another location.

There are positive and negative aspects for using a video-relay interpreter in healthcare settings. VRI can be conducted quickly, may be more private (anonymous), and may be the only way for a patient to communicate with a much-needed specialist.

Still, VRI has many negatives, including occasional technology failure, the quality of the picture may be fuzzy or have pauses, the screen may be small and/or difficult to see, VRI equipment may not be available in all the rooms in a hospital used for diagnosis and treatment, or patients may not be able to lift their heads to see the screen or use their arms or hands well enough for the interpreter to understand them on a screen.

In some communities, only video-relay interpreters are provided. In other areas, a video-relay interpreter may be provided until an on-site interpreter arrives. At that point, there needs to be a transition period in which the video-relay interpreter conveys any needed information to the on-site interpreter who has just arrived. Always keep in mind that an interpreting team (co-interpreters) can also be used, with one interpreter on site and one on VRI. This is one of the many effective ways for Deaf and hearing interpreters to work together.

Using the Domains and Competencies for Healthcare Interpreting

Earlier in this chapter, you were asked to take a few minutes to write down some of the knowledge and skills you think you might need before working in a healthcare setting. In this final section, see how your list compares with the knowledge domains you will find below.

In 2006, as part of a federally funded project, the St. Catherine University CATIE Center undertook an effort to identify the knowledge domains and skill-based competencies needed for medical interpreting. This approach used subject matter experts, and input was gathered from hearing and Deaf interpreting practitioners, Deaf consumers, and interpreter educators. The thirteen knowledge domains the study identified are listed below.

- Healthcare systems
- Multiculturalism and diversity
- Self-care
- Boundaries
- Preparation
- Ethical and professional decision making
- Language and interpreting
- Technology
- Research
- Legislation
- Leadership
- Communication advocacy
- Professional development

These domains and competencies may be used by students and interpreters as a guide for developing needed skills and knowledge. Employers may use these to write job descriptions, and supervisors may use these in job reviews or goal-setting meetings. If you take a healthcare interpreting course, you will examine these domains and competencies more closely. For now, suffice it to know that there are a variety of knowledge domains and skill competencies required for working in the healthcare setting.

Mental health interpreting is also a highly specialized field that requires extensive study. Although there is no national certification for mental health interpreting, the Alabama Department of Mental Health, Office of Deaf Services, created an intensive educational program that leads to a credential (QHMI, due to a lawsuit settled in 2002). Since then, they have developed and offered in-depth training that is attended by interpreters from all over the nation. The initial part of the training program includes an introduction to the following topics, which are essential areas of knowledge for any interpreter working in mental health:

- Mental health systems and treatment approaches
- Diagnostic criteria and disorder types according to the DSM-V
- Sources of language dysfluency and techniques for interpreting
- Secondary trauma stress/vicarious trauma, self-care and safety
- Psychopharmacology
- Psychiatric emergencies
- Support groups and community mental health services

EDUCATION AND CREDENTIALING

How Can I Enter the Profession of Healthcare Interpreting?

Because there is no national certification for healthcare interpreting at this time, each interpreter must demonstrate personal accountability and professionalism in entering the field of healthcare interpreting. One way to do this is to use a career lattice. A career lattice for a particular field helps people understand how to enter or advance in a profession. It also shows the developmental stages within a career. Lattices are often used in practice professions (e.g., physical therapy, social work) to help potential practitioners see the pathway to a specialized career.

Figure 1 depicts a career lattice for healthcare interpreting, located at www.catiecenter.org, for an online version with learning resources. In the online version, you would click on each shape for detailed information and links to learning resources. For example, clicking on the green circle labeled *Pre-requisites for entering the Lattice* would show that entry into this specialty requires a BA/BS degree, certification, inoculations, and experience interpreting in the Deaf community. Clicking on the other green circles gives information about how much time might be required to develop the competencies needed for healthcare interpreting at each level. Learning resources are linked behind each yellow circle. The purpose of this lattice is to give you a general visual picture of how you might progress to becoming a qualified healthcare interpreter.

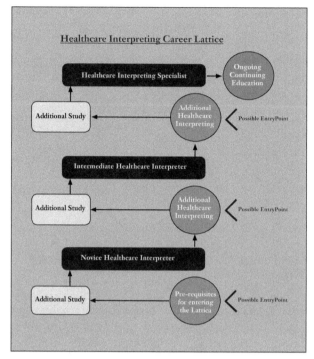

Figure 1: Healthcare Interpreting Career Lattice

Your college or university program may offer general coursework that will help prepare you to advance through the lattice for a future specialization in healthcare. These courses might include healthcare ethics, anatomy and physiology, language and power, medical terminology, abnormal psychology, and death and dying. In addition, some BA and MA interpreting programs offer coursework specifically in healthcare interpreting. Workshops and intensive seminars are available that will aid in your development. Ideally, you would plan and complete a sequence of coursework, which would logically develop the knowledge domains and competencies for interpreting in the healthcare setting. As important as coursework, you must engage in directed observation of healthcare settings. It is instructive to observe healthcare settings both that involve Deaf people and those that do not. Finally, you will need to work under the supervision of a qualified, experienced healthcare interpreter and learn from this combination of on-the-job experience and guidance from an expert practitioner.

Credentials and Licensure

An emergency physician once made the observation that when she is in an emergency room, operating room, triage room, or exam room, every other staff member involved with the patient must have completed a recognized program of study and received a license or certificate in order to practice. This physician remarked that this is true from the phlebotomist, to the X-ray technician, to the respiratory therapist, to the attending physician. However, the interpreter is often the exception and may be there without having completed a course of study approved by an accrediting body. Although some states have licensure or certification requirements for interpreters in the healthcare setting, there is a need for a nationally recognized credential for ASL-English healthcare interpreters. In order for Deaf people to have access to accurate communication in healthcare settings, standards for ASL-English interpreters need to be established. In the absence of a national standard or credential, it is of utmost importance that each interpreter wishing to work in healthcare interpreting carefully study the career lattice, pursue a plan of study, and seek mentorship from an expert healthcare interpreter.

ACKNOWLEDGMENTS

My deep and profound appreciation to those in the Deaf community who have guided me and influenced my work. I would especially like to thank Sheryl Buchholz, Anita Buel, Jimmy Beldon, Janis Cole, Christopher Moreland, Lee Perish, and Beth Siebert. I would also like to thank my colleagues Richard Laurion, Brenda Nicodemus, and Carol J. Patrie for reviewing this chapter.

REFERENCES

Boudreault, P. (2005). Deaf interpreters. In T. Janzen (Ed.), *Topics in signed language interpretation: Theory and practice* (pp. 323–355). Mahwah, NJ: Lawrence Erlbaum Associates.

Crump, C. (2012). Mental health interpreting: Training, standards, and certification. In L. Swabey & K. Malcolm (Eds.), *In our hands: Educating healthcare interpreters* (pp. 54–76). Washington, DC: Gallaudet University Press. Retrieved from http://www.mh.alabama.gov/Downloads/MIDS/MHI_Training_standards_ certification.pdf

Forestal, E., & Clark, S. (2014). The teaming model and transparency for Deaf and hearing team interpreters: Who owns the interpretation? In D. I. J. Hunt & S. Hafer (Eds.). *Proceedings from CIT 2014: Our Roots: The Essence of Our Future.* Portland, Oregon: Conference of Interpreter Trainers.

McKee, M. M., Barnett, S., Block, R. C., & Pearson, T. A. (2011). Impact of communication on preventive services among deaf American Sign Language users. *American Journal of Preventive Medicine, 41*(1), 75–79. Retrieved from http://www.ncbi.nlm.nih.gov/pmc/articles/PMC3117257/?report=reader

Metzger, M. (1999). *Deconstructing the myth of neutrality.* Washington, DC: Gallaudet University Press.

Moreland, C. J., Latimore, D., Sen, A., Arato, N., & Zazove, P. (2013). Deafness among physicians and trainees: A national survey. *Academic Medicine, 88*(2), 224–232. doi: 10.1097/ACM.0b013e31827c0d60.

Olson, A. M., & Swabey, L. (2016). Communication access for deaf people in healthcare settings: Understanding the work of American Sign Language interpreters. *Journal of Healthcare Quality, 39*(4), 191–199. doi: 10.1097/JHQ.0000000000000038.

St. Catherine University CATIE Center. (2008). Medical interpreter: ASL/English domains and compentencies. Retrieved at http://healthcareinterpreting.org/domains-competencies/

Swabey, L., Agan, T. S. K., Moreland, C. J., & Olson, A. M. (2016). Understanding the work of designated healthcare interpreters. *International Journal of Interpreter Education, 8*(1), 40–56.

U.S. Department of Health and Human Services. Office of Disease Prevention and Health Promotion. *Quick Guide to Health Literacy.* Washington, DC: USHHS.

RECOMMENDED READINGS

Beltran Avery, M. (2001). The role of the health care interpreter: An evolving dialogue. The National Council on Interpreting in Health Care Working Papers Series. Retrieved from http://memberfiles.freewebs.com/17/56/66565617/documents/The%20role_of_health_care_interpreter.pdf

Gonzalez, S., Lummer, L., Plue, C., & Ordaz, M. (2018). Community healthcare interpreting. In T. K. Holcomb & D. H. Smith (Eds.). *Deaf eyes on interpreting* (pp. 209–222). Washington, DC: Gallaudet University Press.

Swabey, L., & Malcolm, K. (Eds.). (2012). (Eds.) *In our hands: Educating healthcare interpreters.* Washington, DC: Gallaudet University Press.

6

Interpreting in Vocational Rehabilitation Contexts

LINDA K. STAUFFER

THE VOCATIONAL rehabilitation (VR) system in the United States is funded by the Vocational Rehabilitation Act of 1973 (U.S. Department of Education, 2018) and governed by regulations from the Rehabilitation Services Administration (RSA), an agency within the U.S. Department of Education. Services to consumers are provided by state VR agencies. The VR system is the federal government's program to assist people with disabilities in preparing for, finding, and maximizing employment. During World War I, the government focused on returning young disabled veterans to the workforce. Social policy and broadening legislation during the 20th century expanded the focus to assist all persons with disabilities to achieve employment and community integration.

The VR system, through its state agencies and programs, is one of the largest employers of signed language interpreters today. Interpreters in the VR system work in a range of services from consumers' initial application through post-employment services. Many of these services are provided in community settings, such as doctor's offices, colleges and university classroom, and business environments. This intersection of VR services and community settings may obscure the fact that VR interpreting requires a specialized skill set to be successful.

In many communities, the state VR agency is seen as simply another hiring agency along with referral companies and video-relay services offering employment opportunities to interpreters. Many VR interpreters do not recognize that there is a unique body of knowledge related to this field. A qualified VR interpreter needs to understand specialized skills and knowledge in order to provide high-quality services successfully within the VR system.

Who Does Vocational Rehabilitation Serve?

VR's mission is simple: to assist people with disabilities in finding and maintaining employment, leading to increased independence and improved quality of life. Stated another way, VR helps to remove employment barriers for people with disabilities in order for these individuals to become employed (NCIEC VR Work Team, 2012a).

Persons with disabilities are not employed in numbers equal to their nondisabled peers. According to Bureau of Labor Statistics estimates, in 2011, 28.4% of adults with disabilities, ages 16 to 64, were employed, compared with 71% of persons without disabilities, emphasizing the need for such services (Butterworth, Hall, Smith, Migliore, Winsor, Domin, & Sulewski, 2012). In fiscal year 2012, more than 560,000 individuals applied for VR services across the United States (Institute on Disability, 2014).

Gallaudet University estimates that 38,225.590 people (or 13% of the U.S. population) reported having *hearing problems* (Gallaudet University Library, 2014). This figure includes both deaf and hard of hearing individuals. For working-age individuals who are deaf, Gallaudet estimates that 4,022,334 individuals nationally, ages 16 to 64, have a hearing disability.

VR services work. In fiscal year (FY) 2012, 180,216 VR clients with disabilities successfully achieved employment (U.S. Department of Education, 2014). Of those individuals, approximately 108,440 obtained competitive jobs in the workforce and received salaries plus benefits.

For persons with *significant disabilities* during FY 2012, 167,421 individuals (92.9%) obtained employment after receiving VR services (U.S. Department of Education, 2014). Federal law defines those with significant disabilities as persons with one or more physical or mental impairments that seriously limit functional abilities and who require multiple VR services over an extended time.

VR services are cost-effective. Over a lifetime, for every $1.00 spent on individual receiving services, an individual reduces reliance on government assistance by approximately $7.00. These employed individuals ". . .will pay the cost of their VR services in two to four years" (Council of State Administrators of Vocational Rehabilitation, 2011–2012, p. 1). If these individuals had not received VR services, they may have instead remained unemployed and a substantial drain on taxpayers. Additionally, the improvement in these individual's quality of life cannot be measured in dollars and cents.

HISTORY OF VOCATIONAL REHABILITATION LEGISLATION

The history of the profession of sign language interpreting is intertwined with the passage of VR legislation and the provision of VR services. The federal government's VR program was instrumental in supporting the establishment of the Registry of Interpreters for the Deaf (RID) in 1964. In 1965, while RID was still in its infancy, the Vocational Rehabilitation Act Amendments of 1965 authorized expansion of state rehabilitation services to include spending funds for interpreters, as part of case services to deaf and hard of hearing clients (Public Law 89-333, 1965). In subsequent years, VR provided funding for interpreter training programs that continue today. Federal legislation advanced the rights of persons with disabilities to have access to all aspects of American life, and, at the same time, created the demand for more interpreters. Knowledge of the role of VR federal legislation is key to understanding the growth of the sign language professional in the United States.

Salient Early VR Legislation

The public VR program had its beginning in 1917, with the passage of the Smith-Hughes Act. This legislation created a federal board with responsibility for VR services for disabled veterans. The next year, the Smith-Sears Veterans Rehabilitation Act, also known as the Soldier's Rehabilitation Act, expanded services for WWI veterans returning from war (Colorado State University, 2015). Two years later, the Smith-Fess Act created rehabilitation programs for civilian Americans with disabilities and provided partnership with states to provide such services (Colorado State University, 2015). For the next 33 years, several important acts related to the expansion of VR services were enacted. In 1954, Congress passed additional amendments to the Vocational Rehabilitation Act, to provide training at colleges and universities for rehabilitation professionals and expanded VR services to include persons with mental retardation and mental illness.

Modern VR Legislation and the Impact on Interpreters

By the mid-1960s, VR included services to deaf and deaf-blind individuals. The VR Act Amendments of 1965 (Public Law 89-333, Sec. 9) provided funding to pay for interpreters for the first time, as part of case service expenses. Later, the Vocational Rehabilitation Amendments of 1967 supported the construction and operation of the National Center for Deaf/Blind Youth and Adults.

The decade of the 1970s was a prolific period of legislative progress for persons with disabilities that had a profound impact on their ability to access all aspects of society. One of the most influential laws was the passage of the Rehabilitation Act of 1973 (U.S. Department of Education, (2015) that afforded to persons with disabilities the right to access buildings, transportation, and services receiving federal funds. Section 504 of this act prohibited discrimination on the basis of physical or mental handicap. This became known as the *civil rights act* for persons with disabilities and followed the 1960s civil rights laws that were enacted, prohibiting discrimination of persons on the basis of color or ethnicity, and the early 1970s "women's liberation" movement, prohibiting discrimination based on gender.

The 1978 Rehabilitation Comprehensive Services and Developmental Disabilities Amendments, or Public Law 95-602, Section 115 (d) (1), authorized federal funding for interpreter training programs to prepare interpreters to meet the communication needs of deaf individuals. Funding for interpreter education projects under this act was not appropriated until 1980. The Rehabilitation Services Administration (RSA) continues to fund interpreter education projects today through regional and national center grants.

In 1992, The Rehabilitation Act Amendments increased consumer choice and control in determining goals and services, and presumed that applications were employable unless proven otherwise (U.S. 102nd Congress, 1992). By 2008, amendments to the Americans with Disabilities Act (ADA) broadened the definition of *disability* to include impairments substantially limiting a major life activity (U.S. Equal Employment Opportunity Commission, 2008). Each of these legislative acts has impacted the lives of persons with disabilities and strengthened the federal commitment to equality and the right to access programs, buildings, and services for all persons.

Other Important Federal Legislation

The VR system was not the only important accessibility legislation in modern times that impacted on the provision of interpreting services to deaf and hard of hearing persons. In 1975, the Education for All Handicapped Children Act (Public Law 94-142) was passed, later referred to as *the mainstreaming law* (Colorado State University, 2015). This legislation ensured a free, appropriate, public education in the least-restrictive environment to all school-age children with disabilities. A demand for interpreters in K–12 settings was begun. This law today is codified as the Individuals with Disabilities Education Act (IDEA) (DO-IT, University of Washington, 2017).

One of the most sweeping pieces of legislation impacting the lives of persons with disabilities was the passage of the 1990 ADA. This law extended the rights of persons with disabilities to equal access into the private sector and not just to programs and entities receiving federal funding. The ADA focused on employment, architecture and transportation, public accommodations, telecommunications, and other services having a profound impact in all parts of American life (Colorado State University, 2015).

Deaf Movers and Shakers in the VR System

A history of the impact of VR services on persons who are deaf, hard of hearing, and deaf-blind cannot be complete without mention of a few of the deaf leaders in the VR movement. One individual was Boyce Williams (1910–1998), considered one of the greatest leaders in VR and a founding supporter of the Registry for Interpreters of the Deaf (RID). A current influential deaf leader is Annette Reichman, who has served as an agency

Boyce Williams. Courtesy of Gallaudet University Archives.

director of a deaf center, at state boards for rehabilitation and independent living, and in several influential positions at the federal level.

Boyce Williams became deaf at age 17 from spinal meningitis. He attended the Wisconsin School for the Deaf (WSD) and later Gallaudet College. He returned to WSD to teach math, later also teaching at the Indiana School for the Deaf. There, he became director of vocational training. Later, Mr. Williams became a federal consultant and later the first director of the federal Office of Deafness and Communications (ODC). In 1964, ODC provided funding to support the first workshop on interpreting at Ball State Teachers College that led to the establishment of RID. During the 1960s, thanks to Mr. Williams' efforts, RSA funded the National Leadership Training Program in the Areas of the Deaf and

Annette Reichman

was instrumental in securing funding for the National Interpreter Training Consortium (1974–1979). Boyce Williams was a key player for decades and served in many federal positions, including Board of Fellows for Gallaudet University. He was awarded two honorary doctoral degrees in 1958 and 1972. Dr. Williams died in 1998.

Annette Reichman is a deaf woman who has held influential federal positions within the rehabilitation field. She was the director of the Office of Special Institutions of the U.S. Department of Education and was a 2015 finalist candidate for the President of Gallaudet University. Some of her responsibilities include oversight of special institutions, including Gallaudet University, the National Technical Institute for the Deaf, and the American Printing House for the Blind. Ms. Reichman graduated from Gallaudet University with a B.A. in Psychology and later earned a M.S. degree in Rehabilitation Counseling with the Deaf (University of Arizona) and a Post-Baccalaureate Certificate in Post-Employment Training Administration of Programs Serving Deaf Consumers from San Diego State University. From 1999 to 2005, Ms. Reichman served as Chief of the Deafness and Communicative Disorders Branch of the U.S. Department of Education. She worked with state VR agencies to promote opportunities for deaf, deaf-blind, and hard of hearing persons. She previously served as a project officer for two national interpreter training federal grants, overseeing federal and regional grant centers funded under RSA to increase the quality and quantity of interpreters. She currently is the superintendent of the Arizona State Schools for the Deaf and Blind.

FEDERAL-STATE VR PARTNERSHIP

The RSA works in partnership with state VR agencies to serve individuals with disabilities. RSA awards grants to state VR agencies to provide a wide variety of employment-related services to VR consumers, to prepare for and obtain employment. A federal mandate gives priority services to those with significant disabilities first, if a state has insufficient funding to serve all of its eligible consumers. In 2015, RSA awarded states and U.S. territories more than $3 billion in grants to assist individuals with disabilities in obtaining employment (Rehabilitation Services Administration, 2015a).

Interpreters working within the VR system need to understand not only the goal of VR but also the array of services provided within the VR process. As with any specialized system, there is a body of specialized knowledge, vocabulary, and processes unique to the system. A skilled interpreter needs to be familiar with the knowledge and skills unique to VR interpreting and have an understanding of the VR process.

AN OVERVIEW OF THE VR PROCESS

Application and Eligibility Determination. Although the VR process may vary slightly from state to state, the general process is the same across states. The first step is for an individual to apply to a state VR agency and the determination of eligibility. "Eligible individuals are those who have a physical or mental impairment that results in a substantial impediment to employment, who can benefit from vocational rehabilitation (VR) services for employment, and who require VR services" (Rehabilitation Services Administration, 2015b).

Working with a VR Counselor. Once the consumer is determined to be eligible for services, the individual meets with a rehabilitation counselor. VR counselors may serve a general caseload, that is, serve consumers with one or more disabilities or may specialize in serving a particular group of individuals, such as rehabilitation counselors for the deaf (RCDs). An RCD is a rehabilitation counselor who has graduate education related to the unique needs of deaf, deaf-blind, and hard of hearing individuals and who can communicate with these consumers.

Individualized Plan for Employment. The VR counselor and the consumer will develop an individual plan of employment (IPE). The IPE will describe the specific services needed to achieve a specific employment goal. Emphasis is placed on competitive employment consistent with the individual's strengths, abilities, interests, and that is based on consumer informed choice.

Provision of Services. Once the IPE is complete, the counselor provides the services as proscribed. These services may include employment counseling and guidance, vocational or on-the-job training or postsecondary education, and physical or mental restoration services.

Employment and Case Closure. Once services are completed, the VR consumer is placed in a job. The counselor will provide any needed support services, such as interpreters or other accommodations that the employee needs to succeed. The VR consumer who remains employed for 60–90 days and has achieved the IPE goals will be considered successfully placed, and the case will be closed.

Working with VR Agencies

Interpreters may be called to work with a variety of VR counselors and consumers. Interpreters can be called to provide services anywhere during the VR process, such as intake interviews, eligibility determination, and the development of an IPE. Some hearing VR counselors with general caseloads may hire interpreters for meetings with deaf consumers. Interpreters may also work with RCDs who may have hearing consumers on their caseload, or with a hard of hearing consumer who does not know sign language.

VR interpreters can provide services under several different employment models. Each employment model may have vastly different expectations on how the interpreter provides services. Interpreters can be an employee of a VR agency working in the office or the community with consumers receiving services. Interpreters can be a designated interpreter for an RCD or a hearing counselor with a large number of deaf, deaf-blind, or hard of hearing consumers. Interpreters can also be hired as a private-practice interpreter on an hourly basis by either a VR interpreter referral service or a community interpreter service.

Interpreter as a VR Employee

Many VR agencies that employ deaf professionals and work with deaf VR consumers hire full-time agency interpreters. The full-time VR interpreter may be a *designated interpreter* for one or more deaf professionals. Full-time interpreters may also be employed as *staff interpreters* to provide interpreting services to VR consumers throughout the VR process. The roles and responsibilities of these interpreters may be different from the independent contract interpreter. For example, VR staff interpreters may be expected to report back to the VR counselor, make notes in the case file, and share information about the consumer during case meetings. They can be seen as part of the VR professional team. A designated interpreter may have a more limited scope of responsibilities interpreting only for the deaf professionals and reporting only to these professionals. Both VR staff and designated interpreters are expected to be familiar with the VR process and specialized terminology in addition to being qualified interpreters.

Interpreter as an Independent Contractor

Many VR services are provided in the community, such as doctor's offices, technical schools, colleges and universities, and community agencies, such as local transportation services and technology providers. VR agencies may hire independent contract interpreters either individually, through their own referral office, or through a local interpreter management company to interpret for consumers in community settings. These interpreters may be in addition to staff interpreters or by agencies with no staff interpreters. Contract interpreters may provide services for a one-time assignment or may interpret over a period of time, such as for on-the-job training.

Roles Conflict

Conflicts can happen when there is not a clear understanding of the interpreter's role. Consider the following example based on a real experience:

> A VR counselor has worked with a deaf consumer for several years, preparing this person for employment. Finally, the deaf VR consumer is scheduled for a job interview for an office staff position with a desirable local company that is known to have good wages and benefits. An hourly contract interpreter is hired to interpret the job interview. During the interview, the interviewer says that everyone takes turns making coffee in the mornings. The VR consumer turns to the interpreter and says, "I don't do kitchen duties."
>
> The interpreter voices the comment, and the interview is terminated. The VR consumer is not hired. The consumer is not sure why she wasn't hired. The VR counselor calls the interpreter and inquires what happened during the interview.

Independent contract interpreters may strictly follow the National Association of the Deaf-Registry for Interpreters for the Deaf (NAD-RID) Code of Professional Conduct (CPC), expect to sign or voice all direct statements, and have no expectation to report back to a VR counselor. They may view a request to report as a violation of confidentiality. The VR counselor, however, may have the same expectations of contract interpreters as for VR staff interpreters. Consider the same example with a staff interpreter, as follows:

> A VR counselor has worked with a deaf consumer for several years, preparing this person for employment. Finally, the deaf VR consumer is scheduled for a job interview for an office staff position with a desirable local company that is known to have good wages and benefits. The VR staff interpreter goes to interpret the job interview. During the interview, the interviewer says that everyone takes turns making coffee in the mornings. The VR consumer turns to the interpreter and says, "I don't do kitchen duties."

The interpreter asks for a moment to speak to the VR consumer and further explains that all workers equally share the coffee detail, and the consumer is not being singled out for this task. The VR consumer understands at this point and is willing to share the coffee duty with the other workers as part of her employment. The interview continues and ends with the interviewer being favorable toward the job interview. The staff interpreter reports back to the counselor and makes a note about the coffee question in the case file, so the counselor can later discuss this further with the VR consumer.

Conflicts can happen when the interpreters and the consumers are not aware of roles, responsibilities, and expectations when working with a variety of interpreters throughout the VR process. Additionally, contract interpreters may not have specialized knowledge of the VR system and terminology, rendering them less effective at times than a staff interpreter or an interpreter aware of the VR process.

Essential Skills, Knowledge, and Attitudes for Interpreters Working in VR Settings

Interpreters interested in working in VR settings are expected to be competent interpreters and also possess specialized knowledge of the VR process. Specialization is the provision of services within a defined and focused setting or with a unique population. A specialist is ". . . a practitioner who through advanced training, acquisition of specialized skills and knowledge, and experience distinguishes her/himself as being uniquely qualified for the specialized work" (Witter-Merithew, 2010, p. 9). It is recognized that generalist competence and experience must be acquired before specialization occurs. For example, RID strongly recommends an individual hold a generalist certificate (e.g., National Interpreter Certification [NIC]) and have five years of interpreting experience along with required legal training prior to sitting for the Specialty Certificate: Legal (SC:L) exam; however, the SC:L has been under a moratorium since 2016 (Registry for Interpreters for the Deaf, 2018).

Essential Knowledge for VR Interpreters

Given that the curricula of many interpreter education programs (IEPs) tend to devote considerable time to language learning, the interpretation process, and interpreting practice over two to four years of academic study, often there is little time available to fully expose students to interpreting in VR and related specialized settings. Students graduating from IEPs are prepared at best as entry-level professionals entering the interpreting workforce. Many experience a "readiness to work" gap, whereby additional mentoring and highly supervised experiences are needed to become qualified to work and obtain high-level state or national interpreting credentials and, increasingly, state licensure.

What specialized knowledge is needed to interpret in VR settings? Experts over the past 20 years have highlighted some of the specialized knowledge needed to provide quality interpreting within VR, including:

- A broad understanding of career theory and barriers to employment: attitudinal, architectural, and lack of consumer employment readiness skills
- Knowledge of the VR system and processes both federally and within state VR agencies, such as work readiness, consumer ability and aptitude assessment, employment placement, and on-the-job preparation (NCIEC, 2014a; NCIEC VR Work Team, 2012d; Northwestern Connecticut Community-Technical College and the University of Tennessee, 1995)
- Understanding the unique terminology, jargon and acronyms, and abbreviations used in VR settings, such as those related to the social welfare system (Medicare, Medicaid, food stamps, etc.), audiology testing and evaluations, immigration, etc. (NCIEC VR Work Team, 2012a)
- Understanding of the roles and responsibilities of VR personnel (NCIEC, 2014a)
- Knowledge of the wide variety of community settings in which VR services are provided, such as medical, employment, and mental health, is needed by the VR interpreter (Winston, 2010; Cokely & Winston, 2009)
- Understanding of the wide range of consumer abilities and the impact on communication needs (Winston, 2010; Cokely & Winston, 2009)
- Knowledge of settings in which VR services are provided, such as VR agencies and postsecondary or vocational, medical, mental health, independent living, and legal settings (Cokely & Winston, 2009)
- A strong grasp of assistive technology, such as cochlear implants, hearing aids, videophone, video-relay services, video remote interpreting, and the internet (Cokely & Winston, 2009)

Essential Skills for VR Interpreters

Although general and specialized knowledge is critical for interpreters to provide services in VR settings, skills are also critical. According to the National Consortium of Interpreter Education Centers (NCIEC, 2012), VR competency categories incorporate knowledge of VR systems, general VR knowledge, language and multiculturalism, communication, interpreting skills and knowledge, and professionalism. Some essential skills within these categories identified over the past 21 years include the following:

- Strong ASL and signed English skills (Cokely & Winston, 2009).
- Strong range of communication modalities (signed, oral, written, tactile) (Northwestern Connecticut Community-Technical College, 1995). Interpreters will work with many consumers and professionals within the VR system. The interpreter needs to be able to meet the individual communication needs of each person for whom they provide services.
- Interpreting skills and competencies that meet state/agency requirements and qualifications, such as educational level, interpreting credentials, or certification and licensure (Winston, 2010).
- Ability to apply the NAD-RID CPC (NCIEC VR Work Team, 2012a) in the moment in an ethical manner.
- Ethical decision-making and problem-solving skills (NCIEC VR Work Team, 2012a).
- Ability to apply Demand Control Theory (NCIEC, 2014c), which is one popular approach to ethical decision-making, whereby the interpreter evaluates the demands of the situation (environmental, linguistic, within the individual, between individuals), available controls (responses to the situation), and the resulting effects of each control (decision) when applied.
- Professional behavior (Northwestern Connecticut Community-Technical College, 1995; NCIEC VR Work Team, 2012a), such as appropriate on-the-job behavior, ethical conduct, and commitment to professional development.
- Multicultural competency. VR serves consumers with disabilities from a wide variety of backgrounds, including those from racial and ethnic minorities, those in the LGBTQ community, individuals from remote and

rural areas, and those with little to no work history or those with limited language proficiency (NCIEC VR Work Team, 2012a; Winston, 2010).

- Skill in working with a Deaf interpreters, including CDIs to meet the communication needs of unique populations of consumers who are deaf. (NCIEC, 2014b).
- Soft skills in working with people (NCIEC VR Work Team, 2012b). Soft skills are those involved in relationships with other people or how you approach your work. Soft skills include social graces and etiquette, building rapport, making professional introductions and exits, time management, accepting responsibility, and being a team player.

Essential Attitudes for VR Interpreters

Positive attitudinal traits are not specific to only VR settings and consumers. Some settings, such as mental health facilities, emphasize the need for positive regard. The NAD-RID CPC requires respect for consumers and colleagues. Some of the following attitudes have been highlighted as essential qualities for interpreters working throughout the VR system:

- Respect and sensitivity for diverse populations, including diverse linguistic populations, and individuals with other or multiple disabilities (NCIEC VR Work Team, 2012a; Registry of Interpreters for the Deaf, 2005)
- Unconditional positive regard for the consumer without regard to their circumstances, backgrounds, and mental status (Napier, 2011)
- Professional demeanor (Northwestern Connecticut Community-Technical College, 1995), indicating respect for all parties involved in the interpreted event and a commitment by the interpreter to always display professional behaviors
- Commitment of ongoing advancement of skills and knowledge (NCIEC VR Work Team, 2012d)
- Respect for and commitment to work with deaf interpreters and recognition that they may be best qualified to provide interpreting services, either alone, or with a hearing interpreter, where critical communication is essential or where there is an imbalance of power or experience between the consumer and the interpreter or consumers who are hearing

Issues and Challenges of Interpreting within the VR System

Clarity of Interpreter Role

As mentioned earlier, interpreters within the VR system can be either full- or part-time employees of the agency, designated interpreters for one or more VR professional who is deaf, or hourly contracted interpreters. It is important that the interpreter, the consumer, and the VR counselor have a clear understanding of the interpreter's role. Will the interpreter be expected to report back to the counselor or make notes in a case file? Does the interpreter expect that all assignment-related information is confidential and not reportable to the counselor or anyone? Does the counselor see the interpreter as part of the VR team or as an outside individual contracted interpreter? Does the consumer expect that anything he/she expresses to the interpreter in private will be kept confidential and not be shared with the counselor? Regardless of the model under which the interpreter provides services, everyone that is a party to the interpreted event must have the same understanding in order to avoid conflicts.

Interpreter or Job Coach or Both

Interpreters are sometimes hired as job coaches for VR consumers with limited or no prior work exposure or experience. A job coach is a specialist hired to work alongside a new employee, sometimes performing and demonstrating the job task and helping an employee learn to perform a new job. The job coach may also assist the employee with learning the interpersonal skills needed to succeed on the job and interact and work appropriately with supervisors and co-workers. When needed, the job coach will help the employee to learn and apply social skills. Job coaching responsibilities can also include additional tasks, such as advocacy, employee travel training, and interpreting on the job.

For VR consumers who are in job training, the difference between an interpreter and a job coach who interprets may be confusing. For the interpreter, the responsibilities and expectations of role can be vastly different. The length of the assignment and pay can be quite different between the two roles. Job coaching opportunities open the employment opportunities for interpreters working in the community. It is significantly easier to train interpreters with the skills needed as a job coach than it is to teach job coaches ASL and prepare them to understand the Deaf community. A business that hires a job coach who knows ASL may still need to hire a professional interpreter for a variety of situations, such as awards recognition ceremonies, yearly evaluations, and disputes.

Deaf Interpreter/Hearing Interpreter Teams

More and more Deaf interpreters are working alone to provide translation services (written English document or form to ASL) or together with hearing interpreters. This may be due to a power imbalance, such as in sensitive cases, whereby the number of hearing people (interpreter and one or more hearing service providers) outnumber the deaf consumer, negatively impacting communication. A Deaf interpreter may be the best option when the cultural experiences of the deaf consumer and the interpreter are shared, and interpretation can be more accurate. This can be especially true in mental health and legal settings, but is not limited to any particular setting. The hearing interpreter may be initially approached for an assignment within the VR system. If the hearing interpreter believes that a Deaf interpreter is needed, he or she may need to strongly advocate for such services, especially with hearing general-caseload VR counselors who may not be familiar with what a Deaf interpreter brings to the process. This scenario will continue to be true in many instances until such time that CDIs are available and the community understands the benefits of providing both hearing and/or deaf interpreters.

Research and National Needs Assessments

During 2005–2010, the National Interpreter Education Center, along with the regional centers under the umbrella of NCIEC, conducted and reported on a variety of national interpreter-needs assessments. These included interpreter education needs, practitioner (interpreter) needs, Deaf consumer needs, interpreter referral agency needs, and VR service needs.

The VR needs assessments resulted in four reports, from 2009 to 2011. Below is a summary of these assessment surveys for VR.

VR Needs Assessment Final Report (Cokely & Winston, 2009). State coordinators for the deaf (SCDs), state RCDs, state VR agency leaders, and staff were surveyed to investigate the needs of VR personnel. Eighty state VR agencies nationwide were surveyed, with 34 state VR agencies reporting. Of the agencies, 70% were general VR agencies or combined general blind/visually impaired agencies. All responding agencies served deaf, hard of hearing, deaf-blind, or late-deafened consumers. A majority (91%) of Deaf consumers needed interpreting services, with RSA finding that consumers who are in rural areas, or were "low functioning," were the hardest groups for which to find interpreters. State VR agencies were able to meet the interpreting needs 90% of the time or better for career assessment, employment placement, intake and eligibility, and employment preparation. Many VR settings, however, were provided with unqualified interpreters (12–53%), as reported by the VR personnel. For agencies seeking full-time staff interpreters, 44% reported that they were unable to fulfill these positions. Additionally, 82% of the VR personnel who responded said that interpreters were less available over the past five-year period. Factors affecting interpreter availability included the increase of video-relay service centers, interpreter shortages, less-competitive salaries, and unpredictable time needs, making it difficult to schedule interpreters at the last minute.

VR Interpreter Practitioner Interview Findings (Winston, 2010). Interpreters who directly provide services to state VR agencies were surveyed about their current work status, working conditions, settings in which services were provided, and opportunities and challenges in the VR system. Eighteen VR interpreters responded to the survey. They were fairly evenly divided as to role, with 39% full-time staff interpreters, 33% part-time staff interpreters, and 28% contract/freelance interpreters. VR agencies varied on credentials requirements, with 11% of the interpreters reporting no minimum credential requirements, and 44% requiring national certification. Most (44%) reported that their state had no minimum educational requirements. Interpreters reported interpreting for a wide variety of consumers, including deaf, hard of hearing, deaf-blind, and late-deafened individuals as well as those with limited language. VR settings in which interpreting services were provided most often to least often included:

employment placement, postsecondary, career assessment, medical, mental health, intake and eligibility, independent living, K–12, transition related, and legal. Some challenges and disincentives to working in VR included the wide variety of consumers, including those challenged by immigrant status, low linguistic competence, and limited experience; staff interpreter provides services for a variety of constituents including consumers, VR personnel, potential employers, and other service providers; the addition of other administrative responsibilities in addition to interpreting.

RESOURCES FOR INTERPRETERS

There are a variety of excellent resources for interpreters to learn more about working within the VR system. Many of these can be found online. All current and future interpreters are encouraged to learn about the VR system, which plays such a vital role in the lives of persons with disabilities, include those who are deaf, hard of hearing, late deafened, deaf-blind, and from various cultures and backgrounds.

A. National Consortium of Interpreter Education Centers (NCIEC) of Interpreter Education Centers (NCIEC)
   www.interpretereducation.org/specialization/vocational-rehabilitation/
   This website provides an overview of interpreting in the VR setting, including various documents prepared by the VR Work Team. Links to resources developed through the NCIEC collaborative are provided.

B. Vocational Rehabilitation Glossary, Northeastern University Region Interpreter Education Center (NURIEC) (2012).
   http://www.interpretereducation.org/aspiring-interpreter/mentorship/mentoring-toolkit/vocational-rehabilitation-glossary/
   This searchable database provides an explanation of commonly used vocational rehabilitation terms. Definitions and descriptions of terms are provided in both written English and ASL.

C. National Rehabilitation Association
   www.nationalrehab.org
   This is the website of the National Rehabilitation Association professionals.

D. Rehabilitation Services Administration

http://www2.ed.gov/about/offices/list/osers/rsa/index.html
The RSA oversees grant programs that help individuals with physical or mental disabilities to obtain employment and live more independently through the provision of such supports as counseling, medical and psychological services, job training, and other individualized services.

E.   VR4HearingLoss

www.vr4hearingloss.net/
This website orients VR professionals to the range of needs and services for persons who are hard of hearing or late deafened. Information is provided in written English, and videos are interpreted into ASL.

F.   The National Clearinghouse of Rehabilitation Training Materials

https://ncrtm.ed.gov/
This site is a central repository for accessing and disseminating rehabilitation training resources, such as VR reports, curricula, webinars, and needs assessments developed by RSA-funded interpreter education projects, including those under the NCIEC.

References

Butterworth, J., Hall, A., Smith, F., Migliore, Al, Winsor, J., . . . & Sulewski, J. (2012). *StateData.info - Data Notes: Newsworthy findings from statedata.info and related data sets.* Boston: Institute for Community Inclusion, University of Massachusetts–Boston. Retrieved from https://www.statedata.info/datanotes/

Cokely, D., & Winston, E. (2009). *Vocational rehabilitation needs assessment final report.* National Interpreter Education Centers. Retrieved from http://www.interpretereducation.org/wp-content/uploads/2011/06/FinalVRReport2009.pdf

Colorado State University. (2015). *Resources for disabled students: A brief history of legislation.* Fort Collins, CO: CSU. Retrieved from http://rds.colostate.edu/history-of-legislation

Council of State Administrators of Vocational Rehabilitation. (2011–2012). Investing in America: The public vocational rehabilitation (VR) program—employing the talents of qualified Americans with disabilities in the workplace during challenging economic times. Retrieved from http://www.ct.gov/brs/lib/brs/pdfs/investinginamerica.pdf

DO-IT, University of Washington. (2018). What Is the Individuals with Disabilities Education Act? Retrieved from https://www.washington.edu/doit/what-individuals-disabilities-education-act

Gallaudet University Library. (2014). *Local and regional deaf populations.* Washington, DC: GU. Retrieved from http://libguides.gallaudet.edu/content.php?pid=119476&sid=1029190

Institute on Disability. (2014). *2014 annual disability statistics compendium.* Durham, MA: University of New Hampshire. Retrieved from https://disabilitycompendium.org/sites/default/files/user-uploads/Archives/Previous DisabilityCompendiumReleases/2014%20Compendium%20Release.pdf

Napier, J. (2011). "It's not what they say but the way they say it." A content analysis of interpreter and consumer perceptions of signed language interpreting in Australia. *International Journal of Social Language, 207,* 59–87. doi: 10.115/IJSL.2011.003.

NCIEC. (2014a). *Interpreting in VR settings: Module 1: VR as a federally mandated system study guide.* n.p.: NCIEC. Retrieved from http://www.interpretereducation.org/wp-content/uploads/2014/04/Study_Guide_Module_1_VR_as_a_System.pdf

NCIEC. (2014b). *Interpreting in VR settings: Module 2: Roles and responsibilities study guide, Spring 2014.* n.p.: NCIEC. Retrieved from http://www.interpretereducation.org/wp-content/uploads/2014/04/Module-2-Roles-and-Responsibilities-Study-Guide-5.pdf

NCIEC. (2014c). *Interpreting in VR settings: Module 4: Interpreting for VR clients—knowledge study guide, Spring 2014.* n.p.: NCIEC. Retrieved from http://www.interpretereducation.org/wp-content/uploads/2014/04/Module-4-Interpreting-for-VR-Clients-Knowledge.pdf

NCIEC VR Work Team. (2012a). *Interpreting in VR settings: Domains and competencies.* n.p.: NCIEC. Retrieved from http://www.interpretereducation.org/wp-content/uploads/2012/05/VR-Interpreter-Competencies.pdf

NCIEC VR Work Team. (2012b). *Interpreting in VR settings: Literature review.* n.p.: NCIEC. Retrieved from http://www.interpretereducation.org/wp-content/uploads/2012/05/Interpreting-in-VR-Settings-Lit-Review-FINAL.pdf

NCIEC VR Work Team. (2012c). *Interpreting in VR settings: Annotated bibliography.* n.p.: NCIEC. Retrieved from http://www.interpretereducation.org/wp-content/uploads/2012/05/VR-Initiative-Annotated-Bibliography-5-17-12-FINAL.pdf

NCIEC VR Work Team. (2012d). *Interpreting in VR settings: Expert and focus group findings.* n.p.: NCIEC. Retrieved from http://www.interpretereducation.org/wp-content/uploads/2012/05/Expert-and-Focus-Group-Findings.pdf

Northwestern Connecticut Community-Technical College and The University of Tennessee. (1995). *Professional Development Endorsement System.* National Interpreter Education Project. Winstead, CT: NCCC.

Public Law 89-333. (November 8, 1965). Statute 79, Vocational Rehabilitation Act Amendments of 1965, SEC 2 (a), Sections 1, 2, and 3. Washington, DC: U.S. Government Publishing Office. Retrieved from http://www.gpo.gov/fdsys/pkg/STATUTE-79/pdf/STATUTE-79-Pg1282.pdf

Public Law 95-602. (November 6, 1978). Statute 2955, Vocational Rehabilitation Act Amendments of 1965 SEC 114 (d)(1). Washington, DC: U.S. Government

Publishing Office. Retrieved from http://www.gpo.gov/fdsys/pkg/STATUTE -92/pdf/STATUTE-92-Pg2955.pdf

Registry of Interpreters for the Deaf. (2018). Certificates under moratorium: Specialist Certificate: Legal (SC:L) Retried from https://www.rid.org/ rid-certification-overview/certifications-under-moratorium/

Registry of Interpreters for the Deaf. (2005). *NAD-RID code of professional conduct*. Alexandria, VA: RID. Retrieved from https://drive.google.com/ file/d/0B-_HBAap35D1R1MwYk9hTUpuc3M/view?pli=1

Rehabilitation Services Administration. (2015a). *Vocational rehabilitation state grants*. Washington, DC: RSA. Retrieved from https://rsa.ed.gov/programs .cfm?pc=basic-vr

Rehabilitation Services Administration. (2015b). Vocational rehabilitation state grants: Eligibility. Washington, DC: RSA. Retrieved from https://rsa.ed.gov/ programs.cfm?pc=basic-vr

The Interpreter in Vocational Rehabilitation "Modules 1–4." (1995). The University of Tennessee, National Interpreter Training Center.

U.S. 102nd Congress. (1992). H.R. 5482 - Rehabilitation Act Amendments of 1992. Retrieved from https://www.congress.gov/bill/102nd-congress/house-bill/5482

U.S. Department of Education. (2018). Vocational rehabilitation state grants: Laws, regulations and guidance. Retrieved from https://www2.ed.gov/programs/ rsabvrs/legislation.html

U.S. Department of Education. (2015). The Rehabilitation Act of 1973. As amended. Retrieved from https://www2.ed.gov/policy/speced/reg/narrative.html

U.S. Department of Education. (2014). *Annual report fiscal year 2012: Report on federal activities under the Rehabilitation Act of 1973, as amended*. Washington, DC: U.S. DOE. Retrieved from http://www2.ed.gov/about/reports/annual/ rsa/2012/rsa-2012-annual-report.pdf

U.S. Equal Employment Opportunity Commission (2008). ADA Amendments Act of 2008. Retrieved from https://www.eeoc.gov/laws/statutes/adaaa_info.cfm

Winston, E. (2010). *Vocational rehabilitation interpreter practitioner: interview findings*. Boston, MA: National Interpreter Education Center. Retrieved from http://www.interpretereducation.org/wp-content/uploads/2011/06/FinalVR_ InterpreterReport.pdf

Winston, E., & Dahms, K. (2010). *Vocational rehabilitation—needs assessment synthesis analysis*. National Consortium of Interpreter Education Centers.

Witter-Merithew, A. (2010). *Conceptualizing a framework for specialization in ASL-English interpreting: A report of project findings and recommendations*. Greeley, CO: Mid-America Regional Interpreter Education Center (MARIE). Retrieved from http://www.interpretereducation.org/wp-content/uploads/2011/08/ ConceptFrameworkSpecialization.pdf

7

Interpreting in Legal Contexts

CARLA M. MATHERS

Legal interpreting covers a broad array of settings. When considering the legal interpreting practitioner, one normally envisions courtroom interpreting, interpreting for the police during an investigation, or interpreting at a law office for a consultation. However, many community interpreting assignments, such as educational interpreting and healthcare interpreting, can wander into areas rife with legal implications. For example, when an assault victim is brought into the emergency room, it is likely the police will want to conduct an interview. Likewise, when an interpreter is interpreting a civics course in high school, and the class holds a mock trial. Or, if a Deaf person is admitted to the emergency room and needs to have a consent-to-treatment form sight translated into American Sign Language (ASL). These community assignments quickly turn into assignments with legal overtones or implications. Although training in legal interpreting might be helpful in these settings, it is usually not necessary to hold legal certification to render an effective interpretation in these community settings. The point to remember is that the law permeates society at all levels, and a general understanding of the legal system is helpful for all interpreters regardless of the setting.

GENERALIST COMPETENCIES

In preparing individuals to engage in a practice profession, curriculum developers look to competency-based standards to create a sequence of instruction. Competencies "are statements of the characteristics that graduating students should demonstrate which indicate that [students] are prepared to perform and function independently in professional practice."[1] Professionals use competency-based standards to reflect and discuss their work with peers. Organizations use competency-based standards to evaluate performance and award credentials. National certification is recognized by the Registry of Interpreters for the Deaf. National certification provides "an independent verification of the interpreter's knowledge and abilities allowing them to be nationally recognized for the delivery of interpreting services among diverse users of signed and spoken languages."[2] Hence, competencies are the evidence-based areas of knowledge, skills, and abilities that allow us to identify qualified entry-level practitioners. A critical assumption of the legal interpreting specialist is that she or he has an established and effective generalist practice and has interpreted in a wide variety of general interpreting settings. It is worth a quick inspection, then, at the competency-based standards governing the work of an entry-level interpreter practitioner that must be mastered prior to specializing. These standards apply whether the interpreter practitioner is Deaf or not, although there is an additional set of recognized generalist competency standards developed specifically for Deaf interpreters.[3]

Generalist competencies have been grouped into five domains, each setting forth a unique set of knowledge, skills, and abilities.[4] The domains include interpreting theory and knowledge, human relations, language skills, interpreting skills, and professionalism. The domains recognize that interpreters are human service providers, working within a wide range of interactions between individuals of different cultures who use different languages. Interpreter-preparation programs develop their curricula to build skills and knowledge in each of these domains for their graduates to be considered able to practice in the profession independently and competently.

1. Frere, C. (n.d.). *Developing a competency based curriculum.* Morgantown, WV: West Virginia University. Retrieved from http://www.hsc.wvu.edu/faculty-development/assessment-materials/developing-a-competency-based-curriculum/.

2. Registry of Interpreters for the Deaf, Inc. Certification overview. Retrieved from https://www.rid.org/rid-certification-overview/

3. NCIEC. (2014). Deaf interpreter curriculum. Retrieved from http://www.diinstitute.org/learning-center/deaf-interpreter-curriculum/

4. Witter-Merithew, A., Johnson, L., & Taylor, M. (2004). A national perspective on entry-to-practice competencies. In E. Maroney (Ed.), *Proceedings of the 15th National Convention of the Conference of Interpreter Trainers.* Fremont, CA: Conference of Interpreter Trainers. Retrieved at http://www.cit-asl.org

Once competent as generalists, many interpreters seek to specialize in the legal setting.

As mentioned earlier, evidence-based standards exist, defining the competencies for Deaf interpreters.[5] From 2005 to 2010, the Regional Interpreter Education Center at Northeastern University convened an expert group of Deaf interpreter practitioners who conducted focus groups of Deaf interpreters and educators, to examine the work of competent Deaf interpreters. In three major areas, they found that Deaf interpreter competencies differed from the generalist interpreter competencies and required additional training and attention. Those additional competencies include consumer assessment, language, communication, culture, and interpreting practice.[6] To address these areas, the team created a curriculum designed expressly to educate Deaf interpreters in the practice of interpreting.[7] Although this curriculum addresses domains across content areas, a specialist curriculum for Deaf interpreters in court and legal systems has been developed by the National Consortium of Interpreter Education Centers (NCIEC).

Specialist Competencies

In 2012, led by the Mid-America Regional Interpreter Education Center (MARIE), the NCIEC's Legal Interpreting Work Team drafted a working document entitled *Toward Effective Practice: Specialist Competencies of the Interpreter Practicing within Court and Legal Settings*.[8] The document sets forth five domains in which the legal interpreting specialist must be competent, including court and legal systems knowledge, general legal theory, court and legal interpreting protocol, interpreting knowledge and skills, and professional development.[9] A discussion of the knowledge required

---

5. NCIEC. (2014). Deaf interpreter competencies deaf interpreter curriculum. Appendix A. Retrieved from http://www.diinstitute.org/learning-center/deaf-interpreter-curriculum/
6. Northeastern University Regional Interpreter Education Center. (2011). Deaf interpreter: Effective practices and research findings. Boston, MA: College of Social Sciences and Humanities. Retrieved from http://www.northeastern.edu/riec/projects-activities/deaf-interpreter-initiative/english/
7. *Supra*. n. 2.
8. NCIEC Legal Interpreting Work Team. (2012). *Toward effective practice: Specialist competencies of the interpreter practicing within court and legal settings*.
9. NCIEC Legal Interpreting Work Team. *Toward effective practice*.

in each of these domains provides an understanding of the qualifications, demands, decision latitude, and cultural and linguistic considerations necessary to be a competent legal practitioner.

Court and Legal Systems Knowledge

Having competency in the domain of court and legal systems knowledge suggests that interpreters benefit from a holistic understanding of the American judicial system and how the various subsystems interrelate. Although much legal interpreting involves the judicial system, the American system of government contains three separate branches of government all dealing with the law. Congress drafts laws, and they are implemented and explained by Executive branch agencies. When conflicts arise as to the interpretation of a congressional statute or executive agency regulation, the judicial branch resolves the conflict through litigation of the case or controversy. Interpreters can find themselves interpreting a public hearing in the state capital, an administrative hearing on a Supplemental Security Income overpayment, or a criminal trial. Deaf citizens interact with and legal interpreters must be prepared to interpret in each branch of government. Hence, a healthy appreciation for the structure of government is critical.

Central to the American system of justice is the concept of *jurisdiction*. Jurisdiction is the power that a court has over a specific kind of legal dispute or specific parties in front of it. For the interpreter, this includes, for example, knowing the difference between the federal and state systems of justice and the appellate court systems. It includes an understanding of both substantive and procedural areas of law. Substantive areas of law include criminal law, civil law, family law, bankruptcy law, juvenile justice, and administrative law, among others. Each substantive area can further be broken down into the type of matter heard. For example, in family court, a matter might be a divorce, a paternity case, or a child custody matter. In the criminal system, substantive law includes various crimes, such as homicide, fraud, theft, assault, and battery, among others. In the civil system, substantive law includes causes of action (lawsuits) for malpractice, negligence, breach of contract, and trespass, among others. To say that someone specializes in legal interpreting is almost a misnomer, because the system is vast and contains a multitude of various types of content areas that run the gamut from an appeal in a bankruptcy case to a zoning hearing.

Procedural law is also an area of court and legal systems knowledge with which legal interpreters must be quite familiar. In the criminal context, procedural aspects include the various types of hearings, such as arraignments, status hearings, motions hearings, pretrial conferences, and trials, among others. In the civil arena, procedural aspects include events, such as mediations, discovery, hearings on motions to compel discovery, depositions, pretrial hearings, and trials, among other matters. Interpreters are often thrown into the mix mid-stream, and hence knowing where a case has been as well as what is likely to happen to the case in the future helps situate the interpretation in a manner meaningful to the Deaf participants. Knowing the procedural posture of a specific case also streamlines the legal interpreter's preparatory activities. For example, if a Deaf juror was chosen to serve on a trial, and a consistent team was not available for the duration, it would be ethically proper for the new interpreter to contact the interpreter who had been working the trial previously to discuss the linguistic and content-related information that will assist the new interpreter in rendering an accurate interpretation. Alternatively, if an interpreter was hired for a continued deposition, one liberal decision within the interpreter's latitude would be to reach out to the prior interpreter for contextual background on the content of the deposition. Finally, because Deaf citizens are increasingly chosen as jurors and face the full gamut of substantive and procedural law in both the criminal and civil justice systems, the legal interpreter must be well versed in how jury trials are conducted and the role of a jury in the trial.

Court and legal systems knowledge also compels an appreciation for the vertical structure of courts and how appeals are handled. The most relevant part for the interpreter is to understand the nature of the trial record and how it is used by the attorneys (and the interpreter) to preserve an issue for appeal. The attorney must, at trial, object to any ruling the judge makes that the attorney feels is improper.[10] If the attorney does not object immediately, the ability to file an appeal on that issue is lost. Interpreters are mindful of the record, because at times, the interpreter needs to assert

---

10. Federal Rules of Evidence, Rule 103 U.S. Government Printing Office: Washington, D.C. (2009).

her- or himself into the proceeding to, for example, ask for a clarification or control the pace. In such instances, the interpreter speaks in the third person to make the record clear that the interpreter, not the Deaf person, is interrupting.

A number of areas of legal theory and evidence law also directly affect the interpreter. For example, the interpreter must understand the nature of privileged communications and how it can constrain the various roles that an interpreter can play in a legal case. Privileged communications are confidential conversations between an attorney and a client for the purposes of obtaining legal advice. An interpreter interpreting in a privileged context cannot be compelled to testify, unless the Deaf client grants permission. This is an important parameter, because there are a number of times when it is legally proper to call the interpreter to testify as to a previously interpreted interaction. The evidentiary hearsay rule at times compels that an interpreter be called to testify to a prior interaction.[11] As a result, the doctrine of privileged communications constrains the roles that an interpreter can play in court.

A related area of legal systems knowledge concerns law enforcement at the local, state, and federal levels. When crimes occur or are alleged to have occurred, law enforcement officers engage in an investigation, which can manifest in a number of different ways. For example, detectives in a police department might want to interview a Deaf witness or victim as well as interview a Deaf suspect. This raises ethical conflict-of-interest issues for interpreters who become privy to one side of the story first and may unintentionally appear biased by using the discourse of the victim while interviewing the suspect. If the suspect then refuses to cooperate, believing the interpreter is biased, the goals of the investigation are thwarted. Legal interpreter practitioners carefully weigh all factors in their decision-making process and know how to explain these issues and assist law enforcement in properly staffing an investigation, to avoid these conflicts.

Legal interpreters must be versed in the substantive law governing law enforcement investigations, such as *Miranda v. Arizona*, and the limitations it places on law enforcement as well as the procedural aspects of the

---

11. Federal Rules of Evidence, Rule 602. U.S. Government Printing Office: Washington, D.C. (2009).

investigation and arrest process.[12] While growing up as a consumer of television in the United States, most people have heard the familiar words of the Miranda warnings; however, that incidental learning may be less accessible for some Deaf people. Further, the density of the content of the Miranda and the dearth of equivalent signs mean that legal interpreters must study and train prior to rendering an interpretation of the Miranda warnings in ASL. Other law enforcement procedures, such as grand jury investigations, often require interpreters when they have Deaf witnesses, and interpreters need to be aware of the special rules surrounding grand juries. For example, a grand jury is a prosecutorial tool constitutionally required in certain cases, and it can result in an indictment, which begins a criminal case. Grand jury interpreters essentially then are prohibited from accepting the work in the trial, because of the Court Interpreter Code of Professional Responsibility which disqualifies interpreters involved in the pre-charge phase of an investigation from interpreting for the court in the subsequent case.[13]

In terms of staffing law enforcement assignments, legal specialists know how to assist the investigation by ensuring a Deaf interpreter is retained during the investigation. Certain legal settings, such as law enforcement assignments, juvenile matters, and mental health proceedings, regardless of the consumer involved, are staffed with Deaf interpreters due to the high-stakes nature of the interpreting.[14] Other protocol issues for law enforcement interpreters include ensuring that the interview is preserved on video and that the camera is able to record the signing of both the Deaf person and the interpreting team.

Understanding the nature of courts and the American judicial system, then, forms the basis of the legal interpreter's standing as a specialist. Fortunately, there are many ways to gain competency in this arena that simply require motivation and time on the part of the aspiring legal interpreter.

---

12. *Miranda v. Arizona*, 384 U.S. 436 (1966).

13. Hewitt, William, E. (1994). Model code of professional responsibility for interpreters in the judiciary. In *Court interpretation: Model guides for policy and practice in state courts*. Richmond, VA: National Center for State Courts.

14. Cobb, M., Stewart, K., & Witter-Merithew, A. (Eds.). (2009). *Best practices: American sign language and English interpretation within court and legal settings*. np: NCIEC.

Legal Theory Specific to Interpretation

Much general legal theory relates to interpreters and the impact of various laws and legal theories on interpreting. Legal interpreters need a thorough understanding of the law of privileged communications and its relationship to staffing legal interpreting assignments, and of the law of evidence, which can, at times, compel the interpreter to become a witness in a legal case.[15] Interpreters can be called to testify to any interpreted interaction, unless the interaction was privileged. In a privileged matter, the interpreter cannot be called to testify, unless the Deaf person consents. It behooves the interpreter to know when the setting in which he or she is interpreting is privileged or not. There are several reasons why an interpreter might be called to testify about a prior interpretation. When subpoenaed by defense counsel to testify at a motion to suppress evidence, the interpreter should anticipate having the prior interpretation scrutinized by an expert witness. In this regard, the interpreter understands the legal standards by which the interpretation will be reviewed by the expert.[16] Legal interpreters anticipate being called to testify and have a general understanding of how to respond properly to a subpoena, how to prepare to testify, and how to present their credentials and discuss the prior work in a professional manner.

Finally, legal interpreters should be familiar with interpreter-related legislation, not only at the national level for legislation such as the Americans with Disabilities Act, but also state legal interpreting legislation and licensure statutes. Interpreter legislation typically details the qualifications to practice legal interpreting in a particular area. Many interpreter laws set forth where and when a Deaf interpreter may be required. Knowledge of interpreter-related laws prepares the interpreter to argue for inclusion of a Deaf interpreter, a team interpreter, or any number of other working conditions that might be justified by statute. Legal interpreters should know those seminal court cases that address the right to an interpreter. Most of the case law creating the right derives from spoken language interpreted cases; however, most apply equally to cases interpreted for Deaf people.

---

15. Mathers, C. (2002). To testify or not to testify: That is the question. *VIEWS*. Retrieved from http://www.rid.org/content/index.cfm/AID/70
16. Mathers, C. (2006). The murky waters of testifying in court. *VIEWS*. Retrieved from http://www.rid.org/content/index.cfm/AID/70

In fact, Deaf people have additional laws that provide them more access to justice than limited-English-speaking participants, such as the right to serve on a jury.

Protocol, Ethics, and Decision-Making

The third domain in which legal practitioners demonstrate competent knowledge relates to ethics and protocol. *Protocol* generally refers to that set of guidelines and practices that are expected from a professional in a certain setting. Protocol includes those ethical guidelines that apply specifically to signed language and spoken language interpreters in court. Those guidelines were developed by the courts through committees generally comprised of attorneys, administrators, judges, spoken language interpreters, and some-times, signed language interpreters.[17] Protocol examples include speaking in the third person for the record when asserting an interpreting need, routing all communications with a Deaf witness who is testifying through the court, asking for a clarification, and knowing when certain discourse in court is not to be interpreted, even though it might be heard by the interpreter. Protocol is not debatable, although there is room for a range of decisions, both liberal and conservative, to be made. Legal interpreters support their decisions with legal theory, case law, protocol, and ethics.

Most courts and ethical codes define interpreters as officers of the court.[18] This designation carries with it a number of duties and obligations that may be unfamiliar to interpreters not trained in legal interpreting. For example, as a court officer, the interpreter's primary duty is to preserve the integrity of the interpreted proceedings. Because an interpreter is typically the only one who knows sign language in the room, when something within the realm of signed language or Deaf culture happens and compromises the proceedings, the court interpreter's duty to act and inform the court is trig-gered. The power to interrupt the proceedings is not to be taken lightly and must be used cautiously and not abused, or the credibility of the entire pro-fession is threatened. Officers of the court must also avoid appearing overly friendly with any of the participants, to retain the semblance of neutrality. The interpreter might appear to a Deaf person to be aloof or even rude.

---

17. NCIEC Legal Interpreting Work Team. *Toward effective practice.*
18. NCIEC Legal Interpreting Work Team. *Toward effective practice.*

Legal practitioners must also know when the designation of *officer of the court* does not apply and ensure that the proper ethical guidelines are followed. For example, as discussed below, the officer of the court is required to disclose prior knowledge of a Deaf litigant under certain circumstances on the record in open court.[19] This is required protocol. However, if the same specialist is interpreting in a law office or other setting in which the officer of the court designation does not apply, then any disclosure of prior professional contact with the Deaf individual would constitute an obvious breach of the National Association of the Deaf-Registry of Interpreters for the Deaf (NAD-RID) Code of Professional Conduct's confidentiality requirement. Knowing which rules and principles apply in which setting and making decisions accordingly is a critical skill area for legal interpreters.

Legal practitioners take various roles in court. When hired by the court for a proceeding in which a Deaf person is involved, the role is typically defined as a proceedings interpreter who serves as an officer of the court, as mentioned above. There are other roles that legal interpreters play both in court and in investigations leading up to a criminal or civil case. When counsel does not use sign language, then there is a role for the interpreter, as a part of the litigation team, to interpret privileged communications between the attorney and client and to monitor the court interpreters for accuracy. In the profession, this role is called the *table interpreter* or the *interpreter who provides access to counsel.* This last function of monitoring the proceedings interpreters for accuracy preserves the attorney's ability to object to interpreted errors for appeal. Both sides have the right to have an interpreter present and monitoring the court interpreters. Legal interpreters often interpret in law enforcement investigations and then remain associated with the prosecution to serve the function of interpreting conversations between the prosecution and deaf witnesses and of monitoring the court's interpreter for accuracy. Good legal practitioners anticipate the need for these other roles and assist the hiring party in both identifying their staffing needs and providing resources to enable appropriate staffing.

Court interpreting protocol also defines a *conflict of interest* somewhat differently for legal interpreters than for non-legal interpreters. Certainly, the most obvious example of a conflict occurs when an interpreter has a financial interest in the outcome of a court case. Yet, courts are hyper-concerned

---

19. NCIEC Legal Interpreting Work Team. *Toward effective practice.*

about relationships and appearances of favoritism. When one is working within such a small community as the Deaf community, conflicts of interest arise frequently for the legal interpreter who arrives at court only to find that she or he has previously met the Deaf individual. Cultural considerations come into play here. For example, common greeting strategies, such as hugging a Deaf acquaintance, are not permitted in court and legal settings, because the impression of favoritism created.

Not all conflicts, however, are created equal. Interpreters are required to use discretion in considering how the nature of the prior contact with the Deaf person would look to an outsider. If the relationship would make a neutral outsider think the interpreter might somehow skew the interpretation in favor of the Deaf person, then the interpreter should decline the assignment. If however, the nature of the contact would not suggest an improper relationship, a conflict still exists, but it must be disclosed, on the record, before the judge and the parties in order to permit an exploration of the nature of the relationship through examination and cross-examination.[20] If the court, on the record, determines that the prior contact does not constitute a conflict, then the interpreter can be sworn to interpret the legal matter. Obviously, in order for the interpreter to engage in this conflicts analysis, the interpreter must know who the Deaf part(ies) may be in the matter. Ethical legal practice demands adequate preparation for the interpreter. It would be inefficient, wasteful, and harmful to accept an assignment and then ask to be recused upon discovering an impermissible conflict.

Legal interpreters are adept at navigating the labyrinth of obtaining preparation materials. Interpreters may have to contact attorneys ahead of time or do online case searches to find the docket of a case to which they are assigned. A common myth is that the court will not cooperate in providing preparation materials. Legal cases are public, and the files are public documents for the most part. Any citizen with time can walk into any court in the country and review a case file and make copies. Hence legal interpreters have the additional duty and overhead associated with trips to the court prior to the day of the case to review the case file and get an idea of the alleged facts in the case, in order to prepare for interpreting the trial.

Ethical legal practice also requires a high level of maturity and professionalism, as it is quite possible that one will have to turn down lucrative

---

20. NCIEC Legal Interpreting Work Team. *Toward effective practice*.

assignments if such a conflict exists. Finally, there are implications for our relationship with the Deaf community, and legal practitioners are particularly sensitive to their place in the community. Many of the requirements to competent legal interpreting practice require the interpreter to explain to the Deaf person, in the presence of the attorney, the ethical limitations and protocol requirements, for example, of the required disclosure of prior contact. Legal interpreting ethical limitations also seemingly violate a commonly held value that Deaf people should be able to request and receive their interpreter of choice. In the court's view, the Deaf individual is simply choosing someone who they feel will interpret more favorably to their side. Legal practitioners make time to inform Deaf consumers of these limitations.

As mentioned earlier, in recorded proceedings, a transcript is prepared, typically by a court reporter. The interpreter has an important relationship to the record and needs to know how to interact with it. For example, if the interpreter needs to ask a Deaf witness for a clarification, the interpreter must ask the court for permission rather than asking the witness directly, as is often practiced outside of court. The associated protocol to avoid confusion of the transcript is for the interpreter to speak in the third person. A request for clarification would sound like, "Your Honor, the witness has used a term the interpreter is unfamiliar with. May she ask for clarification?" Once permission is received, the interpreter can ask the witness directly for that specific item of clarification. The record then is clear that it is the interpreter asking for clarification rather than the Deaf witness asking for clarification. The process is also transparent to both the court and the consumer.

Power permeates the courtroom. The courtroom physically manifests power spatially, and each and every person has a specific place in court—from the attorneys, to the jury, to the clerk. The judge's bench is elevated, and the audience is physically separated from the litigants by a short wall. The jury is confined to a "box." Witnesses are slightly elevated on the "stand." Some defendants are locked up in a cell just outside the court or may even be physically separated from the court by a wall, with a window built in for communication. At times, defendants only appear in court through video projection from an offsite jail. When a private conversation occurs between the attorneys and the court, they huddle at the judge's bench, and a white noise machine is turned on to mask the conversation. Other times, the jury is sent out of the room in order for the attorneys' and the judge to talk. In extreme cases, the attorneys, the reporter, and the judge retire to the judge's chambers for a more private and in-depth conversation.

As opposed to ASL interpreters, courts are far more familiar with spoken language interpreters who sit next to the limited-English-proficient person, facing the judge and whispering the interpretation quietly to the party. No one, except sometimes the court reporter, is allowed to walk through the middle of the courtroom (called the *well*) at will. Even attorneys ask permission from the court to cross the well to approach a witness. Signed language interpreters, however, must not only stand in the sacred well, but also do so with their back to the judge—a traditional sign of disrespect. Legal practitioners new to a courtroom must be prepared to explain the logistics of interpreting. They reassure the court that although they need to stand in the well, they will not block the view of the judge or of the jury to the witness. Further, as a result of the unique positioning of signed language interpreters, they often are in a position to overhear the conversation at the bench, even when the white noise machine is used. Those conversations are intended to be private, and legal practitioners are not permitted to interpret the conversations, even if others in the courtroom can hear.

This brings up another difference between community and legal interpreting: Some dialogue in court is not interpreted, and some interpreters feel that that is not fair to the Deaf person. Again, protocol was created and court interpreter ethics were written by the court committees on language access to apply to all interpreters who work in court. It is important to keep in mind that some of the protocol conflicts with community interpreting perspectives. For example, when the interpreter is taking the oath, the interpreter does not also interpret for the Deaf party. Or, when the interpreter asks permission to approach the bench to discuss an interpreting issue, the interpreter does not also interpret the conversation for the Deaf person, because those conferences are intended to be private. Proactively, however, the interpreter can prepare the Deaf party, in the presence of the attorney, to alert them to the unique protocol the court requires of legal interpreters.

LEGAL LANGUAGE, LEGAL DISCOURSE, AND INTERPRETING STRATEGIES

Legal language is well known for being dense and inaccessible, and legal interpreters constantly study to keep up on the various linguistic nuances of the discourse they interpret. Much research has been conducted on the comprehensibility of legal discourse. Many legal scholars have argued on behalf of the validity of the Plain English movement for writing legal materials.[21] Signed language interpreters draw from the fields of forensic linguistics to further their knowledge of an appreciation for the intricacies of legal English.[22] During the existence of the National Consortium of Interpreter Education Centers, a signed language legal dictionary was produced. The dictionary contains approximately 300 common legal terms with an ASL interpretation and a sample of the term used in context.[23] Natural ASL legal discourse is readily available in the Deaf press and on YouTube, where Deaf commentators discuss legal topics. Legal interpreters continue to hone their linguistic skills as language changes over time.

Legal discourse is governed primarily by the Rules of Evidence, as interpreted by the courts. Attorneys are constrained in how they frame questions, phrase objections, and present arguments. Specific rules relate to the sentence structure of how direct and cross-examination questions are constructed, as well as the types of responses that are admissible or objectionable.[24] Legal interpreters navigate these form-based parameters and obtain the expected type of response, given the great differences in syntax between ASL and English. For example, the phrase "do you enter into this agreement freely and voluntarily" often is restructured into ASL to convey the concept that no one is forcing the agreement. As a result, the ASL version usually elicits a negative response, to wit: "no." The expected response, however, is "yes, I am entering into this freely and voluntarily." Hence, the legal interpreter needs to anticipate and restructure

21. Tiersma, P. (1999). *Legal language*. Chicago, IL: University of Chicago Press.
22. Charrow, R., & Charrow, V. (1979). Making legal language understandable: A psycholinguistic study of jury instructions. *Columbia Law Rev.*, 79, 1306–1374.
23. National Consortium of Interpreter Education Centers. Legal terminology. Retrieved at http://www.interpretereducation.org/specialization/legal/terminology/
24. Federal Rules of Evidence, 611(c). U.S. Government Printing Office: Washington, D.C. (2009).

the interpretation to obtain a positive response, such as by rendering the English as "yes, no one is forcing me."

Legal interpreters work in a variety of modes. The type of discourse to be interpreted in a specific mode is governed by statute, practice, and policy. Consecutive interpreting is mandated by federal law in federal proceedings when a Deaf witness is on the stand. The court recognizes that consecutive interpreting is more accurate, and when the court is the recipient of the interpretation, it insists upon the highest standard of accuracy. From spoken language interpreting colleagues, signed language legal interpreters have borrowed the technique of note-taking while interpreting. As an aid to memory, note-taking assists the interpreter's short-term memory to retain units of information that might not be dense and easily retrievable, such as numbers, addresses, and dates. The majority of proceedings, however, are conducted in the simultaneous mode. Deaf interpreters must likewise be able to interpret simultaneously or semi-simultaneously in accordance with the oath to interpret accurately. Sight translation is a method of interpreting a written text to a Deaf person. Sign translation is commonly used by spoken language interpreters when a letter or other document is presented into evidence, but is written in a foreign language. Signed language interpreters typically offer to perform a sight translation of the form used at an arraignment that a defendant must fill out regarding their finances, in order to obtain free or discounted attorney services. A variety of other commonly interpreted forms exist as well.

Legal interpreters constantly strive to learn more legal vocabulary, learn how it is used in authentic discourse, and improve their interpreting ability in all of the modes used in court. Lifelong learning is a core value of legal interpreters and manifests as the final domain in *Toward Effective Practice: Specialist Competencies of the Interpreter Practicing within Court and Legal Settings*.

LIFELONG LEARNING

It bears repeating that lifelong learning is a core value of legal interpreters. As practitioners in a specialty field, many interpreters hold legal certification. Legally certified interpreters, as a group, advocated for and implemented an RID requirement that 2.0 of their certificate maintenance units must be in the field of legal interpreting, in order to maintain their certificates. Legal practitioners, under the auspices of the Legal Interpreter Member Section of the RID, have a long-standing collaboration through an online forum in which to share experiences and learn from others. Legal interpreters typically hold a national legal interpreting conference or event annually through partnership with various organizations. The RID Legal Interpreter Member Section (www.rid.org/legal-interpreters) is active in providing information, resources, training, and opportunities for collaboration to its members. Legal interpreting skills, as in all practice professions, stagnate if not exercised vigorously and often.

There are a number of resources available for interpreters who want to become legal interpreters. Although the website is no longer maintained, the NCIEC has numerous resource materials available for aspiring and working legal interpreters that were created during the life cycle of the NCIEC and may be accessed at www.interpretereducation.org. Interpreters interested in legal settings can identify specialists through the RID member section or through their local RID subchapter events. Furthermore, courts are public institutions, and it is a founding principle of the United States that we maintain a free and public judiciary. Aspiring interpreters should go to their local courts and observe proceedings. They should seek out the court interpreter program manager and ask to observe interpreted proceedings. Nearly every courtroom in most American cities has spoken language interpreters present, functioning, and available to observe. Many legal interpreters form study groups when preparing to be legal interpreters and engage with experienced mentors. Study groups can observe court together or seek out speakers from the bar or judges' associations on criminal law or civil procedure. It is another core value of legal interpreters that a period of supervised induction is a necessity to build the foundation of competent practice. Legal interpreters can seek out more experienced legal interpreters and work with them to develop skills. Finally, with the internet, real trials and legal procedures can be watched from the comfort of home on YouTube. In sum, there is no limit to the amount of information that is available to one who seeks to enter the specialty area of legal interpreting.

8

Interpreting for People Who Are DeafBlind

SHERRY SHAW

Describing the Diverse DeafBlind Community

As with the term *Deaf*, we avoid saying *the Deaf* or *the DeafBlind* without referring to the fact that we are talking about people. It is appropriate to say *Deaf people, people who are Deaf, DeafBlind people*, and *people who are DeafBlind*. The term *sighted* describes a person who has functional vision, such that activities of daily living (such as driving) are not hindered. *Congenital* means something present at birth; whereas, *adventitious* means something acquired later in life, possibly as a result of a syndrome, illness, accident, or the natural aging process. A person who is adventitiously deaf and blind will have distinct communication needs from the person who learned American Sign Language as a child and later became blind, so for this reason, understanding a bit of the person's history will inform the interpreter about how he or she will best work with the DeafBlind person. In other words, the age people become deaf or blind affects how they communicate, and the combination of congenital and adventitious conditions affects language acquisition. If a person becomes deaf after acquiring language (adventitiously), that person will either maintain the original language and make adjustments to access it differently or learn a new language altogether (such as a signed language). Take for example a person who was hearing and sighted at birth, but loses his or her hearing at the age of 11 from an acute illness. This person may retain spoken language and use "oral" skills (lipreading) as the adjusted mode of communication; however, it is also possible the person would become a user

131

of signed language as the primary form of communication. It is common for adventitiously DeafBlind people to be non-signers, but everyone has his or her own preferences for communication that "works." Some people who are congenitally deaf may be signers from infancy and identify with Deaf culture, especially if they were born into Deaf families. Already having a form of visual communication, these people will have access to a versatile language that will allow them to communicate, if they need to transition from accessing the language visually to receiving the language tactilely.

DeafBlind, *Deafblind*, and *deafblind* are all terms that involve dual sensory conditions, but they are slightly different from each other. *DeafBlind*, without a hyphen, with or without upper case, is the preferred notation in the international community and represents a single condition more complex than the combination of vision and hearing loss. The hyphenated term *Deaf-Blind* is widely accepted by consumers who are congenitally deaf and adventitiously blind (usually after language development). People who use signed language and maintain cultural-linguistic ties to the Deaf community may also prefer the hyphenated designation. When referring to children who are deaf and blind at birth or in early childhood, *deafblind* is used. Whichever term is used, it is important to note that *DeafBlind* seldom means a person is totally without visual or hearing sensation. *Residual* hearing or vision refers to the amount of sensory input that is usable, or *functional*, for the person's daily living.

In summary, people who are DeafBlind can be born deaf and later become blind, born blind and later become deaf, born deafblind, or become deaf and blind later in life. Any combination of vision and hearing abilities, including the degree of residual hearing and vision, determines how a person communicates, achieves independence, and navigates within the environment. Each person requires unique skills from the interpreter based on the degree to which residual hearing and vision are used to comprehend information and fully participate in a situation. There is not one standard description of someone who is DeafBlind; rather, the population is known as *heterogeneous*. In a heterogeneous population, one size does not fit all, as each person brings a unique set of vision and hearing abilities to the communication process.

Focusing on Communication Needs Rather than Conditions

The primary concern of the interpreter is successful communication with the individual, not the causes or implications of the person's condition, unless of course, these condition-related topics affect how the interpreter will provide the essential functions of the job. A DeafBlind person is likely to offer information to the interpreter that will help the two understand each other and work as a team. For example, a person may offer that he or she has Usher syndrome, which usually means the person was born deaf and has progressive vision loss that starts during young adulthood. The interpreter can use this information to formulate appropriate questions for the consumer, such as "Where would you like me to sit?"; "What type of interpreting works best for you?"; or "Is it helpful for me to sign in a smaller space?" In another scenario, a DeafBlind person may tell the interpreter he or she has macular degeneration and will watch the interpreter through peripheral vision. The interpreter would then ask, "Do you prefer I sit on one side over the other?" and "Is there a distance that is most beneficial for you?" Formulating questions related to communication, rather than asking about a condition, contributes to an interpreter's professional presentation. Asking probing questions, such as "How long have you been blind?" or "Can you see me now?" can be perceived as insensitive and intrusive, so interpreters would be more likely to build a positive rapport with the consumer by avoiding questions that are unrelated to the specific need for efficiency in interpreting.

Considerations of onset (the actual time in a person's life when a condition impacts vision and hearing) and stability (consistent degrees of hearing and vision) are factors that will determine how much functional vision or hearing one has at any given moment. Some conditions are notorious for changing, or being volatile—sometimes changing gradually over a period of years and sometimes rapidly; sometimes changing bilaterally and sometimes unilaterally. Stability affects language choice (signed or spoken), use of technological supports (cochlear implants, assistive listening devices, computer applications), receptive and expressive communication, employment, quality of life, leisure, relationships, independence, and education (Registry of Interpreters for the Deaf, Inc., 2007).

It is common for a person to have stable vision and hearing for a long time before experiencing a decrease in peripheral vision, central vision, or visual acuity (clarity) and/or changes to the ability to discern speech or hear certain frequencies. Likewise, degenerative conditions can stop progressing, and the conditions do not always result in a person becoming totally deaf and blind. Most conditions are unpredictable, which means interpreters need to guard against making assumptions about how a person prefers to communicate based on the interpreter's prior experience with the person. Previous strategies that resulted in successful communication in one setting and on one particular day do not automatically apply to the next day. Interpreters make communication assessments each time they meet a DeafBlind person, even if the two of them already know each other and see each other frequently.

Age of onset affects a person's concept development, spatial awareness, and language acquisition, among many other aspects of development. The critical milestones in auditory and visual development center on two major events: language-learning and unhindered movement, or travel, within the environment. Prior to these events, vision and hearing contribute to development in a different way than development occurs in a child who is born deaf and blind. We can expect touch to be the primary connector of all DeafBlind children and adults to the world, but touch may be the only way a child orients him- or herself. Later in the chapter, I discuss the value of touch more in depth; however, the key point to understand now is that interpreters observe, analyze, and consult with the consumer about the different mechanisms for communicating concepts based on how an individual is processing information. We learn about a person's conceptual organization the more we interact and work with that person, and sometimes the interpretation is trial and error until we can gain a firm sense of what is effective and not effective in our interpreting methods. An example of how onset affects the interpreter is related to one of the role extensions associated with interpreting for a person who is DeafBlind: visual description.

THOUGHT WORLDS AND LIVED REALITIES

Terms such as *thought worlds* and *lived realities* relate to the psychological adjustment and experiences of people who identify themselves as DeafBlind.

The risk of isolation is inherent to people who rely on touch to form relationships to the outside world. Interpreters are challenged to consider the daily life of a DeafBlind person, thinking about how everyday tasks are accomplished and problems are resolved. The physical and mental stamina to manage household business tasks, obtain and maintain employment, and live independently can lead to common phenomena within the DeafBlind community: fatigue and grief. Grief is often the result of a loss, such as independence, friends, jobs, and cultural identity. Stages of grief can occur throughout a person's life, if the conditions impacting that person are progressive. Expressions of grief include anger, frustration, impatience, depression, and withdrawal. Interpreters may be involved throughout the grief cycle, especially if the DeafBlind person is receiving psychological counseling.

Art, sport, and leisure are excellent means for alleviating fatigue, coping with loss, and creating a balanced life for all of us, and in the DeafBlind community, these activities can contribute to identity and belonging within the community. Camps, or *retreats*, occur around the world for DeafBlind people to experience a fun, safe, and educational environment that provides all the support services needed to fully participate. There are several camps across the United States, but the longest-running camp is the Retreat for DeafBlind Adults (www.deafblindlh.org/seabeck/), sponsored by the Seattle Lighthouse and held in Seabeck, Washington, each summer. Seabeck attracts DeafBlind people domestically as well as internationally for five days of relaxation, games, dancing, socials, arts and crafts, and outdoor adventure, and there is always a demand for qualified interpreters and support service providers (SSPs) at camps like Seabeck. Leisure is a documented component of quality-of-life indicators for people who are DeafBlind, and it would be an understatement to suggest that DeafBlind people are often in a state of emotional and psychological adjustment. Adjusting, facing challenges, combating isolation, and overcoming barriers are facilitated by a healthy dose of leisure, socialization, and relaxation.

MULTIPLE SOURCES OF INFORMATION AND PERSONAL POWER

Thus far, you have learned the ways that conditions, timing, and exposure to language affect an individual's access to the environment during times when conditions may fluctuate. To reiterate about concept development, a child who has any amount of hearing and vision at birth, the brain perceives the world differently than that of a child who is born without sight or hearing. A person who begins experiencing vision changes during the teenage years will have an extensive visual memory that facilitates his or her interaction with the environment. A Deaf teenager may have had a driver's license for several years before losing night vision and later peripheral vision, causing the need to suspend driving for safety reasons. Although diagnosis of Usher Syndrome (typified by the example of congenital deafness and adventitious blindness) may not occur until there is an experience of night blindness or peripheral vision loss, generally known as *tunnel vision*. This person would probably have a good sense of direction. Another case in point would be a DeafBlind person who is congenitally deaf and adventitiously blind and who loves fashion and wants to be alerted to the latest styles worn by others in a group setting. Therefore, in addition to interpreting between languages, the interpreter provides details from the environment that allow the person to visualize the information he or she expects to receive from the interpreter. In all interactions with the DeafBlind community, whether as an interpreting student or a qualified interpreter, empowering the person to make autonomous decisions and participate fully in his or her environment should be the interpreter's goal.

The concept of empowerment cannot be overemphasized when working with the DeafBlind population, and it will be reiterated throughout this chapter. It is easy to slip into the role of a helper and decision-maker, because it saves time and effort on the part of the interpreter. At all costs, interpreters are required to leave the decision-making to consumers and not accept responsibility for making choices that rob another person of the opportunity to function independently. If the interpreter identifies where a person will sit or what a person will eat by filling a buffet plate and giving it to the DeafBlind person, the interpreter is exhibiting a form of oppression by disempowering the consumer from making his or her own decisions.

INTERPRETER SKILL SET

Interpreting for the heterogeneous DeafBlind population is a complex specialty requiring competence in communication methods beyond those required for signed language interpreting with the general Deaf population. Of course, one needs excellent language skills (signed and spoken language); however, the additional skills needed by the interpreter include the ability to (1) physically guide a person, (2) inform the person about people and places in the environment, and (3) use a variety of communication tools and methods to be the most effective interpreter possible. Just as in interpreting for the broader Deaf community, the interpreter who brings to his or her interpreting a vast variety of life experiences and *schema* is better equipped to interpret effectively. DeafBlind people may work in such capacities as conference presenters, scientists, technology specialists, attorneys, professors, rehabilitation counselors, and many other professions, and the interpreters who partner with them have the responsibility to accurately represent what these consumers are expressing with appropriate terminology and *register* (level of formality). Skill sets that meet the needs of DeafBlind consumers certainly include signed and spoken language competency and a basic knowledge of different interpreting techniques; however, interpersonal skills, disposition, physical and mental stamina, and a sense of humor are also valuable skills to develop.

Language-related characteristics that describe an effective interpreter for people who are DeafBlind include sign clarity and coherence. Although, these two characteristics are important for all interpreters, those who work with tactile signed language will be more readily understood if they concentrate on clear formation and logical development of ideas when interpreting. Regardless of the excellent skills an interpreter might have, attitudes determine whether or not an interpreter is received into the DeafBlind community enthusiastically. Interpreters working for DeafBlind persons need flexibility in adjusting to personal communication preferences and varying degrees of consumer independence, and they must be comfortable with close interaction and touch. Remaining open to personal growth, accepting feedback and making the necessary changes, staying alert to the environment, and prioritizing another person's inclusion in the interpreted event are all essential to the interpreting process.

Let's talk for a moment about humor as a skill set. In reading the "Thought Worlds and Lived Realities" section, you learned about the ways leisure contributes to quality of life for people who are DeafBlind. The difference between simply well-trained interpreters and those who have reputations for being most valued in the DeafBlind community is the diligence devoted to developing trust and participating frequently in community activities. These interpreters develop a receptivity to the needs of consumers, whether individually or in organizations, and they commit to building community alliances. As trust develops between individuals, usually over long periods of time, interpreters-as-allies learn how humor, in the right place and at the right time, contributes to a DeafBlind person's ability to reflect positivity and enjoy a situation. Research on humor validates that it reduces stress, promotes well-being, is essential for dealing with adversity, and helps facilitate social situations. Naturally, a good sense of humor can help interpreters overcome any awkwardness, fear, or hesitation about working in the DeafBlind community. An interpreter who enjoys a challenge will also enjoy this kind of interpreting!

INTERPRETING PROCESS

The interpreting process, which typically involves facilitating communication between a hearing person who does not sign and a sighted Deaf person who uses a signed language, becomes more complex when a consumer is DeafBlind. Beyond interpreting an auditory message, the interpreter becomes responsible for monitoring the visual environment and supplementing the traditional interpretation with information that assists the person in orientation to physical surroundings. For example, information about the people who are present, what people are doing, where people are seated, the room layout, and the general mood and ambience of a room contributes to a person's full participation. Descriptions of the environment are also important for a person's safety. The interpreter should describe the location of exit doors, obstacles in pathways, changes in the terrain, and other indicators that could affect a person's ability to exit a building safely. In addition to safety, a rich environmental description empowers the consumer to make his or her own decisions and express preferences. Without this environmental description, a consumer does not have the necessary information to control the environment according to personal needs.

During professional meetings or classes, interpreters not only provide consumers with general environmental information, they also provide specific information about what people are doing. It may not seem important to a sighted person that people are whispering in the corner or using personal technology instead of attending to a presentation, but this kind of detail allows a consumer to assess the levels of attention and engagement of others. The interpreter needs to be alert to these kinds of details and provide as many details as possible before, during, or after providing the interpretation. Visual information, combined with auditory information, promotes consumer independence and reduces a sense of isolation within group settings. The same combination of visual and auditory information is needed in all community settings, including one-on-one consultations (e.g., doctor's appointment, counseling), small group meetings (e.g., family counseling, advisory boards), formal venues (e.g., courtrooms), or large gatherings (e.g., conferences, performing arts venues). Whatever the situation, the interpreting process involves communicating multiple sources of information to the DeafBlind consumer.

It is sometimes difficult to know how much information a particular consumer might want in a certain setting. Amount of visual detail depends on the individual, and preferences are related to personal interest, the amount of vision the person is able to use, and the degree of long-term visual memory that contributes to a person's ability to conceptualize characteristics of people, places, and objects. One example would be a DeafBlind woman, age 70, who had full visual abilities until the age of 15, when she slowly began to lose her vision. Always interested in fashion and personal presentation, when the woman became dependent upon Tactile American Sign Language for communication and environmental information, she wanted specific information about what people were wearing. Another person might have no interest in this type of visual information. Requests for more specific details, beyond, for example, the room layout, will vary from person to person, and the only way for an interpreter to know what information is beneficial to an individual is to ask that person.

Among many other skills, an interpreter needs the ability to adjust pace, negotiate turn-taking, modify signs and fingerspelling, and discern a message's key points to successfully communicate complex concepts and minimize information deprivation. The relationship between the interpreter and the DeafBlind consumer determines the degree to which understanding is communicated, clarification is provided, and pace is adjusted to accommodate any fatigue or other barriers to communication. Trust and rapport between interpreters and consumers result in the development of a comfortable system of providing feedback (called *backchanneling*), and oftentimes a signal system is developed, so gaps in information exchange are can be remediated.

IMPORTANCE OF TOUCH

Without touch, access to the physical world is limited for a person who is DeafBlind, and touch used for communication takes on a function that is different from touch in the general population. Typically, people have a specific distance with which they are most comfortable, and they become uncomfortable when someone violates that "personal space." This is often referred to as the *bubble*, and that bubble is nonexistent when interacting with DeafBlind people who communicate tactilely. Touch is used for signifying your presence (gentle shoulder touch), getting someone's attention (tapping the back of a person's hand), guiding a person (consumer taking your elbow), and interpreting tactilely (your hands under the consumer's hand/s). It is common for the interpreter to maintain some form of light contact when standing or sitting beside a person who is DeafBlind during periods of rest or breaks in meetings or classes. Constant contact signifies presence.

Research extensively documents the importance of human touch across life stages (birth to old age) and cultures, and the functions of touch are magnified in the DeafBlind population because touch equals access. Disconnecting from a DeafBlind person by removing touch happens frequently when changing interpreters, taking breaks, or moving to another task with another person. When the interpreter is working in a group setting, such as a conference session, meeting, or class session, and leaves the presence of the DeafBlind person, it is important to first anchor him or her to something tangible, if the person would otherwise be left without a sense of being grounded in the environment. *Anchoring* a person to a nearby table, chair, or wall means gently guiding the person to a tangible object, thus contributing to his or her security and orientation in space.

CULTURAL NORMS AND ETIQUETTE

Within the Deafblind community, there are cultural norms that guide interactive behaviors, attire, and protocols. The most prevalent norms within the community include always identifying yourself by name (regardless of how briefly you stepped away), anchoring a person to a tangible object before stepping away, and informing someone when you are leaving the room or stepping away from the person's field of vision. To get a person's attention, it is inappropriate to wave in front of someone's eyes. The appropriate way to get attention is to touch someone gently on the shoulder or back of the hand.

Cleanliness and grooming take on additional importance when you are in close proximity to another person, and for interpreters, this involves nail care, breath, and hand sanitizing. The appropriate attire for interpreters in the DeafBlind community includes a solid shirt that contrasts skin tone, three-quarter-length sleeves, limited-to-no jewelry, high neckline, and trousers, while avoiding any other garment or accessory that can be visually distracting to a person with low vision. Tattoos should be covered, colognes should be avoided, and facial piercings should be removed. Other preferences may be added to the list of attire recommendations based on an individual's visual condition, and these preferences should be respected. For example, some people have difficulty seeing shades of purple and ask interpreters to avoid this color. Others are distracted by simple wedding rings and will ask for them to be removed prior to interpreting. It is good practice to dress conservatively and simply, so you are able to move freely to accommodate a person's visual field and alleviate any barriers to effective communication.

COMMUNICATION STRATEGIES

Each DeafBlind person communicates differently, and the person's preference may depend on lighting, fatigue, or content of the message being interpreted. Sometimes, finding the exact method or technique that is most effective for the moment requires experimentation, allowing the consumer to try different ways and selecting what best works for him or her. Tactile interpreting, interpreting within a restricted field, tracking, and Print on Palm are commonly used in the United States for people who have varying degrees of vision and hearing. People who do not sign (and some who do), may prefer to use an oral transliterator nearby in conjunction with assistive listening devices, hearing aids, and cochlear implants. When interpreters are hired to work with a DeafBlind person, they are typically informed of the communication modality used by the consumer prior to the assignment. However, keep in mind that the interpreter always makes an independent assessment ahead of time, in collaboration with the consumer, in case context, fatigue, lighting, content, or other determining factors change the consumer's typical communication modes.

Tactile interpreting involves placing your hands under the consumer's hand or hands and signing naturally. Sometimes, the person can "read" signs using one hand (usually with his or her nondominant hand on the interpreter's dominant hand) and seated side-by-side and slightly angled toward each other. Sometimes, the person reads with both hands and is seated in front of the interpreter (possibly with knees interlocking) and with or without a table for resting elbows. If a DeafBlind person has residual vision and the ambient lighting in the room is good, he or she may require the interpreter to sit closer or farther away than usual and sign within a restricted field of vision, keeping signs closer to the body and within a smaller space. This method is called *restricted field interpreting*.

When lighting changes, as when lights are dimmed to show a video, the consumer with low vision may cue the interpreter to switch from restricted field interpreting to tactile interpreting or *tracking*, which involves the DeafBlind person lightly placing his or her hands on the interpreter's forearm or wrists to control the sign space and keep the signs within a field that can be seen. Certain circumstances lend themselves naturally to modality changes. For example, it is common for tactile communication to change when the topic involves numbers, such as a general discussion about checking accounts moving into the exact amounts in a checking and savings account. Numerals that may be more difficult to differentiate tactilely may be more readily understood by drawing the numbers on the person's palm in a technique called *Print on Palm*. Print on Palm is also used for writing letters in block-print style on a person's nondominant, open palm, when the person is not a signed language user. The technique provides opportunities for people to communicate when they share a written or spoken language, but do not share a signed language, as with DeafBlind people from other countries. If a person has limited sensation in the hands, perhaps due to a condition called *neuropathy* and associated with diabetes, Print on Palm can be done on the person's back, arm, or any place the person has sensation.

In countries other than the United States, communicating with DeafBlind people can be accomplished through methods that do not require knowledge of a formal signed language, such as Lorm (more prevalent in Europe than North America), tactile braille, and tactile fingerspelling. Awareness about the many communication methods on the part of the interpreter, along with flexibility and willingness to shift methods and modalities, ensures consumers receive successful interpreting services.

Role Expansion

The interpreter's role extends beyond interpreting auditory information and providing environmental details into areas that affect a person's mobility, navigation, and independence. Guiding a person, often referred to as being a *sighted guide*, is a common role for the interpreter when a person needs to move from one environment to another. The interpreter needs training from an orientation and mobility specialist to learn the safest way to guide a person and should pursue this training as soon as he or she determines readiness to begin working in the DeafBlind community. Keeping in mind that the interpreter should focus on the consumer's right to make personal decisions, proper guiding allows the DeafBlind person to travel.

When preparing to work as interpreters within the DeafBlind community, learning how to provide support services to the DeafBlind community (aside from interpreting) is an excellent way for students to acquire the extra skills needed for the interpreter's expanded role. Interpreters can become involved as SSPs, who assist DeafBlind community members with everyday tasks, such as shopping and reading the mail. The American Association of the Deaf-Blind explains that SSPs are not used to provide personal care, run errands, or interpret for appointments. Rather, SSPs can accompany a person to a grocery store, family gathering, sporting event, or other community function.

The SSP is a trained person, sometimes a volunteer or agency-supported worker, who can assist the DeafBlind person with daily tasks. Interpreting students can become excellent SSPs because they are familiar with concepts around culture, access, and independence as a part of their educational programs. SSPs have some of the same responsibilities as interpreters (providing environmental information and guiding); however, SSPs are not necessarily qualified interpreters. Both SSPs and interpreters are bound by the ethical constraints of confidentiality and respect for the DeafBlind person's privacy (Nuccio & Smith, 2010), and many interpreters begin their DeafBlind specialty training as SSPs.

Providing sighted guide services, or *guiding*, involves first making the DeafBlind person aware that you are present, and then offering to guide the person to his or her seat, the restroom, the buffet line, etc. Asking a person if assistance is needed is the appropriate way to offer guiding services. If the person is trained in guiding techniques, he or she will reach out for your elbow to be led. If the person is not familiar with guiding techniques, the interpreter can simply say, "Please hold my elbow, and I will take you to the water fountain." The person should walk a step behind you, so if there is any change in the terrain, the person can sense from the guide that there are changes ahead. When guiding a person who is DeafBlind, it is best not to talk or sign at the same time you are traveling (although there are some people who are quite good at this). Keeping the person safe during guiding is the primary goal of the interpreter. It is inappropriate to push or pull a DeafBlind person when guiding. When there is an emergency and an immediate need to evacuate without providing the usual explanation about what is happening in a room, there are signals to alert a person of the emergency. In the United States, making a large "X" on a person's back serves the purpose of alerting the DeafBlind person, and once everyone is in a safe place, explanations can follow.

Another way the interpreter's role may be expanded is through touch signal systems for conveying information in real time about the environment to a DeafBlind person. Touch signal systems accompany interpreting, or they facilitate social interaction between DeafBlind people. One system is known as *haptic signals* or *haptics* (derived from the Greek *Haptikos*, or sense of touch), which refers to providing visual information primarily on a person's back, arm, or leg (when seated), so he or she can participate more fully in social interaction. For example, the interpreter or SSP can inform the DeafBlind person how audience members are responding (smiling, laughing, frowning, nodding in agreement or disagreement), what people are doing (raising a hand for questions), and how a room is laid out (tables, chairs, refreshments, materials). By combining pressure, repetition, movements, and drawings as they are happening, inclusive conversations and interactions are possible. The foundations of haptics apply to Pro-Tactile, a vibrant cultural movement within the American DeafBlind community that promotes empowerment and autonomy through total contextual access and immediate feedback, or backchanneling. The premise of a supplementary touch signal system is that DeafBlind people do not have to solely rely on interpreted messages to absorb environmental information that sighted people receive through visual channels.

Power and Oppression

I have discussed many of the ways the interpreter's role and responsibilities differ between interpreting in the DeafBlind community and interpreting in the general Deaf community. However, there is a caveat to new interpreters learning how to apply all these extra responsibilities, such as providing visual and environmental information and guiding a person. That caveat is to avoid patronizing a person by making assumptions about what he or she can and cannot do and providing more information than the person may need or desire. Allowing our assumptions to guide our actions, no matter how noble our intent, leads to *oppression*, which means taking unnecessary control and exerting power over another person who is considered unequal to oneself. The ethics associated with interpreting with people who are DeafBlind include not wielding power over a person who is dependent upon another person for communication and environmental access. Usually, this power is demonstrated through making decisions for DeafBlind people, because we assume we know more or because it seems to be quicker to decide for someone rather than to let the person do the deciding.

Deaf(Blind) Plus

The term *Deaf Plus* refers to children or adults who are Deaf with other conditions that may affect communication and daily living and does not usually refer to people who are DeafBlind. Although this term might be used generically to include DeafBlind people, usually Deaf Plus means the person is Deaf with complicating cognitive or physical disabilities. A DeafBlind person who experiences traumatic brain injury, for instance, might have very different communication needs than were evident prior to the injury. Likewise, a DeafBlind person who is autistic might have a communication system that is idiosyncratic, or unique, such that an interpreter would need access to family members and caretakers to develop an understanding of how the person communicates without typical language. Deaf Plus populations require additional resources (e.g., programs, caretakers, service coordination, support networks) to maximize the potential to live independently, receive an education, and work. Because this group is considered to be low incidence within the general population, services that are specifically designed for Deaf Plus people may be limited. The importance of highly trained interpreters and SSPs having training to work with Deaf Plus individuals is based upon the fact that 39% of deaf youth in the United States have additional conditions (Gallaudet Research Institute, 2011). The likelihood that interpreters will encounter children and adults with multiple conditions that warrant modifications to traditional interpreting methods is fairly predictable, and training in these particular skill sets is usually obtained through in-service (workshops) rather than preservice (college programs) interpreter education programs.

RESOURCES AND REFERENCES

Websites

American Association of the Deaf-Blind	http://www.aadb.org/
Helen Keller National Center	https://www.helenkeller.org/hknc
Deafblind International	http://www.deafblindinternational.org/
National Center on Deaf-Blindness	https://nationaldb.org/
National Family Association for Deaf-Blind	http://nfadb.org/
Perkins School for the Blind (Deafblind education)	http://www.perkins.org/school
Sense: Connecting Sight, Sound, and Life	https://www.sense.org.uk/
Welcome to Pro-Tactile: The DeafBlind Way	http://www.protactile.org/

References

Berge, S. (2014). Social and private speech in an interpreted meeting of deafblind persons. *Interpreting, 16*(1), 82–106.

Berge, S., & Raanes, E. (2013). Coordinating the chain of utterances: An analysis of communicative flow and turn taking in an interpreted group dialogue for Deaf-Blind persons, *Sign Language Studies, 13*(3), 350–371.

Danish Association of the Deafblind. (2012). *103 haptic signals: A reference book.* Retrieved from http://wasli.org/wp-content/uploads/2013/07/103-Haptic-Signals-English.pdf

Gallaudet Research Institute. (2011). *Regional and national summary report of data from the 2009–2010 annual survey of deaf and hard of hearing children and youth.* Washington, DC: GRI, Gallaudet University. Retrieved from https://research.gallaudet.edu/Demographics/2010_National_Summary.pdf

Metzger, M., Fleetwood, E., & Collins S. D. (2004). Discourse genre and linguistic mode: Interpreter influences in visual and tactile interpreted interaction, *Sign Language Studies, 4*(2), 118–137.

National Task Force on Deaf-Blind Interpreting. (2014). *An annotated bibliography on deaf-blind interpreting.* Retrieved from http://www.unco.edu/marie/pdfs/Resources/Deaf%20Blind/2014NTFDBIBiblioStandardPrint.pdf

Nuccio, J., & Granda, A. J. (2016). *Pro-tactile: The deafblind way.* Retrieved from http://www.protactile.org/

Nuccio, J., & Smith, T. (2010). *Providing and receiving services: Comprehensive training for deaf-blind persons and their support service providers.* Retrieved from http://wctest.seattledbsc.org/wp-content/uploads/2014/04/sspdbcurriculum_tagged.pdf

Northwest Connecticut Community College. (2001). *The national curriculum: An introduction to working and socializing with people who are Deaf-Blind.* San Diego, CA: DawnSignPress.

Palmer, R., & Lahtinen, R. (2005). Social-haptic communication for acquired deaf-blind people and family: Incorporating touch and environmental information through holistic communication. *DbI Review, 35,* 6–8.

Registry of Interpreters for the Deaf, Inc. (2007). *Interpreting for individuals who are deaf-blind.* [Standard practice paper]. Alexandria, VA: RID Publications. Retrieved from http://rid.org/about-interpreting/standard-practice-papers/

9

Credentialing and Regulation of Signed Language Interpreters

ANNA WITTER-MERITHEW

The quality control of signed language interpreters is a frequent topic of discussion in the Deaf and interpreter communities. Deaf consumers want assurance that the individuals who provide them with linguistic access—often in the most personal aspects of their lives—are linguistically and culturally competent and professional. They want to know that from one interpreted interaction to the next, the behavior and performance of different interpreters is reliable and sufficiently standard to meet their needs. Interpreter practitioners want to be valued and respected in the marketplace. They want credentialing systems that are based on the work they actually do and that measure knowledge and performance in a fair, professional, and equitable manner. The general public wants to know that when they hire or work with a professional interpreter, they can trust that communication access will be achieved. In response to these expectations, the interpreting industry and the national and state governments have set various standards and regulations related to who is qualified to work as an interpreter.

WHY REGULATION OF PROFESSIONS IS IMPORTANT

Professions are typically distinguished from other types of occupations based on the degree of expertise the practitioner needs and complexity of the work they perform. Generally, it is assumed that the general public does not hold the knowledge and skills held by professionals. That is

149

certainly true in terms of sign language interpreting—few people hold the knowledge, skills, and abilities necessary to be a professional interpreter. Typically, the competence of professionals is acquired through formal study focused on the acquisition of a complex set of skills, higher-order thinking and decision-making skills, ethical standards of practice, and a body of specialized knowledge. Society and consumers of professional services expect that the professional will *do no harm* and that they will not use their professional position in a manner that is detrimental to those individuals who rely on their services. These two expectations form the cornerstone of trust that the general public relies on and extends to professionals.

At its core, regulation of any profession seeks to protect the safety and interests of the consumers, as well as to safeguard practitioners. The goal of promoting professional competence through regulation is a worthy one, because it protects the public by helping consumers readily identify competent practitioners and simultaneously aids the profession or field by encouraging and recognizing the standardization of practice.

Professions are regulated for three primary reasons: Ensure minimally acceptable standards of competence, provide accountability and assurances to consumers, and improve the quality of service provision by providing guidance about best practice and fostering continuing education (Sutherland & Leatherman, 2006). These purposes are promoted through regulatory processes.

The Starting Place

Although sign language interpreting is an emergent profession, efforts to regulate the work of interpreters have been associated with the industry since its early inception. The three primary ways the field of sign language interpreting is regulated is through the accreditation of interpreter education programs, certification of practitioners, and licensure of practitioners. The focus of this chapter is on certification and licensure, but it is important to briefly address the issue of program accreditation.

Prior to the passage of federal laws related to the rights of disabled Americans or laws relating to linguistic access, Deaf people led the process of vetting interpreters. This assured Deaf people that those who served as interpreters were sufficiently connected to the community, its values, and its expectations. Potential interpreters were recruited from interested family members, coworkers, and friends. Deaf community members would commit time and energy to guide the acquisition and mastery of ASL by these potential interpreters. They would immerse interpreters into the community and induct them into interpreting. Deaf community members would share feedback and observations with one another as a way of monitoring which interpreters were the best fit, in terms of the community's expectations and needs (Mathers & Witter-Merithew, 2014).

As the demand for interpreters exceeded the supply, the need to establish training and education programs increased. And with the shift to academic preparation of interpreters came a decrease in the level of involvement of Deaf people in determining who should and should not interpret. This shift also initiated the need for more formal ways to regulate the practice of interpreting.

Accreditation of Interpreter Education Programs

Accreditation, unlike the testing of individual practitioners through certification or licensure, evaluates and judges institutions or specialized programs. The accreditation of interpreter education programs is under the purview of the Commission on Collegiate Interpreter Education (CCIE). It was founded in 2006 for the purpose of promoting professionalism in the field of interpreter education. This entity is the result of leadership and development led primarily by the Conference of Interpreter Trainers (CIT). CIT is the professional association of interpreter teachers and trainers in the United States.

The overarching goal of accreditation of interpreter education programs is to help ensure that graduates are *qualified* to enter the workforce and work successfully as practitioners. The CCIE accreditation process requires programs to evidence compliance with a robust set of standards. The standards address policies on entry requirements, curricular goals, faculty selection, teaching methods, assessment, and projected student outcomes. So, when aspiring students of interpreting seek a program, selecting one that is accredited provides assurance that the program has met national standards and engages in both an internal and external review of its quality and effectiveness.

Currently, 13 baccalaureate degree and five associate degree interpreting programs have been accredited. This is a just over 10% of the 140+ programs currently offered in the United States. So, although national standards exist and have been adopted, the accreditation system is still relatively new, and it may take years to achieve the intended impact. This is just one example that reinforces the emergent nature of interpreting as a profession.

WHAT IT MEANS TO BE QUALIFIED

At the root, the term *qualified* means fit or competent for a specified purpose or a given job. It denotes that someone has complied with some set of specific requirements or conditions necessary for a given job and has been determined to be eligible to do the job by some recognized mechanism or entity.

Interpreter qualifications can be viewed through more than one lens. For example, the U.S. Department of Justice, in defining the regulations implementing the Americans with Disabilities Act (ADA) for title II (state and local government services) and title III (public accommodations and commercial facilities) defines a qualified interpreter as the following:

> A "qualified" interpreter means someone who is able to interpret effectively, accurately, and impartially, both receptively (i.e., understanding what the person with the disability is saying) and expressively (i.e., having the skill needed to convey information back to that person) using any necessary specialized vocabulary. (U.S. Department of Justice, 2014)

Because the definition indicates that the interpreter can convey the message both expressively and receptively, it means the interpreter must be competent in both languages—English and American Sign Language. To do this both effectively and accurately, a qualified interpreter needs to understand the interpreting process, how equivalency between two languages is achieved, the sociocultural norms that impact different types of communication events, and the manner in which equivalency of meaning is achieved in each language. Additionally, to interpret in an impartial manner means a qualified interpreter is someone who understands how an interpreter is to conduct themselves in a range of situations. They know how to apply the ethical framework from which the role and responsibility of an interpreter is conceived and implemented.

However, being qualified to interpret in a general sense does not necessarily translate to being qualified to interpret in all situations. For example, a person who is qualified to teach does not mean they are qualified to teach every subject or to address the unique or individual needs of a given student. A qualified teacher is someone who has the general competence necessary to engage in the task of teaching in designated content areas.

Consumer Perspectives

To appreciate this distinction as it relates to interpreters, it is important to give consideration to the direct and personal experiences of deaf individuals. One only needs to view any number of ASL vlogs posted on the internet or to engage in a conversation with a consumer to gain their perspective. Generally, deaf consumers are open to sharing the impact of working with interpreters who do not possess sufficient competence to meet their needs. Sometimes, the impact is significant. The general experience of deaf consumers indicates that there are some inherent challenges to their access to competent practitioners.

A Deaf consumer needs assessment, conducted by the National Interpreter Education Center (NIEC, 2009), indicates that although deaf consumers generally know how to access interpreters and use interpreters regularly, they continue to struggle to secure qualified interpreters. This is particularly true in settings like health care, employment, and legal. And, even when they are able to secure interpreters, they report inconsistent satisfaction with their services.

Consider the following statements from consumers about one aspect of a qualified interpreter's effectiveness—their attitude. These deaf consumers were interviewed as part of a national project to define entry-to-practice competencies (Witter-Merithew & Johnson, 2005).

> Consumer 1: There is concern in the Deaf community that interpreters do not always reflect attitudes consistent with Deaf community norms. I believe advance-screening individuals who aspire to become interpreters could reduce this situation. We want to ensure that they possess qualities of empathy, compassion, interest in humanity and improving society, and

open-mindedness. Although these qualities can be inspired through life experiences and exposure to deaf people, they cannot be totally learned and must be inherent in the individual to some degree.

Consumer 2: When I think about what constitutes an appropriate attitude for an interpreter, I think of many things—the most important being respect for the right of deaf people to be self-determined. Entering interpreters need to appreciate the importance of power as a part of interpreting and how their attitude can foster the right of deaf individuals to take control of the little decisions involved in the process (e.g., what language will be used, where the interpreter will sit or stand, introduction of the interpreter) as a precursor to taking control of the bigger decisions involved in the process (e.g., comprehensibility of the interpretation, turn-taking, power imbalances).

Consumer 3: There is a community-wide concern among Deaf people regarding the attitude of interpreters. It shows itself in a sense of powerlessness among deaf consumers. Interpreters convey the impression to deaf consumers that interpreters are "owed" or that the Deaf community is obliged to the interpreter. This expression of superiority that is expressed by some interpreters makes many deaf people uncomfortable and perpetuates the notion that interpreters' attitudes are not aligned with the expectations of the Deaf community. Their behavior is not based on mutual respect, or a mutual goal of improving communication access. This sense of entitlement impacts the entire interpreting dynamic.

These critical experiences from deaf consumers help practitioners to gain an appreciation that what constitutes *qualified* often depends on the lens through which you view interpreting. Such experiences compel us as interpreters to maintain open and consistent dialogue with deaf people, so we develop a keen awareness of their point of view. It also underscores the importance of interpreters using discretion and respect in accepting assignments. Although interpreters may be deemed qualified in terms of the standards of their state, they may not be qualified for a specific assignment or a specific consumer.

DISTINGUISHING CERTIFICATION AND LICENSURE

Society's reliance on the expertise of professionals has contributed to the growth and development of certification programs and licensure standards nationwide. Such systems guide the work of a wide range of professionals, including interpreters. Employers view certification and licensure as a mechanism for determining that the professionals they hire have met minimum standards of competence. Consumers view certification and licensure as a stamp of approval by a recognized entity—one that provides a level of gatekeeping that is intended to protect their interests. In the case of national certification offered by the Registry of Interpreters for the Deaf (RID), sign language interpreters view it as a portable credential that enables them to work in most any state.

Although the goal of both licensure and certification is to recognize who is qualified to provide a specific professional service, the two systems differ in the following ways:

- Licensure is overseen by government agencies. Certification is typically overseen by an association related to the specialized work of a group of professionals or the testing and certification industry.
- Licensing is a mandatory credentialing process established by a state government. Certification is a voluntary credentialing process established by a private, typically nonprofit, professional association. However, it is possible that part of the licensure process requires an individual to hold the voluntary professional certification. That is certainly the case in terms of sign language interpreting.
- In states with licensure requirements, it is a violation of the law to work without a license. This provides employers and consumers with an additional remedy for addressing efforts of nonqualified individuals to provide professional services. Government regulation strengthens gatekeeping. In states where there is no licensure requirement, the certification credential is commonly a requirement to work. However, because credentialing associations only have authority for oversight of those individuals who hold certification, the association can do little when uncertified individuals provide services. They only have authority to self-regulate. So, the combination of certification and licensure provides a much stronger foundation for protecting the interest of consumers, employers, and a qualified workforce.

Although there are differences in each system, licensure and certification both serve the common purpose of determining who is minimally qualified to practice a particular occupation or profession. And, in some instances such as sign language interpreting, the two systems can work in concert to ensure that the rights of consumers are protected. In fact, states that require licensure for interpreters to minimally register to work, certification is one of the associated qualifications that must be provided.

Certification as Self-Regulation

Private organizations establish certain criteria for certification, and a person becomes certified after meeting that criteria. Certification is a form of self-regulation, in that it is voluntary and operates without governmental oversight. Certification does not provide a legal mechanism to practice an otherwise governmentally regulated profession, but it does allow certificate holders to accurately promote the fact that they are certified by the private entity. There are no governmental penalties for failure to achieve certification or for losing certification recognition.

In the case of sign language interpreting, the most widely recognized certification program is that of RID. It is one of only a few national professional associations of signed language interpreters and the only one that currently offers certification. Eligibility for taking the certification examination involves meeting a variety of criteria, including, but not limited to, education and experience. The examination process includes both a written and performance test. A candidate must pass the written exam before being eligible to sit for the performance exam. RID certification must be maintained annually and requires participation in a Certification Maintenance Program (CMP) that requires certified practitioners to earn a minimum number of continuing education units over a 4-year cycle. At the end of each cycle, assuming renewal standards have been satisfied, practitioners must begin a new cycle and continue to fulfill the established requirements.

Certification as Professional Standing

From the consumer perspective, certification is a way in which consumers may or may not draw an inference about the quality of a practitioner's work. Because certification is based on satisfying a minimum standard of competence, and the ability of practitioners will range from meeting the standard to performing well beyond the standard, it may not be a clear indicator of the standard of competence to consumers. Although professional certification cannot guarantee competence, it is nevertheless widely used by the general public or by employers as a measure of competence. Typically, practitioners who aspire to professional standing and want to advance in a profession desire certification.

Enforcing Ethical Practice

The only potential method of public protection is through enforcement of ethical standards of practice by the private organization that confers the certification. In the case of RID, this regulation occurs through the Ethical Practices System (EPS) that upholds the integrity of ethical standards among interpreters by maintaining and implementing a process of reviewing and resolving complaints of ethical violations. When practitioners are found in violation, they are subject to a variety of disciplinary actions, ranging from censure to suspension or revocation of certification. Violations are published by RID, giving the name and state of the practitioner, the certification they hold, the specific violation and the related disciplinary action.

Table 1 offers a sample of how that information is published. In accordance with Standard 3.10 of the *EPS Manual*, when a violation of the National Association for the Deaf-Registry of Interpreters for the Deaf Code of Professional Conduct has been determined, regardless of the sanction, the interpreter's name, location, violation, and a summary of the sanction are printed in the journal *VIEWS*.

National Certification Programs

RID certification is not the only nationally recognized interpreter certification. From the early 1990s until late in 2002, the National Association of the Deaf (NAD) offered certification, and practitioners in numerous states were awarded certification from the NAD. The NAD system involved five levels—the higher the level, the greater the competence of the practitioner. This system is no longer available for newly entering practitioners; however, those who already hold the credential may still be recognized as certified, depending on their state regulations.

In 2003, NAD and RID entered into an agreement that RID would recognize NAD Level III, IV, and V interpreters as RID-certified members, if they held an active certification, joined the RID prior to June 30, 2005, and complied with the organization's CMP requirements. Level I and II practitioners were determined to not hold sufficient competence to be recognized by RID as professionally certified practitioners, and so this agreement did not extend to individuals holding those levels.

Another nationally recognized credential is the Educational Interpreter Performance Assessment (EIPA) administered by Boys Town National Research Hospital in Omaha, Nebraska. It is unique in several ways. First, it tests individuals at either the elementary or secondary level of educational interpreting. Second, the candidate can be tested in their ability to interpret in one of the following four ways: spoken English and ASL, spoken English and Manually Coded English, spoken English and Contact Signing (Pidgin Signed English [PSE] or English-like signing), or spoken English and Cued American English (cued speech). So, for example, an individual interpreting in a K–12 setting might choose to be tested at the secondary level between

Table 1. Sample EPS Published Decisions.

Interpreter	Credentials	State	Tenets	Sanction
John Doe	NIC	Mississippi	Violation of CPC Tenet 1: Confidentiality, Tenet 3: Conduct, and Tenet 4: Respect for Consumers	Suspension of NIC certification for a period of 6 months and completion of prescribed mentoring, ethics training, and readings to be completed within 9 months. Effective Sept. 30, 2015.
Jane Doe	CI and CT	Vermont	Violation of CPC Tenet 2: Professionalism, Tenet 3: Conduct, Tenet 4: Respect for Consumers, and Tenet 6: Business Practices	Certification revocation, effective November 1, 2015

spoken English and ASL, or to be tested at the elementary level between spoken English and Cued American English.

In 2007, RID entered into an agreement with Boys Town to recognize certain EIPA-assessed individuals as RID-certified members. Individuals who possess a 4.0 or above on the EIPA (which provides a score on a 5-point scale) are eligible for Ed:K-12 Certification, if they are a current RID member, meet the EIPA written and performance requirements, and meet RID's educational requirement. Once recognized as a certified member, these interpreters must participate in the same CMP as any other certified member of RID. Effective June 2016, RID ceased the agreement with Boys Town regarding recognition of the EIPA for RID certification designation. Although no additional EIPA-assessed individuals can achieve the RID-certified designation at this point in time, RID continues to honor the certification designation for those individuals who satisfied and continue to comply with the terms of the 2007 agreement prior to the June 2016 date.

It is not uncommon for certified interpreters to want to assert that they are more qualified than someone who is not certified. However, in reality, the most that can be factually said is that certified individuals have taken the initiative to measure their own qualifications against the profession's consensus criteria, standards, or principles of competence; other individuals have not. As previously mentioned, certainly consumers and employers depend on the profession's standards to assist them in identifying competent practitioners. So, to this end, holding professional certification serves as an advantage when seeking work.

State Certification Systems

Some states choose to administer their own certification programs. Unlike national certification, state certification establishes a mandatory process for practitioners working in the state and is administered by a government agency or entity. Three states require state certification to work as an interpreter. The Texas Bureau of Evaluation for Interpreters (BEI) is one such state.

The Department of Assistive and Rehabilitation Services (DARS) Office for Deaf and Hard of Hearing Services (DHHS) Board for Evaluation of Interpreters (BEI) certification program is responsible for testing and certifying the skill levels of individuals seeking to become certified interpreters in Texas. It is a level system, offering five designations—Level 5 designating the highest degree of competence. Maintaining certification with the BEI requires accrual of continuing educations and annual renewal. As well, the BEI is recognized and administered locally by several other states.

Other states, such as Missouri, have what is called a Quality Assurance Screening (QAS) as an additional pathway to becoming state certified. In some cases, this testing instrument is also used to meet licensure and registration requirements.

Certification as Part of Registration

Some states require professional interpreters to register in order to work. Registration is procedurally similar to obtaining a license, although it does not typically carry the same ability to enforce compliance that comes with licensure. To be eligible to register, typically, the interpreter needs to satisfy certification and education requirements. Other states maintain a registry—a list of individuals who are qualified to work as an interpreter. This is not unlike the RID database that lists members, their certification(s), and how they can be contacted.

Registration and registry laws vary in scope and application. For example, Kansas requires interpreters to be registered, but their law does not provide for the enforcement of the requirement. Conversely, Nevada's registration law provides for both criminal and civil penalty. Table 2 further illuminates how registration and registry works in four states that recognize RID certification as part of the process. There are both similarities and differences in each of these registration or registry systems. For example, all recognize multiple testing and credentialing systems— RID certification being the consistent system across all of the examples. Another similarity is that all of the states have a Commission for the Deaf or other specialized social service agency for the deaf that is responsible for the registration process or maintenance of the registry. However, the period of renewal varies for each state, with 3 years being the longest period. As well, not all require evidence of continuing education. However, for those individuals with RID certification, participation in the CMP is mandatory, even though it is not required by the state regulatory system. Another difference is the approach to enforcement. Three have some degree of enforcement—with Nevada being the most stringent. Kansas has no enforcement. These variations demonstrate how each state tailors the process to meet its individual needs.

STATE LICENSURE AS A FORM OF REGULATION

The focus of state licensure is on those occupations or professions where the good of the public is potentially at risk and must be protected. Accordingly, governmental agencies establish licensure requirements, and when those requirements are met, grant to practitioners the right to practice.

Typically, the process of licensure for a given occupation or profession is administered by a state board that oversees the application, approval, renewal, and compliance process. Licensure is usually based on a combination of requirements, including education, testing of competence by some type of examination, and experience. Typically, requirements for maintaining currency through continuing education are included. These requirements, which can vary from one state to another, set what the state determines is the minimum standard of competence necessary to protect the interests of society. License to practice must be renewed on a schedule set by the state. For example, in North Carolina, sign language interpreters must renew their license to practice each year by September 30th. At the time of renewal, the practitioner must submit application, evidence of continuing education, and annual payment of the licensure fee.

As previously mentioned, licensure to practice is mandatory. As a result, the laws and regulations associated with licensure may provide for criminal or administrative penalties for practicing without a license. For example, in the state of Utah, interpreting without a license is considered a Class B misdemeanor. That means unlicensed practice is a criminal violation. In other states, an administrative penalty may be imposed—a civil monetary fine.

In terms of sign language interpreting, licensure is an expanding trend. Although less than 15 states currently have licensure, at least that many more are engaged in amending or introducing interpreter legislation. Table 3 highlights four state licensure systems—all geographically dispersed.

Table 2. Sample of State Registration Laws.

State	Law	Registration Process	Categories	Practicing without Registration
Kansas	75-4355b: All interpreters for the deaf, hard of hearing, and speech impaired, secured under the provisions of K.S.A. 75-4355a through 75-4355d, shall be certified by or registered with the Kansas commission for the deaf and hard of hearing or an agency designated by the commission.	Individual making application to register -Must complete and submit an application -Include a copy of certification(s) -Must engage in continuing education	1. Nationally certified—RID, including NIC 2. State-certified Kansas Quality Assurance Screening Level IV and V (This certification is no longer available but still recognized.)	No penalties identified in the statute or available regulations or published procedures
Nevada	NRS 656A.080: The Aging and Disability Services Division of the Department of Health and Human Services is to establish a registry of persons engaged in the practice of interpreting or the practice of real-time captioning	Individual making application to register - Must be at least 18 years of age - Submit an application - Payment of fees - Evidence compliance with the requisite criteria for the category for which they seek registration, including education, training, experience, and certification	1. Apprentice [can demonstrate intermediate competence] 2. Skilled Practitioner [possesses national certification] 3. Advanced Certified Practitioner [possesses advanced national certification]	A person who violates the provisions of the law - Is guilty of a misdemeanor - May be assessed a civil penalty of up to $1,000

State	Legislation	Requirements	Classifications	Disciplinary Authority
			4. Apprentice Educational Interpreter [possesses an EIPA of 3.0]	
			5. Intermediate Educational Interpreter [possesses an EIPA of 3.1–3.9]	
			5. Advanced Educational Interpreter [possesses an EIPA of 4.0 or higher]	
Pennsylvania	PL 492, No. 57: Providing for state registration of individuals providing sign language interpreting and transliterating services to individuals who are deaf or hard of hearing, and imposing duties on the Office for the Deaf and Hard of Hearing in the Department of Labor and Industry.	Individual making application to register - Must be at least 18 years of age - Submit an application - Payment of fees - Evidence of knowledge and proficiency certification by an approved entity - Renewable every 2 years	1. Registered sign language interpreter 2. Registered provisional sign language interpreter	The department shall have the authority to impose disciplinary or corrective measures or levy civil penalties on a registrant or an individual who has obtained a provisional registration for violations.

(Continued)

Table 2. (Continued)

State	Law	Registration Process	Categories	Practicing without Registration
		Provisional registration is allowed for individuals who have graduated within 5 years from an interpreter education program from an accredited college or university and who has passed an approved written exam.		
West Virginia	WV Code 5-14-5 9(b): The Commission for the Deaf shall establish, maintain, and coordinate a list of qualified and certified interpreters for the deaf.	Individual making application for registration must - Submit completed application with resume with three references - Copy of all certifications - Copy of current RID membership card - Copy of transcripts or certifications from an interpreter education program, if applicable - Renewable every 3 years	1. RID Certified, including CI, CT, NIC and CDI 2. NAD-certified Level II, IV and V 3. K–12 interpreters who met the Board of Education Policy 5202	Violation can lead to suspension, revocation, reprimand, or requirement that the interpreter complete additional training.

There are both similarities and differences in each of these state licensure systems. For example, all require a continuing education requirement as part of the renewal process. All have some civil or criminal action associated with working without licensure. All have a board that oversees the licensure process. All recognize national certifications. However, some only recognize RID's certification, whereas others include the NAD's or EIPA's. In addition, at least one of the states offers a multilevel testing system as an alternative to recognizing national certifications. Two others have an alternative system of classification in lieu of certification. These variations are representative of all of the licensure laws currently in place—they are tailored to the needs of the given state.

RECOGNIZING THE SPECIALTY COMPETENCE OF INTERPRETING PRACTITIONERS

As the needs of deaf Americans for linguistic access and inclusion become more complex and/or heightened opportunities for their involvement in more aspects of society increase, so does the potential need for interpreter practitioners to specialize. *Specialization* has been defined as the narrowing of practice based on specific events, populations, or functions (Witter-Merithew, 2010). Specialization offers practitioners an opportunity to gain higher levels of competence in specific areas of practice.

Essentially, there are two ways in which interpreter practitioners seek recognition as a specialist— self-designation or achieving some sort of endorsement by a recognized entity. Given that there are currently only a few areas of practice where specialty endorsement exists, self-designation processes are more prevalent.

Self-designation of specialized competence typically occurs when an individual practitioner acquires specialized knowledge of a certain setting and makes a concerted effort to gain a high level of experience working within that setting. Common examples of this can be seen in the area of K–12, health care, legal, and performing arts interpreting. But, specialization competence is not limited to setting—it could also involve working with a specific population or in a particular function. For example, a practitioner may hold specialized competence in working with individuals who are DeafBlind or with deaf immigrants who do not yet possess competence

Table 3. Sample of State Licensure Programs.

State	Law	Requirements to Obtain Licensure	Licensure Renewal Requirements	Penalty for Working without License
New Hampshire	RSA 326-1 became effective in 2003. Interpreters must hold a license in order to receive remuneration and to practice in most settings, except religious, or by waiver signed by the consumer.	- Must be 18 or older - Meet education and competence standard evidenced by either national certification (such as RID, NAD or EIPA) or the state classification system - Be of good moral and ethical character - Pay licensing fee	- Renew every 3 years by way of application - Proof of continuing education through RID's certification maintenance system - Renewal fee	Class A misdemeanor and may, in addition, be subject to a civil penalty of up to $2,000 per offense or, in the case of a continuing offense, $250 for each day the violation continues
New Mexico	NMSA §61-34-1, Signed Language Interpreting Practices Act, requires interpreters to have a license in order to work.	Three designations—community, educational, and provisional. - All require individual to be 18 or older, be of good moral and ethical character, and submit an application.	- Community and educational license renews every 2 years by way of application. - Proof of compliance of RID's CMP. - Renewal fee.	Violations to the Licensure Act are considered a misdemeanor.

		- Community and educational require RID certification. - Provisional requires proof of completion of an interpreter education program.	- Provisional renews annually for four cycles (5 years total) then must move into certified category or lose ability to work. - Proof of continuing education as an associate member of RID. - Renewal fee.	
North Carolina	Statute 90D-14 of General Statute 8B became effective in 2002. Must be licensed to work in all settings, except K–12, which is regulated by standards set by the Department of Public Instruction (DPI)	Must be 18 or older and do the following: - Meet education and competence standard evidenced by either national certification (such as RID, NAD or EIPA) or a state classification system - Be of good moral and ethical character - Go through a fingerprint and criminal background check - Pay licensing fee	- Renew annually by way of application - Proof of at least 20 contact hours of approved continuing education - Renewal fee	Board has the authority to assess civil penalties not to exceed $1,000 for the violation of any sections of 90D or any rules adopted by the Board. The Board may also assess the costs of disciplinary actions against the interpreter.

(Continued)

Table 3. (Continued)

State	Law	Requirements to Obtain Licensure	Licensure Renewal Requirements	Penalty for Working without License
Utah	Utah Code 53A-26a-101 became effective in 1994.	- Must be 18 or older - Must have at least a high school diploma, GED, or equivalent - Must be certified by a recognized entity, such as RID, EIPA, or NAD, or by state certification. - State system awards three levels of competence—professional, novice, and provisional. - Be of good moral and ethical character. - Pay an administrative fee.	- Renewal is done annually - Requires submission of an application - Proof of at least 20 hours of approved continuing education - Payment of renewal fee	Class B misdemeanor

in ASL. Or, in terms of function, practitioners may specialize as video-relay interpreters, where their work is done primarily through the use of technology, or as designated interpreters, where their work is done primarily in collaboration with a single deaf professional. Practitioners may declare their specialization using business cards, websites, reputation, recommendation, employment, or other ways in which they promote their work.

Conversely, formal endorsement of specialization is the result of external recognition by some recognized entity. It typically includes successful completion of a specialized course of study, some period of supervised work, and validation of minimum competence through certification or other endorsement. For example, formal preparation in the areas of legal, healthcare, and public school interpreting exists at several universities in the United States. Specialty programs typically involve advanced coursework that assumes generalist competence prior to specialization. This is particularly true in the area of legal and healthcare interpreting—less so in K–12 interpreting.

Further, currently, specialized endorsement is conferred through assessment or certification for both K–12 and legal interpreters. Historically, RID offered the Special Certificate: Legal (SC:L) to individuals who already possess generalist certification and then meet training, experience, and supervised work experience requirements. This certification program is currently under moratorium as of January 1, 2016, due to the need for test revision. Boys Town National Research Hospital offers the EIPA that awards one of several designations to interpreters working in K–12 settings. Both of these credentialing entities require passing both a knowledge and performance test.

For a limited amount of time, RID also offered the Special Certificate: Performance Arts (SC:PA). It was not determined to be a sufficient priority in the area of specialized practice to sustain a testing and certification system, and so the offering of the exam ended. And, for many years, there has been pressure from practitioners for RID to establish a testing and certification system for healthcare interpreters and/or to collaborate with other such systems external to RID. Although such endorsement does not yet exist, it remains an ongoing part of the public discourse among RID members and interpreter practitioners.

REFERENCES

Barnum, B. (August 13, 1997). Licensure, certification, and accreditation. *Online Journal of Issues in Nursing, 2*(3). Retrieved from https://www.researchgate.net/publication/26406345_Licensure_Certification_and_Accreditation

Cokely, D., & Winston, E. (2009). Phase II deaf consumer needs assessment: Final report. National Consortium of Interpreter Education Centers (NCIEC). Retrieved from http://www.interpretereducation.org/wp-content/uploads/2011/06/FinalPhaseIIDCReport.pdf

Ferguson, R. F., & Brown, J. (2000). Certification test scores, teacher quality, and student achievement. In D. Grissmer and J. M. Ross (Eds.), *Analytic issues in the assessment of student achievement* (pp. 133–156). Washington, DC: National Center for Education Statistics.

Harvey, L., Mason, S., & Ward, R. (1995). *Role of professional bodies in higher education quality monitoring.* Birmingham, UK: Quality in Higher Education Project.

Gardner, H., & Shulman, L. S. (2005). *The professions in America today: Crucial but fragile* (pp. 13–14). Cambs, UK: Daedalus.

Jacobs, J. (2012). Certification of professionals. *Association law handbook: A practical guide for associations, societies and charities.* 5th edition. Washington, DC: Association Management Press, pp. 398–405.

Jacobs, J. (2012). Certification of professionals-administration. *Association law handbook: A practical guide for associations, societies and charities.* 5th edition. Washington, DC: Association Management Press, pp. 406–415.

Mathers, C., & Witter-Merithew, A. (2014). The contribution of Deaf interpreters to gatekeeping within the interpreting pofession: Reconnecting with our roots. In *Our roots: The essence of our future CIT conference proceedings* (pp. 158–173). Fremont, CA: Conference of Interpreter Trainers. Retrieved from http://www.cit-asl.org/new/2014-23-mathers-and-witter-merithew/

Schoon, C. G., & Smith, I. L. (Eds.). (2000). *The licensure and certification mission: Legal, social, and political foundations.* New York, NY: Forbes Custom Publishing.

Sullivan, William M. (2005). *Work and integrity: The crisis and promise of professionalism in America.* 2nd ed. Indianapolis, IN: Jossey Bass.

Sutherland, K., & Leatherman, S. (August 2006). Does certification improve medical standards? *British Medical Journal, 333,* 439–441.

U.S. Department of Justice. (2014). *ADA requirements: Effective communication.* Washington, DC: USDOJ. Retrieved from http://www.ada.gov/effective-comm.htm.

Witter-Merithew, A., & Nicodemus, B. (2010). Toward intentional development of interpreter specialization. *Journal of Interpretation,* 55–76.

Witter-Merithew, A. (2010). *Conceptualizing a framework for specialization in ASL-English Interpreting: A report of project findings and recommendations.* National Consortium of Interpreter Education Centers (NCIEC). Retrieved from

http://www.interpretereducation.org/wp-content/uploads/2011/08/Concept
FrameworkSpecialization.pdf

Witter-Merithew, A., & Johnson, L. (2004). Market disorder within the field of sign
language interpreting: Professionalization implications. *Journal of Interpretation*,
pp. 19–56.

Witter-Merithew, A., & Johnson, L. (2005). *Toward competent practice: Conversations
with stakeholders*. Alexandria, VA: RID Publications.

10

International Perspectives on Interpreting: Isn't Everything Just Like at Home?

DEBRA RUSSELL

The field of signed language interpreting continues to experience rapid changes, and in recent years, significant events in many parts of the world have contributed to this evolution. Governments have recognized the national signed language(s) used in their countries, signed language interpreters now have access to greater opportunities for learning at postsecondary institutions and within interpreter organizations, and the scholarship and research about signed language interpreting continues to grow, producing a body of evidence upon which to support the profession (Bontempo, 2015).[1]

A TRIP AROUND THE WORLD: THE CURRENT STATE OF INTERPRETING AS A PROFESSION

Napier (2009) identified that the state of educational opportunities for signed language interpreters varies considerably around the world, ranging from countries having no training available, to short-term workshops and courses that last a few weeks, to college-level 2- and 3-year programs, up to countries such as the United States, which has programs based at universities offering bachelor's, master's, and PhD programs in American Sign Language interpreting. Within this context of dramatically different

---

1. Signed languages are visual-gestural languages that are not universal, but rather evolve within specific Deaf communities and the people who use the signed language to communicate with each other.

opportunities for learning to become a signed language interpreter, there are also no standard requirements for becoming certified as and working as an interpreter; nor are there professional bodies that represent interpreters in some countries (Bontempo, 2015).

The World Association of Sign Language Interpreters (WASLI; http://wasli.org) was founded in 2005, with the assistance of the World Federation of the Deaf (WFD; https://wfdeaf.org) in order to globally support the development of the field of professional signed language interpreting. The organizational structure includes the selection of regional representatives, who then work at the multicountry regional level to support the training of interpreters and the development of interpreter associations. As of 2015, there are eight such regions, which also mirror the regions chosen by the WFD. WASLI and WFD signed a Memo of Understanding (MOU) in 2007, which was then updated in 2017, and since 2005, the organizations have worked closely on several projects that have resulted in increased training opportunities and the development of standard practices and standards.[2] In 2011, WASLI released a philosophy statement on the education of signed language interpreters and created a framework for interpreter education, in order to respond to the numerous requests for information about how best to start the education of interpreters (see www.wasli.org). This framework has been useful to countries, especially those that may have recently ratified the United Nations Convention on the Rights of Persons with Disabilities (UNCRPD). The UNCRPD addresses Deaf people's rights to participate in all aspects of society, including education, justice, government, and culture, and sign language is addressed in several of the tenets. Countries that have signed and ratified the UNCRPD are then held to account for the ways in which the rights of their Deaf citizens are supported through professional interpreting services. This then requires countries to implement sign language research and opportunities for interpreter training. As Bontempo (2015) emphasizes, opportunities for WFD and WASLI to influence education and training for signed language interpreters is crucial to the implementation of the UNCRPD.[3]

---

2. A Memo of Understanding (MOU) is an agreement that sets out the terms and conditions of mutual collaboration between two organizations.

3. See Napier (2009) for further information on international developments in interpreter education.

Oceania

The region known as *Oceania* includes Australia, New Zealand, Fiji, and the Solomon Islands. Australia and New Zealand have long-standing interpreter associations, and Fiji has also very recently formed a professional organization. There are well-established paths to interpreter education in both Australia and New Zealand, with programs available at the college and university levels. Napier (2004) and Napier, McKee, and Goswell (2006) describe the context of professionalizing the field of sign language interpreting in Australia and New Zealand, with sign language interpreting emerging in the 1980s, following similar paths as the United States and the United Kingdom. During that time, several factors supported the creation of formal training programs, including anti-discrimination legislation, the lobbying efforts of Deaf organizations, the burgeoning linguistic research about the signed language used in Australia (Auslan), and the formation of interpreter associations. Interpreters in Australia can engage in interpreter education through Macquarie University and in New Zealand at the Auckland University of Technology. Macquarie University is a unique model, in that it includes signed and spoken language interpreters taking some classes together at the postgraduate diploma level. Students who wish to pursue a master's program can transfer into the translation and interpreting program, which is offered by blended delivery format, making it accessible online and in intensive learning blocks. In addition to the postgraduate diploma route, the WASLI Oceania representative, Angela Murray, reports that prospective interpreters can pursue a 1-year diploma in five Australian states, and Deaf interpreters can pursue training in two states (personal communication, April 20, 2017). Australia has traditionally had a two-level accreditation system that certifies both Deaf and hearing interpreters through the National Authority for the Accreditation of Translators and Interpreters (NAATI), and more recently they have added a conference level of accreditation.[4]

New Zealand offers professional training for interpreters and has done so since 1992 (Napier et al., 2006), and it has evolved into a 3-year bachelor's degree program. Given the bilingual nature of the country, additional efforts have been made to recruit interpreter students who are speakers of

---

4. See Spring (2000) for a further discussion of the evolution of this system.

Maori, in order to meet the demand for interpreters who can interpret between Maori, New Zealand Sign Language (NZSL), and English. Since 1997, the interpreter association, Sign Language Interpreters Association of New Zealand, known as SLIANZ, has been active and has well-established links with interpreter associations in other countries, as well as with the New Zealand Society of Translators and Interpreters.

Fiji does not yet have a formal pathway to educate signed language interpreters; however, during 2015, WASLI and the interpreter associations in the region were able to support some short-term training, which built on previous workshops and seminars given by consultants from the region, in a similar approach to the one described by Nelson, Tawaketini, Spencer, and Goswell (2009). The community is focused on providing training for Deaf community members who can then teach their language to others, and this is a key step for any country developing a solid approach to the training of signed language interpreters. A significant event for Fiji occurred in 2015, when their interpreter president was selected by WASLI as a delegate to be sponsored to attend the WASLI conference at Istanbul. These types of opportunities serve to build capacity within the region, as the interpreter delegate establishes a network of international support, acquires new knowledge, and builds confidence as an interpreter leader. In 2018, Fiji will host the first WASLI Oceania regional conference, further supporting interpreter development in the region.

Each of the countries of the region experiences challenges, and the key issues facing Australian interpreters were described by the Oceania representative at the WASLI General Meeting of July 15, 2017, as pay rates, working conditions, recognition for the work performed, length and breadth of interpreter training programs, and quality control and monitoring. New Zealand faces three primary challenges: a shortage of trilingual Maori interpreters, a lack of interpreting standards and regulations, and having only one location for training interpreters. By contrast, the Fijian concerns center on the lack of available interpreter training, the poor remuneration for interpreting, and the lack of full-time interpreter positions that can serve the community. Numerous other islands also comprise this region; however, little is known about the Deaf and interpreter communities in some of these remote locations.

Like WASLI and WFD, both the Australian and New Zealand interpreter associations have signed MOUs with the national Deaf associations of their respective countries, strengthening the joint collaboration and accountability for addressing shared issues and challenges, as they relate to interpreting and the Deaf community.

Asia

Asia is one of the largest WASLI regions with 38 countries, including Japan, India, Philippines, Mongolia, Nepal, Malaysia, and Thailand, all of which have national associations. Some countries, such as Japan and India, have two national interpreter associations. Numerous countries do not have interpreter associations, and some countries' interpreter associations have dissolved due to a lack of interpreter leaders. Singapore, Hong Kong, and Bangladesh have groups of signed language interpreters that operate within the national Deaf associations. The WASLI regional representative, Etsuko Unemoto, reports that a major challenge is communication among the interpreters in the region, as there is limited internet access in some countries, and the linguistic and cultural diversity of the region also makes it difficult to find a common written or spoken language that can be used for communication purposes (personal communication, July 11, 2017). This region has enjoyed considerable success in having interpreters attend meetings that are imbedded within the WFD Regional Secretariat (WFD-RS) conferences that are held in the region every 2 years. By cooperating with WFD, the program committee includes a day of learning for signed language interpreters from the region, and these events have been significant for all, but especially for those interpreters coming from countries with no formal training opportunities. Forty signed language interpreters participated in the 2016 WFD-RS conference, making it the largest gathering at the regional level to date. These events allow for face-to-face exchanges of information that are more helpful than accessing each other via email or other technological options.

Training varies throughout the region, from short-term trainings, to longer private diploma programs, such as the one offered in Malaysia through RC Missions, to graduate diplomas in interpretation and translation offered through Deakin University in Hong Kong. Some examples of the diversity of approaches within the region include interpreter associations, such as the Indian Sign Language Interpreters Association (ISLIA), which provides short-term training for signed language interpreters, in addition to the 1-year interpreting program that has been recognized by the Rehabilitation Council of India. The 1-year program is offered by the Indian Sign Language Research and Training Centre (See http://205.147.97.190/islrtcapp/) and at three regional associations. Another example of how training can emerge from short-term training and evolve into postsecondary institutions can be found in Nepal, where international interpreter trainers have been working with Thai interpreters to develop their skills and knowledge, and over the past few years, this has resulted in collaborative relationships between Mahidol University and the Deaf community, leading to the creation of their first sign language interpreting bachelor's degree program (Zane Hema, personal communication, April 15, 2018.

Signed language interpreters in the region who know at least one other signed language report that they have accessed formal sign language interpreter education programs in Canada, the United Kingdom, the United States, and Australia, and upon their return, they have worked with the communities in order to enhance the knowledge and skill level of interpreters who have not had the privilege of formal education.

Some of the challenges that signed language interpreters experience in Asian countries stem from the lack of awareness that country governments have about Deaf people and their human rights. Many Deaf people have no idea that they have a right to access information through a sign language interpreter, and even if their country is a signatory to the UNCRPD, it does not mean that the national and/or local governments have implemented policies and processes to support access in the way intended by the UNCRPD. Further challenges stem from the fact that in many countries, Deaf people cannot access education beyond the most basic years, resulting in unemployment, underemployment, and poor literacy rates. This then impacts their ability to mobilize and lobby their governments for better training of signed language interpreters and access that is equitable in order to support their human rights. Further, many countries in the region report that schools for the Deaf are being closed as governments adopt a Western educational policy of "inclusion," which further exacerbates the educational problems faced by Deaf people.[5] Finally, interpreters have identified that interpreting is not well recognized or supported, especially when the national signed language is not recognized. When interpreters do attempt to organize a professional association, they face numerous barriers, including societal attitudes, a lack of remuneration, insufficient knowledge and experience needed to sustain an association, and insufficient financial resources to operate the association, which then results in people leaving the voluntary posts, leading to the ultimate closure of the association (Monica Punjabi, personal communication, April 2, 2018).

Finally, Japan and India have signed MOUs between Deaf and interpreter associations, and the level of cooperation between associations and governments is high, resulting in advancements in those respective countries.

Africa

The Africa continent comprises another WASLI region, and at this time, there are eight interpreter associations that represent the countries of Ghana, Ivory Coast, Kenya, Tanzania, Nigeria, South Africa, Zambia, and Namibia. At the 2011 WASLI conference held in Durban, South Africa, interpreters from the region met to identify a set of common priorities. A top priority for the region was training for signed language interpreters and instituting a train-the-trainer model, so that Deaf community members and interpreters who live and work in the country could develop the capacity to deliver regular training. One strategy for developing this approach was to partner with the National Alliance of Black Interpreters (NAOBI) based in the United States, to access trainers who could work with other countries on the development of curriculum and resources.

The 2008 WFD Regional Survey identified the following issues that are pertinent to the status of sign interpreting profession in Africa:

- Lack of interpreter training and education
- Lack of a proper remuneration system for sign language interpreting services

---

5. For further reading on educational access, see Russell and McLeod (2009) and Russell and Winston (2014).

- Absence of interpreter associations in many countries
- Absence of legislation to make the provision of sign language services available
- Lack of mutual working relationships between signed language interpreters and Deaf communities

These issues have led interpreters in Africa to focus on establishing associations in countries where there are none and organizing training programs. For example, Ghana created a professional association in 2011, and three of their interpreters participated in leadership training with Nigerian signed language interpreters. As well, they have offered joint training with the national and local Deaf associations, which has then had a positive impact on the relationships between Deaf and interpreter community members. Further, interpreters have worked with Deaf communities to achieve common goals, such as creating awareness about the need for professional interpreting services. By comparison, the Ivory Coast also established an association in 2011; however, no interpreter training events have been held to date, and instead the emphasis has been to work in partnerships with other nongovernmental organizations (NGOs) to advocate for the implementation of the UNCRPD. Kenya also has an association that offers short-term workshops to interpreters. In Kenya, Ethiopia, and Tanzania, there is training at the university level; however, it is not part of a language practice degree, but is instead a module or short course as part of another degree, exposing the students to sign language. Nigeria has had an interpreter association since 2009 and has more than 150 signed language interpreters registered as members. There are formal interpreter programs based at two Nigerian universities, and several international NGOs have supported the development of interpreting. For example, the Swedish Association of the Deaf has collaborated with NGOs to offer mentoring opportunities for Nigerian Deaf leaders and signed language interpreters. In April 2018, the Educational Interpreters Association of Nigeria (ESLIAN) held a conference, focusing specifically on the needs of interpreters that work in school settings. Tanzania does not have any formal training approaches, although their interpreter association reports that through advocacy efforts, they are seeing increased salary levels for their work. Interpreters and Deaf leaders, from within and outside of the country, are playing a role in mentoring the interpreters. One of the newest interpreter associations is the South

African Association, formed in 2014, that has already achieved a major accomplishment in that they participated in the creation of the South African Language Practitioners Council Act, ensuring signed language interpreters were also covered by the legislation. Like Nigeria, South Africa has programs that train interpreters at the university level, offering diplomas, postgraduate diplomas, and master's degrees at three universities, including the University of Witwatersrand, University of the Free State, and University of the North West.

The major challenges cited by the WASLI regional representative, Natasha Maliko (personal communication, July 10, 2015), include the lack of human and financial resources to move interpreting forward as a profession in many of the African nations. Further, she cites a lack of cooperation and collaboration among interpreter and Deaf associations, which then impacts the accomplishments of both organizations. Similar to the Asia region, South Africa needs leadership training for interpreters, to sustain and grow the regional activities. Finally, a key issue, stressed by Akach (2006), is that African Deaf communities have a long history of colonization, and as such, national signed languages need to be supported, because the indigenous sign languages were lost as a result of the imposition of sign languages from other countries, such as American Sign Language. Akach (2005) states the following:

> As WASLI members we need to protect our members against abuse that comes as a result of bad training, and in particular the imposition of a foreign signed language that recipients of the service do not understand. We should advocate and encourage proper training of our members. (p. 43).

As African signed language interpreters look to the future, they have expressed a goal of creating an African Federation of Sign Language Interpreters as one vehicle to foster greater collaboration within the region and to coordinate training opportunities. There is a desire for more equitable access to human, financial, and material resources, to continue to develop the profession of interpreting on the African continent.

Balkans

At the 2007 WASLI conference, a motion was put forward to create a new region: the Balkans. The rationale for this change was that the developmental stages of Serbia, Kosovo, and Albania were very different from those of European countries, and as such, the region required a different focus when compared to other countries where signed language interpreter recognition and training was well established. Emerson and Hoti (2007) describe the steps taken in Kosovo to create the first training project for interpreters. The funding for the work came from the Finnish Deaf Association, and 10 interpreters were chosen as the first cohort. Eight of the ten interpreters came from Deaf families and as such knew the national signed language. The training was comprised of two levels, with the second level compressed into a five-day training program with an international interpreter educator. From these early roots of interpreter education, there is now a mechanism to offer regular interpreting education, delivered by the Kosovo Association of the Deaf in collaboration with a university. In addition, the government has recognized the national signed language and funded interpreting services. In Serbia, a similar approach has been taken, and interpreter education has been delivered by the Deaf association and in more recent years, by the interpreter association in an intensive, 6-day format, which focuses on the role of the interpreter, professionalism, ethics, and interpreting techniques. The Balkans has made tremendous progress, as countries in the region ratify the UNCRPD and recognize the national signed languages. However, the lack of interpreter recognition and the availability of training materials that are accessible in languages other than English are two examples of the problems that are present in the region.

Transcaucasia

This region of the globe comprises the countries of the former Soviet Union, including Armenia, Azerbaijan, Belorussia, Georgia, Kazakhstan, Kyrgizia, Moldova, Russia, Tajikistan, Turkmenistan, Ukraine, and Uzbekistan. One of the distinct advantages of this large region is that many of the signed languages share a common grammatical structure based on Russian Sign Language (Anna Komorova, personal communication, July 11, 2017), so when Deaf citizens and interpreters meet, there is an effective way to communicate, unlike in the Asian region. Russia is the only country in the region that has a university-based program for training interpreters; the other countries have short-term training available on an intermittent basis, usually offered by the Deaf associations. Most, if not all interpreters in the other countries have Deaf family members, and although some may have additional university education, it is not in interpreting. Countries such as Armenia, Ukraine, Georgia, Russia, and Tajikistan have programs on television with signed language interpreters, raising awareness of sign language and interpreting services. Turkmenistan has an organization of nearly 5,000 Deaf and Deaf-Blind people; however the number of signed language interpreters is unknown. Uzbekistan reports a Deaf population of 30,000, with approximately 10 interpreters registered in the association.

The challenges in this very large region include the lack of systematic and regular training for signed language interpreters, working conditions for interpreters, and the recognition of signed languages in order to implement policies. In 2014, a conference was held in Moscow on the linguistic rights of Deaf people, and WFD, WASLI, and the Russian Deaf association signed a declaration that is being used to lobby the government for significant changes to policies and practices.[6] Russian Sign Language has been recognized, but the resources needed to provide equitable communication access are not yet in place.

Europe

Europe and the United Kingdom have enjoyed a long history of providing formal learning opportunities for interpreters at the postsecondary level. Interpreter associations exist in many countries of the region and are also well established. The European Forum of Sign Language Interpreters (efsli; http://efsli.org) was officially formed in 1993 as a vehicle for information-sharing and training among its interpreter members and interpreters at large. Each year, their annual conference includes a training seminar and draws delegates from throughout Europe, the United Kingdom, and around the world. The organization offers summer and winter schools as one approach to supplementing the education that interpreters take at other institutions. In 2014, WASLI and efsli renewed their collaborative working agreement, and efsli is now able to be a regional

---

6. The declaration can be viewed on the websites of WASLI and WFD in International Sign and in English.

member of WASLI. This change required WASLI to adjust its constitution, which previously only allowed national members.

One of the unique approaches to training that has been offered since 2009 is the European Master in Sign Language Interpreting (EUMASLI; www.eumasli.eu) study program. This is a joint effort across three universities based in Germany, Scotland, and Finland.[7] One other unique university program is the initiative undertaken by the University of Hamburg under the direction of Dr. Christian Rathmann. This program specifically educates Deaf interpreters and is the only one of its kind in Europe, as other universities combine programming for Deaf and non-deaf interpreter students. Training across the region is available at the diploma, postgraduate diploma, bachelor's, and master's degree levels, and the accreditation processes vary across the countries. For example, in the United Kingdom and the Netherlands, an interpreter can become a nationally registered sign language interpreter upon successful completion of their interpreting studies, whereas in other countries, there are not yet accreditation processes established to determine quality of service. Some countries have ratified the UNCRPD, and others have not, which also creates challenges in providing linguistic access for Deaf citizens.

Within the European context, although many gains have been made for signed language interpreters, several areas still require development. Legislation at a European level filters down to a national level with varying success. Countries in the north of Europe tend to have better-established interpreter education programs within polytechnics and universities. In southern Europe, interpreter training tends to be based within traditional institutions, such as local/regional or national Deaf associations. Similarly, accreditation varies between lists held by national associations to lists held by government organizations. With the joint work between the European Union of the Deaf (EUD) and efsli, there is, however, some common understanding as to the goals of interpretation and the standards that should be achieved for accreditation. Future work at a transnational level should ensure that Deaf citizens' mobility is not impeded by lack of interpreter access (Dr. Christopher Stone, personal communication, July 11, 2017).

---

7. For further information about EUMASLI, see Hessman, Salmi, Turner, and Wurm (2011).

North America

The North American region of WASLI is comprised of Canada, the United States, and Mexico. Arguably, the U.S. has led in many developments in sign language research, the training of interpreters, and the creation of organizations to represent interpreters. The national body for U.S. interpreters is known at the Registry of Interpreters for the Deaf (RID) and has over 16,000 members.[8] RID offers several testing and accreditation processes, including a certification for Deaf interpreters. Several states require licensure, which can require evidence of maintaining interpreter certification through RID and ongoing and regular professional development, in order to ensure that the standards of interpreting remain high. In addition to RID, another organization, known as Mano a Mano (https://manoamano-unidos.org), represents the interests of the growing number of trilingual interpreters, who use English, ASL, Spanish and/or Spanish, Mexican Sign Language (LSM), and English. The National Consortium of Interpreter Education Centers (NCIEC; www.interpretereducation.org) has also placed a priority on trilingual interpreting in the United States, developing a standardized curriculum and other resources to train ASL/Spanish-English interpreters.

Many universities offer interpreter education programs at the bachelor's, master's, and more recently, PhD levels. The Conference of Interpreter Trainers (CIT; www.cit-asl.org/new/) is an organization that supports the professional development of interpreter educators, and there is an accreditation process available to interpreter programs through the Commission on Collegiate Interpreter Education (CCIE; www.cit-asl.org/ccie.html).

Canada has had a national interpreter association since 1979, known as the Association of Visual Language Interpreters of Canada (AVLIC; www.avlic.ca/), which is organized in such a way that there are chapter affiliate organizations based at the provincial level, and working interpreters must be members of both their national and provincial organizations. AVLIC offers a national certification program and provides a forum for discussion of issues at the national level. Canada currently has three postsecondary programs that train signed language interpreters over 3 years: one program that is a part-time program for French-LSQ interpreters, one program

---

8. For more information on RID, see www.rid.org.

that has recently changed from a 3-year program to a 4-year degree in ASL-English interpreting, and one program that results in a degree in linguistics with a minor in interpretation.

Mexico has recently established a national association for signed language interpreters and is working toward having greater opportunities for the training of interpreters. As in other regions of our world, most of the training occurs within the context of Deaf associations, and there is one initiative close to Tijuana that has offered interpreter training at the postsecondary level. This program addresses some of the realities associated with living close to the U.S./California border and the need for trilingual interpreters. However, the challenges in Mexico are numerous, including a lack of formal training opportunities for interpreters and no formal qualification, which means that interpreters are not seen as professional (Daniel Maya Ortega, personal communication, April 2, 2018). As well, it is estimated that there may be as many as 500,000 Deaf citizens who use LSM and only 350 interpreters working regularly in the country. Deaf people are regularly excluded from essential services, such as education, health care, and the justice system. AVLIC and RID are collaborating and supporting the efforts of their Mexican colleagues in lobbying for solutions to address the many issues.

The interpreters and Deaf associations of this region have established MOUs between them, and Mexico has signed an MOU with the spoken language interpreters and translators association. What remains a challenge is continuing to maintain the relationships between the leaders of the associations in order to achieve collaborative gains for the interpreting profession.

Latin America and the Caribbean

Like Asia, this region is comprised of some 38 countries, 11 of which have active interpreting associations. University programs train signed language interpreters in Brazil, Colombia, Uruguay, Argentina, Chile, and Venezuela, and Panama will open a postsecondary program in 2016. Brazil, Peru, and Colombia have legislation in place that recognizes signed language interpreting as a profession, and 10 countries have recognized the national signed language. These countries include the Domincan Republic,

Panama, Venezuala, Brazil, Uruguay, Chile, Peru, Ecuador, Colombia, Costa Rica, and Nicaragua. However, legislation does not always result in policies that support Deaf people or the provision for professional interpreting services. Currently, interpreters provide services in educational, legal, political, television, arts and culture, and religious settings. In 2009, 2013, and again in 2017, Latin American interpreters hosted regional conferences that brought together 300 interpreters from the area, and in addition, WASLI has also provided training in a number of countries. The presidents of the interpreter associations meet virtually on a regular basis, and there is incredible cooperation among the countries to support each other. One of the major barriers is that the majority of published interpreter research is in English or Portugese, which is inaccessible to the large number of Spanish countries. To this end, Latin America is collaborating with an interpreter association in Canada that is raising funds to cover the cost of translating key interpreter education materials. The economic reality is also a large challenge for the development of interpreting in Latin America and the Caribbean, in that many countries simply do not have the resources to create systems that could provide professional interpreting services.

One of the major issues that WASLI and WFD face in El Salvador and the Dominican Republic is the imposition of ASL by well-meaning missionaries and interpreters, and a lack of support for the national signed language. The region is also affected by the religious beliefs of interpreters, who are not able to separate their personal beliefs from the interpreting role. The WFD is offering human rights training in many of these countries, in an effort to raise awareness of the importance of national signed languages and the role that professional interpreters play in accessing human rights.

ARE THERE OTHER ORGANIZATIONS BESIDES WASLI AT THE INTERNATIONAL LEVEL?

WASLI was created for the purpose of developing the profession of sign language interpreting by advancing standards for training and helping to create professional bodies in countries where there are none. WASLI works closely with WFD, which is an essential aspect of the organization's approach, and this modeling is helpful to countries where Deaf associations and interpreters may have difficulties in cooperating. One of the key aspects of their shared agenda has been to recommend standards for International Sign (IS) interpreters working at UN events and to implement a process whereby WFD and WASLI can now accredit IS interpreters, who may be Deaf or non-deaf.[9] As well, WASLI and WFD have produced standard position papers that can be effective tools for countries in need of support to lobby their governments for communication access. For example, the statement on communication access for Deaf people during times of national emergencies, such as an earthquake or tsunami, have led the way to proactive policy development and planning in several nations (http://wasli .org/wp-content/uploads/2012/11/WFD-and-WASLI-Communication -during-natural-disasters-and-other-mass-emergencies-for-deaf-people -who-use-signed-language-Jan-2015-FINAL.pdf).

The association internationale des interprètes de conference (International Organization of Conference Interpreters; AIIC; http://aiic -usa.com), formed in 1953, is the global association representing conference interpreters. In more recent years, AIIC has broadened its mandate, based on its working relationship with efsli and WASLI. In 2012, it adopted a resolution to include membership for signed language interpreters who work as conference interpreters. AIIC created the AIIC Sign Language Network, and shortly after, Ms. Maya de Wit of the Netherlands was admitted as AIIC's first signed language interpreter member.

In 2015, the Federation of Interpreters and Translators (FIT; www .fit-ift.org) and WASLI signed an MOU, and the two organizations began developing policies and practices that can affect interpreters working in

---

9. International Sign has been described as a contact phenomenon (Stone & Russell, 2016) and a situational pidgin (Locker-McKee & Napier, 2002), although its features do not make those of a pidgin (see Lucas & Valli, 1992). It is ostensibly an extension of foreigner talk; that is, it incorporates the same types of language modification native signers use to interact with non-native signers. Foreigner talk includes "slower rate of speech, louder speech, longer pauses, common vocabulary, few idioms, greater use of gesture, more repetition, more summaries of preceding utterances, shorter utterances and more deliberate articulation" (Gass & Madden, 1985, 4). IS has no single globally established form, although there does exist some organizational-established lexicon (Supalla & Webb, 1995). Greater mobility of deaf people within some transnational regions (e.g., Europe) results in greater frequency of exposure to Deaf people from other countries within those regions, greater knowledge of the lexicon of other signed languages, and more frequent use of "international" signing strategies.

conflict zones, as well as a common code of conduct that can be used as an example for countries that are developing their own standards.

One other international organization that has welcomed signed language interpreters has been Critical Link (www.facebook.com/CriticalInternational/), a Canadian organization that hosts international conferences for community interpreters. The conferences are held every 4 years and showcase practical training and community-based research from both spoken and signed language interpreters and educators.

WHAT TYPES OF SERVICE MODELS EXIST AT THE INTERNATIONAL LEVEL?

In countries where there are well-developed supports and services, we can see vibrant Deaf associations with strong relationships with interpreters. In some countries, the Deaf association manages the interpreting services. For example, in Colombia, the Deaf association screens and selects the interpreters that work in the public education system. In Ukraine, the Deaf association represents some 60,000 Deaf and hard of hearing members, and interpreters have traditionally worked for the association. However, as the country moves to a civil democracy model, the association is working toward a future where the government and universities provide the interpreters. Countries that have Deaf associations that are members of the WFD are able to access information and support that strengthens the local or national work, whereas countries that are economically challenged struggle to attend congresses where they can create knowledge networks and access partnership opportunities.[10] In countries such as these, there can be considerable tension, as interpreters attempt to move to a model of payment for their interpreting services and/or try to emulate practices that work well in developed countries with a long history of developing the profession of interpreting, such as North America or Scandanavian countries. When the practices and approaches do not suit a country's stage of development, the relationships between Deaf people and the interpreters who serve them is damaged, ultimately leading to mistrust.

---

10. Countries that are less developed, emerging economically, and creating stable and civil societies are called *emerging countries*. These countries have often been referred to in the past as *third-world countries*.

Countries that are well-off have examples of for-profit interpreter services and a range of choices. However, in these countries, the relationship between interpreter and Deaf consumer can become strictly a business relationship, which is also very detrimental, and as such, there has been a push to regain that sense of connection to the Deaf community and to preserve what is known as a "Deaf Heart." For emerging countries that may not be at the same stage of development, the question WASLI is often asked is how is it that Deaf and interpreter communities could ever be this far apart. These perspectives are important reminders of the importance of Deaf people and interpreters working collaboratively to find solutions that work in the country in which they live.

One aspect of interpreting service delivery that has dramatically changed our world has been the implementation of video-relay services (VRS).[11] Once more, we see a range of service models, from the Deaf association operating the services within their centers, to Deaf-owned companies that employ freelance interpreters, to platforms that use Skype and have interpreters on demand, to nationally regulated services, such as the U.S. models. Most countries do not have such services, again, often due to economics and/or the stage of development of the country. If the country's infrastructure cannot support such a service (limited internet; natural disasters such as earthquakes, etc.), or there is very little awareness of human rights or the recognition of national signed languages, then the priorities of the country are very different. If a country has very few interpreters, and the Deaf association places a priority on face-to-face service delivery, then the development of VRS may come at a much later stage of development. However, it is common for Deaf people in the majority of the world's countries to be able to access text-based communication through cell phones, applications like Facebook, instant messaging, WhatsApp, etc. When the internet is stable and reasonably priced, they can access video-conferencing tools in order to communicate effectively.

---

11. A video-relay service (VRS) is a video-telecommunication service that allows Deaf, hard of hearing, and speech-challenged individuals to communicate over video telephones and similar technologies with people who can hear and do not know sign language, in real time, via a signed language interpreter.

So What Can We Learn from This Brief Journey Around the World?

When it comes to the education of interpreters, we can see that some countries considered less developed may actually have stronger models of true collaboration among Deaf people and interpreters. The model of developing an interpreter program from scratch, such as what happened in Kosovo, is an excellent example of how the training can be relevant and meaningful for the country and remain firmly embedded in the Deaf community. The country began by gaining support from the Finnish Association of the Deaf, who assisted them in documenting their signed language in linguistically sound ways. Deaf linguists worked with local Deaf leaders to video the language in natural contexts, to be able to identify the structure, lexicon, and variation within the language. From this crucial first phase came the development of an interpreter program, using a local interpreter who was well-respected in the Deaf community as the first interpreter educator, supported by an international advisor. By strategically pairing these two people, the country was able to prepare their first cohort of interpreters, eight of whom were already fluent in Kosovo Sign Language, to move into providing community-based interpreting, something that had been unavailable during the civil war in the Balkans area in the 1990s. Since this work began, the community has expanded its program to a longer format that is still delivered by the Deaf association and local interpreter educators (both Deaf and hearing), which grounds the interpreting practice firmly within the Deaf community. This model also involved creating an Interpreter Working Group to design a professional code of conduct and documents that described suitable working conditions for interpreters and best practices for educating the wider community on working with an interpreter. The group produced valuable documents that were suitable for the context in which the interpreters found themselves working.

Although this model may be viewed as nontraditional by countries that have long-established education at the college and university level, it is a model that works well and can be replicated at the international level in countries where there are no interpreter programs. It is in keeping with WASLI's Philosophy for Interpreter Educators, which stresses the need for international educators to work together to design effective practices and deliver quality education in a manner that recognizes and includes local expertise in the cultural, linguistic, social, and political conditions.[12] Although programs in North America are discussing the growing disconnect between interpreter education programs and the Deaf communities involvement in the instruction and management of those programs, here we see models of education that do not require service learning, as the Deaf community is an active player in the selection of students and the delivery of the program (Shaw, 2013). The other benefit of this model is that there is no reliance on international educators after the program is implemented, as the advisor effectively works with the local community to build capacity and knowledge at the local and national level. The international advisor has the ethical responsibility to ensure that the students are going to the local educator for all of their needs and questions to be addressed, so that the community sees that it has the ability to meet its own needs and find solutions to its own problems. The WASLI Interpreter Education Guidelines contain other similar models that highlight the work in Colombia, Mexico, New Zealand, and Kenya, all of which describe how these alternate pathways can and do produce effective interpreters. So, one of the most important takeaway messages from these examples is that there are many culturally and linguistically sensitive ways to educate interpreters, and that more developed countries can learn from lesser-developed countries.

I WANT TO DO SOME INTERNATIONAL WORK—A WORD TO THE WISE

Occasionally, interpreters from other countries that have longer histories and experiences with interpreter education will travel and offer training in countries where they are invited. Although this approach can be helpful, it also can be problematic if the training is not offered in a way that is linguistically and culturally sensitive, does not support local sign language recognition, and/or does not help to develop locally based trainers who can continue the work. As we saw in the above section, it is not possible to begin with creating university-based interpreter programs in countries of

---

12. See http://wasli.org/special-interest/interpreter-trainers for the complete statement.

emerging economic means and political awareness of the human rights of the Deaf community. Often, the most helpful first step is to encourage the national association to work with Deaf linguists with international experience who can help them to document their national signed language while simultaneously educating the Deaf community on their human rights.

How, What, Whom—Working with Local Deaf and Interpreter Communities

If you are interested in travel and work in another country, it is critical to assess what you can offer. Here are some questions to ask yourself: Are you a fluent user of your own national signed language? What type of interpreting experiences have you had that would be useful to the country you are going to? What are your own beliefs and perspectives that might create an impact in another location? How aware are you of the geopolitics and the ethnic, linguistic, and religious practices that shape the region? Are you comfortable visiting a region where there is the threat of violence and/or political conflict; where the governments may be corrupt and/or unstable; and/or where you may not be afforded the same rights and treatment you enjoy in your own country? What are your abilities to manage very divergent views of the world that may ultimately conflict with your moral and/or personal beliefs? How aware are you of the national Deaf associations and the issues that may be impacting local Deaf and interpreter interactions? Can you suspend judgment and teach from a frame that reduces the impact of your Western-developed world experiences? Have your travelled outside of your home country, beyond taking in an all-inclusive holiday somewhere? By answering these questions honestly, you will be in a better position to determine your readiness to work internationally.

Qualifications

In terms of qualifications, if you are going to be placed in a teaching and learning environment, you will need to be able to demonstrate your academic qualifications and your work experience. In countries where visas are required, you may need to submit a resume and a full description of the teaching event that you will deliver. As an international guest, you will likely be expected to attend high-level meetings with government and/or university officials and participate in media interviews, in order to support the local Deaf community's agenda. Often, countries that have less experience with formal education will place you in a position as "expert," and this position of power and privilege needs to be balanced with the need to work with local Deaf community members and interpreters in order for them, and the local officials, to come to value their own expertise and support their own goals.

Some practical questions also must be considered, such as the language in which will you be expected to teach. Will you be working with spoken language interpreters? If so, do they have a contextual understanding of what you will teach? Often, the spoken language interpreters have had little or no access to formal education, or they may be exceptional written translators but be completely ill prepared for handling the simultaneous interpreting of a workshop or presentation. Will you have access to electricity while teaching, or should you prepare for teaching without relying on computer equipment? You may be billeted or stay at a local dormitory. It may mean you do not have regular access to power, water for bathing and/or drinking, and food that you are comfortable eating, so you need to plan for these aspects, again in culturally sensitive ways.

Working with Local Deaf and Interpreter Community Members

Experienced international educators will need to collaborate with relevant stakeholders, including, but not limited to, Deaf and hearing community members, Deaf and hearing interpreters, national Deaf and Deaf-Blind representatives, spoken language community and translation/interpreting organization representatives, government representatives, and educational institution representatives. The aim of these collaborative efforts is the development of expertise and the empowerment of local personnel to lead the establishment of interpreter education, in whatever format that it is to take in their respective countries, and to support existing and developing national associations of signed language interpreters.

In some countries, there can be more than one national Deaf association and more than one national interpreter association, so it important to understand the local and/or national Deaf community politics that may also be impacted by your visit. You will need to know what kinds of local training have occurred previously. It can be very helpful to reach out to other sojourners who have visited the country and may have also offered training, to get their perceptions on the stage of development of the community.

There are many parallel processes that may be taking place in the country, such as the development of materials, resources, and partnerships with other nongovernmental organizations, so try to determine what processes may be co-occurring with your visit.

Now, How Do I Learn International Sign?

IS is a contact variety of sign language used in a variety of different contexts, particularly at international meetings, such as the World Federation of the Deaf (WFD) congress, events such as the Deaflympics, in video clips produced by Deaf people and watched by other Deaf people from around the world, and informally when travelling and socializing. It is not as conventionalized or as complex as natural sign languages and has a limited lexicon (see www.wasli.org).

What is most important is that a travelling educator must be very fluent in a country's national signed language and preferably have exposure to a second signed language. IS fluency is not the goal to aspire to, even though it may be the default communication approach, if you do not know the local signed language. Moody (2002) reminds us there is a misconception that one can learn IS by studying a list of frequently used IS signs used at international conferences. There are no formal classes or academic programs where you can go and learn IS; interpreters who have been working in IS since the 1970s have learned to communicate effectively by travelling and meeting Deaf people from as many different countries as possible. The first requirement for becoming fluent in IS is to be very fluent in at least one national signed language, and preferably in two or three other signed languages as well. That way, the more signed languages you know, the more linguistic strategies you have to adapt to the lexicon used in other countries. Experience communicating with Deaf people in other countries can help to broaden your awareness of the visual lives of Deaf people and the different cultural views that Deaf people hold on a range of topics, from politics, to religion, family, education, culture, work, and so on.

Earlier in this chapter, I emphasized the need to respect the national signed language and reduce the influence of other signed languages from your teaching method. This is a key component of any international development work, and although there is a great deal of mobility today, and Deaf people do communicate across cultures and countries, it is also true that English and dominant signed languages, like ASL, can replace or reduce the status of national signed languages. Similarly, IS can find its way into a national signed language in a way that is inappropriate. Hence, you will need to work with local Deaf and interpreter educators, remain linguistically and culturally sensitive, and, as much as possible, allow yourself to be led by people in the local Deaf community with the support and guidance of an international educator.

REFERENCES

Akach, P. (2006). Colonization of sign languages and the effect on sign language interpreters. In R. L. McKee (Ed.), *Proceedings of the inaugural conference of the World Association of Sign Language Interpreters* (pp. 32–43). Douglas McLean Publishing: Coleford, UK.

Bontempo, K. (2015). Signed language interpreting. In H. Mikkelson and R. Jourdenais (Eds.), *The Routledge handbook of interpreting* (pp. 112–128). London, UK: Routledge.

Emerson, S., & Hoti, S. (2007) The beginnings of Kosovo interpreter training and the impact of international advisors. In C. Roy (Ed.), *Diversity and community in the worldwide sign language interpreting professional—Proceedings of the second WASLI conference held in Segovia, Spain* (pp. 115–122). Coleford, UK: Douglas McLean Publishing.

Gass, S., & Madden, C. (1985). *Input in second language acquisition.* Rowley, MA: Newbury House Publishers.

Hessman, J., Salmi, E., Turner, G. H., & Wurm, S. (2011). Developing and transmitting a shared interpreting research ethos. In B. Nicodemus and L. Swabey (Eds.), *Advances in interpreting research* (pp. 177–198). Amsterdam: John Benjamins.

Locker-McKee, R., & Napier, J. (2002). Interpreting into International Sign Pidgin: An analysis. In *Sign Language and Linguistics*, 5(1): 27–54.

Moody, B. (2002) International signs: A practitioner's perspective. *Journal of Interpretation*, (2), 1–47).

Napier, J. (2015). Comparing signed and spoken language interpreting. In H. Mikkelson and R. Jourdenais (Eds.), *The Routledge handbook of interpreting* (pp. 129–143). London, UK: Routledge.

Napier, J. (2004). Sign language interpreter training, testing and accreditation: An international comparison. *American Annals of the Deaf, 149*(4): 350–359.

Napier, J., McKee, R., & Goswell, D. (2006). *Sign language interpreting: Theory and practice in Australia and New Zealand.* Annandale, Australia: The Federation Press.

Nelson, K., Tawaketini, I., Spencer, R., & Goswell, D. (2009). Isa Lei: Interpreter training in Fiji. In J. Napier (Ed.), *International perspectives on sign language interpreter education* (pp. 171–189). Washington, DC: Gallaudet University Press.

Ramsey, C., & Pena, S. (2010). Sign language interpreting at the border of the two Californias. In R. L. McKee and J. Davis (Eds.), *Interpreting in multicultural multilingual contexts* (pp. 3–27). Washington, DC: Gallaudet University Press.

Russell, D., & McLeod, J. (2009). Educational interpreting: Multiple perspectives of our work. In J. Mole (Ed.), *International perspectives on educational interpreting* (pp. 128–144). Brassington, UK: Direct Learned Services Ltd.

Russell, D., & Winston, B. (2014). Tapping into the interpreting process: Using participant reports to inform the interpreting process in educational settings. *Translation and Interpreting, 6*(1): 102–127.

Spring, M. (May 2001). *Evolution of language services: The Australian scene from infant to teenager.* Paper presented at the Critical Link 3 conference, Montreal, Canada. Retrieved from https://criticallink.org/s/Cl3_Spring.pdf

Shaw, S. (2013). *Service learning in interpreter education—Strategies for extending student involvement in the Deaf community.* Washington, DC: Gallaudet University Press.

SouthAfricanLanguagePractitioner'sAct(2014).Retrievedfromhttps://en.wikipedia .org/wiki/South_African_Language_Practitioners%27_Council_Act,_2014

Stone, C., & Russell, D. (2016). Comparative analysis of depicting signs in IS and ASL interpreting. In R. Rosenstock and J. Napier (Eds.), *International sign: Linguistics, usage and status* (pp. 65–83). Washington, DC: Gallaudet University Press.

Supalla, T., & Webb, R. (1995). The grammar of international sign: A new look at pidgin languages. In K. Emmorey and J. Reilly (Eds.), *Language, gesture and space* (pp. 333–352). Mahwah, NJ: Lawrence Erlbaum Associates.

Valli, C., & Lucas, C. (1992). *Linguistics of American Sign Language: A resource text for ASL users.* Washington DC: Gallaudet University Press.

APPENDIX

Objectives, Keywords, Questions, Activities

In an effort to provide students and instructors with support as this text is used within the context of a course or program of study, the editors and chapter authors have created learning objectives, identified key words, and developed discussion questions and activities to apply what has been learned through the chapters. These components can be incorporated into a formal course through learning modules and integrated into weekly class sessions.

Chapter 1. Interpreting: An Overview, Len Roberson

Objectives

After studying this chapter, students will be able to do the following:

1. Define key terms about who interpreters are and what interpreters do
2. Explain the differences between in-person interpreting and interpreting via technology
3. Compare various types of interpreting positions, such as independent contractor, staff, video, and designated interpreter.
4. Describe the settings in which interpreters work.
5. Compare and contrast simultaneous and consecutive interpreting.
6. Explain each of the primary models of interpreting.

Keywords

Interpreting, transliterating, translation, interpreter, independent contractor, staff interpreter, designated interpreter, video relay service, video remote interpreting, simultaneous interpreting, consecutive interpreting, sight translation

Discussion Questions

1. Based on what you have just read in this chapter, and what you brought with you to this class through prior learning and experiences, how would you describe who an interpreter is and what an interpreter does?

2. This chapter presented information about how we deliver our services as interpreters. Interpreting in person and via technology are both options for an interpreter in considering how they will work. What could be considered the pros and cons of these two delivery models? Which do you see yourself doing in the future and why?

3. In addition to "general" interpreting, three specialized settings were discussed in this chapter. What are they? Based on your reading and perhaps classroom discussions, how might the work of the interpreter differ in each setting? What additional skills and knowledge might you need in each of the specialized areas above beyond those needed for effective work as a generalist in the interpreting profession?

4. This chapter presented information on several models of interpreting. Describe how the field of sign language interpreting has changed over the years based on these models.

Activities

1. Interview a few local interpreters in your own community to learn about their work and why they chose to become an interpreter. Based on what you have read in this chapter, ask them some questions about which aspects of their work they enjoy the most, which do they find most challenging, and what advice they would offer you as a student of interpreting.

2. Arrange to observe at least two different interpreters working in two different situations. As you observe, note what you see that relates to the information you have read in this chapter. Be prepared to highlight what you saw in action that further enhances your understanding about the work of interpreters.

3. Working with at least one other person, develop a visual representation of the interpreting process as you understand it. Do not worry

about using the right terms, but focus on what you believe the process of interpreting is and what happens during that process. Be prepared to share your visual model with the class.

CHAPTER 2. HISTORICAL FOUNDATIONS OF A TRUST-BASED PROFESSION, CAROLYN BALL

Objectives

1. Students will be able to understand the role that Deaf people have played in the establishment of interpreting as a profession.
2. Students will be able to describe key theories and people in the field of American Sign Language Interpreting and Interpreting Education.
3. Students should be able to synthesize social, political, and legal perspectives that have influenced the development and implementation of spoken and signed language interpreter education.

Keywords

Egyptian hieroglyph, International Federation of Translators, Paris Peace Conference, Nuremburg trials, Laurent Clerc, William Stokoe, Vocational Rehabilitation (VR), Boyce Williams, Registry of Interpreters for the Deaf (RID), Interpreters, Interpreter Educators, Lou Fant, Lottie Riekehof, Virginia Lee Hughes, Babbidge Report, Ball State College, National Interpreter Training Consortium (NITC), National Technical Institute for the Deaf (NTID), American Deafness and Rehabilitation Association (ADARA).

Discussion Questions

1. Of all the events relayed in this chapter on the development of Deaf education in the United States in the 1800s, which do you feel was the single, most influential event that led to the realization that more interpreters would be needed?
2. Compare the relationship between Clerc and Gallaudet to present Deaf–hearing interpreter relationships.

3. Why was Boyce Williams such a critical part of the establishment of professional interpreting in the United States?
4. What role did the Babbidge Report play in helping to establish the critical need for qualified interpreters in the United States?

Activities

1. Write a history of the interpreter training program in your state. Be sure to include the following:
   a. Names of pioneers who established the program.
   b. Names of Deaf community members who were key to the establishment of the program.
   c. What laws were passed in the state to provide funding for the program?
   d. What year was the program established?
   e. What degree was offered when the program was first established?
   f. List the faculty who have taught at the college/university since the program's inception.
   g. What national/state organizations has the program been involved in through the years?
   h. How many students are in the interpreter training program?
   i. How has the interpreter training program influenced the Deaf/Hearing community?
   j. What are your thoughts and feelings about the program now?
   k. Compare the curriculum of the program today and determine if this curriculum has changed over the years.
   l. Publish the history of the interpreter training program on Wikipage.

2. Discover two pioneers in your interpreting community, and conduct a historical interview with these pioneers.
   a. Determine the questions you will ask the pioneers.
   b. Send the questions to the individuals, and ask them if they would like to change or edit the questions.
   c. Video the interview.
      i. Make sure to have the person you interview sign a waiver.

    d. Make note of the date, time, and place of the interview.

    e. Search online for oral history interviews, and discover which method will suit this interview the best. Organizations such as the Oral History Organization or the American Historical Association will be beneficial.

3. Make a PowerPoint presentation or keynote presentation to include the historical information that you have gathered about the interpreter training program and the Deaf community in your area, and include the interview you conducted in the presentation.

    a. Apply for local, state, and national Deaf and interpreting organizations to present the history that you have gathered.

CHAPTER 3. PROMOTING THE USE OF NORMATIVE ETHICS IN THE PRACTICE PROFESSION OF COMMUNITY INTERPRETING, ROBYN K. DEAN AND ROBERT Q POLLARD, JR.

Objectives

After reading this chapter, you will be able to do the following:

1. Explain how signed language interpreting is a specialty within the broader field of translation and interpreting and what makes signed language interpreting and community interpreting unique.

2. Define these ethics terms: *normative ethics*, *descriptive ethics*, *deontology*, and *teleology*.

3. Describe how and why community interpreting moved away from normative ethics and adopted a descriptive ethics approach.

4. Identify terms (other than *role*) that more effectively convey ethical concepts in interpreting practice.

5. Explain how identifying a profession's values is necessary when moving away from descriptive ethics and toward normative ethics.

6. Identify the four core principles (values) all service-based professions consider and apply in their practice.

Keywords

Community interpreting ethics, decision-making models, interpreter's role, values-based decision-making

Discussion Questions

1. Normative messages (what an interpreter should do) can be found in ethical material, such as codes of ethics, textbooks (e.g., Frishberg, 1986; Stewart & Witter-Merithew, 2006), and standard practice papers, as well as within professional discourse, such as that which occurs in classrooms and interpreting workshops.
   a. Identify some of the normative messages you have received from authors, teachers, and peers.
   b. Discuss those messages through the lens of deontology versus teleology.
   c. Choose one of those normative messages and identify the value that is underpinning it.
   d. Construe a situation where that value may need to be forfeited in favor of another value. Explain your reasoning in light of the competing values.
2. In this chapter, we have highlighted the normative ethical constructs of responsibility and consequences. We have further suggested that professional values should be the standard by which consequences are measured and how the term responsibility is understood. Identify an interpreting situation where an interpreter would be justified in prioritizing or upholding the values of the setting and forfeiting one or more values traditionally associated with interpreting (we gave an example of this on pages 42–43).
3. From your personal experience, identify a time when you had to choose between two conflicting values. Did you use the idea of specified principlism—where you tried to apply a broader value to a given situation and then modified your decision to mitigate negative outcomes? Describe that situation in these terms.

Activities

1. Download a copy of AVLIC's Code of Ethics (http://www.avlic.ca/ethics-and-guidelines) and a copy NAD-RID's Code of Professional Conduct (http://www.rid.org/ethics/code-of-professional-conduct). Review both documents, identifying the similarities and the differences in terms of normative ethics and descriptive ethics and the matter of values.

2. Consider the list of values offered on page 60 for community interpreters (those that include interpreting values and the values of the setting). Interview a practicing interpreter by asking them to tell you about a situation where she or he prioritized the values of the setting over interpreting values. You may need to explain to him/her what these terms refer to, because most interpreters are used to rule-based or descriptive ethics approaches.

3. Ask a peer, an interpreter educator, or a practicing interpreter to respond to the following ethical dilemma (explored in Dean, 2015):

   You are called to interpret for a terminally ill patient and his family members at a "family meeting," comprising the team of healthcare professionals who are caring for the patient. Some family members pull you aside before entering the room and expressly ask you not to mention the word *cancer* in your interpretation, but to refer to it vaguely as "an illness."

4. Ask a peer, an interpreter educator, or a practicing interpreter what they would do and how they would justify their decision. Write down what they say, and analyze it in light of the material explored here. Consider the following questions:
   a. Did they respond with "well, that depends" and then offer some examples of salient factors or demands (from DC-S: environmental, interpersonal, paralinguistic, intrapersonal demands)?
   b. Did they respond with normative ethical material (e.g., "You should always make sure that . . .")?
   c. Did they use the term *role* or a role metaphor to justify their reasoning?
   d. Did they mention consequences, and were those consequences a function of values from interpreting and/or values of the setting?

CHAPTER 4. APTITUDE AND DISPOSITION: LEARNED VS. NURTURED CHARACTERISTICS OF STUDENT INTERPRETERS, SHERRY SHAW

Objectives

After reading this chapter, students will be able to do the following:

1. Identify key linguistic, cultural, motivational, and dispositional characteristics to begin learning the interpreting process.
2. Distinguish between the hard and soft skill sets needed to enter an interpreter education program and to learn the interpreting process.
3. Identify personal characteristics that are represented by professional interpreters.
4. Conduct a self-analysis of readiness to learn the interpreting process.
5. Describe the historical attempts to screen interpreters for aptitude and motivation.

Keywords

Aptitude, motivation, disposition, interpreter education, working memory, source language, target language, cognitive capacity, simultaneous interpreting, consecutive interpreting

Discussion Questions

1. Discuss the difference between soft skills and hard skills. Think of examples of either skill type that would enhance or detract from the ability to interpret.
2. Why is it important for interpreter education programs to be able to predict who will succeed in learning the interpreting process?
3. How do students know they are ready to enter an interpreting program?
4. What strategies might be applied to a person who self-assesses as "not yet ready" for program admission?

Activities

1. Form groups of three or four students. Each group selects one article from the reference list to analyze. Summarize the article, and report your findings to the larger group.
2. Perform a self-assessment of mindset and discuss the outcome with a partner (http://mindsetonline.com/testyourmindset/step1.php).
3. Keep a week-by-week journal about world knowledge you attain, vocabulary you learn, cultural awareness you experience, and other steps you make in the areas that are deemed to be critical for learning the interpreting process (soft or hard skills). At the end of each week, summarize your experiences and construct a plan for the following week to enhance your personal growth in areas needing further development. Continue this self-assessment cycle for six weeks.

CHAPTER 5. INTERPRETING IN HEALTHCARE SETTINGS: MORE THAN NEEDLES, BLOOD, AND TERMINOLOGY, LAURIE SWABEY

Objectives

After studying this chapter, you will be able to do the following:

1. Describe how healthcare interpreting is different from other types of interpreting.
2. List the variety of people you may work with, including Deaf and hard of hearing patients, their family members, and the healthcare professionals involved in caring for these patients.
3. Identify the types of settings in which healthcare interpreters work.
4. Describe the specialized knowledge and skills required to interpret in a healthcare setting.
5. List the recommended entry-level qualifications for interpreting in health care, and summarize the types of experiences and education needed to advance in this specialized area.

Keywords

Health literacy, doctor-patient communication, domains and competencies for healthcare interpreters, CDI (Certified Deaf Interpreter), vicarious trauma, "do no harm," healthcare interpreting career lattice, designated interpreter, self-care, medical terminology, credentialing in health care

Discussion Questions

1. Imagine that you are an interpreter in a rural community. Your regular job is interpreting at public school for an eighth-grader. However, if there is a need for an interpreter at the Urgent Care Center, you are usually the person they call, as there are very few interpreters within a 50-mile radius. Do you take these jobs, or do you suggest alternatives? If you do take the job, what influences your decision? If you do not take the job, what recommendations do you make? Why? Would this situation spur you to study healthcare interpreting? Why or why not?

2. Often, new interpreters think that they can accept jobs in healthcare settings, because they have personal experience going to the doctor's office. Suppose you are a recent graduate from an IEP, and an agency asks you to take an interpreting job for a Deaf patient who has a nagging cough. You have had lots of bronchial infections and have seen several doctors about nagging coughs. Would you take the job? If yes, under what circumstances? If no, why?

Activities

1. Look at the list of domains and competencies on p. 88. As you review the list, which domains would you like to learn more about? Select three and then find the full document online. Read the competencies under those three domains. What did you learn?

2. Write down three aspects of healthcare interpreting that you find appealing; then write down three aspects of healthcare interpreting that you find unappealing. From that, and using what you have learned from your textbook so far, do the following:

    a. Provide a two- to three-paragraph rationale as to why you would consider becoming a healthcare interpreter.

b. Provide a two- to three-paragraph rationale as to why you would not consider becoming a healthcare interpreter.

    Note: You must complete both a and b. Share your responses with a partner and discuss.

3. Think about your interactions with the healthcare system during your life. Think of a situation that involved you, a family member, or a close friend in the healthcare system that has had an impact on you. Tell the story of this experience to a small group of other students. What made that interaction memorable, in a positive or negative way (or both)? As you listen to the stories in your group, are there any themes that you can identify for what makes a healthcare experience memorable? Make a list of themes to share with the class.

4. As a class, identify several lawsuits that have been filed related to language access for Deaf people in healthcare settings. (Find a list on the NAD website: http://nad.org/issues/health-care). Divide into groups of three students and have each group select a lawsuit to investigate. Why was the lawsuit filed? What was the outcome? Report your findings back to the class.

5. Divide into groups of six. In each group, two people will review each of the following websites and report back to the group. The organizations you will learn about are the National Council on Interpreting in Health Care (www.ncihc.org), the California Health Interpreters Association (www.chiaonline.org), and the International Medical Interpreters Association (imiaweb.org). Report back on the following:

a. When was the organization established?

b. Who does the organization serve?

c. Is certification offered? If so, what are the requirements to become certified?

d. Does the organization have a professional code of ethics or professional practice? If so, how does it compare to what you have learned about the NAD-RID Code of Professional Conduct (https://www.rid.org/ethics/code-of-professional-conduct/)?

e. Are there resources on the website that you would recommend to your peers?

f. How might you use this website in the future?

6. Read the NAD's position statement on VRI interpreting at http://nad
   .org/issues/technology/vri/advocacy-statement-medical-setting. Find
   out what the policy is for using VRI at the hospitals/clinics in your area
   or state. Do the policies reflect that of the NAD? Why or why not?

Chapter 6. Interpreting in Vocational Rehabilitation Contexts, Linda K. Stauffer

Objectives

1. Describe the integral relationship of VR services to the growth of interpreting in the United States.
2. Identify the VR mission, eligibility requirements for services, and major processes of the VR system.
3. Describe the unique skills, knowledge, and attitudes interpreters need to demonstrate to successfully interpret in VR settings.
4. Describe the differences in the roles and responsibilities of the VR staff interpreter, the VR designated interpreter, the VR independent contract interpreter, and the job coach, who is also an interpreter.

Keywords

Vocational rehabilitation (VR), rehabilitation counselor, rehabilitation counselor for the deaf (RCD), individualized plan of employment (IPE), staff interpreter, designated interpreter, private practice/freelance/hourly contract interpreter, general VR caseload, interpreter specialization, competitive employment, NAD-RID Code of Professional Conduct (CPC), demand-control schema, job coach, Certified Deaf Interpreter (CDI)

Discussion Questions

1. Describe the overall purpose of vocational rehabilitation (VR) and how VR serves consumers who are deaf and hard of hearing.
2. Discuss how services provided by and funded by VR has changed over the years. What do you believe is the overall impact of these changes?

3. What do you believe VR should consider moving forward with in regard to services provided to consumers who are deaf and hard of hearing? If you were asked what changes to VR services should be made, what would you offer as ideas for the future?

4. Imagine that you are an interpreter who is called by a VR counselor to interpret a job interview for a VR consumer who is deaf. What questions would you need to ask the counselor before accepting this assignment?

Activities

1. Divide the class into small groups, and have each group provide a report on a major federal law positively impacting the lives of people with disabilities. You may select a law highlighted in this chapter or some of the many others that have been enacted. Alternate activity: Divide the class into small groups, and have each group report on a law in your state related to accessibility for persons who are Deaf, DeafBlind, or hard of hearing.

2. Role-play an on-the-job situation with a new deaf employee who is not aware of the workplace rules, such as punctuality, break times, and eating on the job. Develop a short skit using the same scenario, but where an interpreter is hired to facilitate the communication. In a second scenario, there is a full-time job coach who is also an interpreter. How would the "interpreter's" role be different in each scenario?

3. Imagine a person who is deaf, age 45, an ASL user, who has lost his assembly line job due to a plant closure in his small rural town. There are no similar jobs in his town or any nearby towns. This man applies to the local VR agency in order to receive services. He wants VR to help him get training and find a new job in a new field. Role-play interpreting within each of the primary phases of the VR process to become familiar with the language, terminology, and typical services provided at each step of the way.

4. Role-play the following situation: You have been called by a hearing general caseload VR counselor to interpret for her first meeting with a 17-year-old girl who is deaf with deaf parents in order to determine VR eligibility. The girl just graduated from the school for the Deaf located across the state, and you are not familiar with her signing skills or

communication needs. You are a graduate of an interpreter education program and hold a state interpreting credential meeting VR's minimum qualification requirements. You are willing to take the assignment, but feel strongly that a CDI team interpreter is needed. Make the case to the hearing VR counselor, who is not familiar with the Deaf community, that s/he should provide two interpreters for this assignment.

Chapter 7: Interpreting in Legal Contexts, Carla M. Mathers

Objectives

1. Describe the qualifications necessary for an interpreter working in legal settings, including courtrooms.
2. Compare the general and specialized competencies needed for interpreting in legal settings.
3. Explain the differences between criminal and civil court systems.
4. Describe the reasons an interpreter should clearly understand the structure and protocol of courts and court processes.
5. Explain the legal foundation that supports the provision of an interpreter in legal settings.
6. Identify best practices, principles, and protocols associated with interpreting in legal settings.
7. Explain the various roles of an interpreter in legal settings.

Keywords

Competencies, jurisdiction, substantive areas of law, procedural law, privileged communications, Miranda warning, proceedings interpreter, table interpreter, conflict of interest, legal discourse, consecutive interpreting, simultaneous interpreting, sight translation, sign translation

Discussion Questions

1. Based on your reading of this chapter, and after considering the other materials you have reviewed, discuss what level of understanding and

familiarity of legal interpreting interpreters should have as a professional. Provide several reasons why.

2. Identify two to three interpreting assignments that might not necessarily be "legal" in nature at the onset, but could change during the assignment to be more legal in nature than assumed. How should this affect your work as an interpreter? What could you do in each situation to provide for a successful interpreted interaction?

3. What are competencies in relation to the work of an interpreter? How are specialized competencies different? Based on your reading, what is special or unique with regard to skills or competencies you should consider relative to work as a legal interpreter?

4. Identify the various roles an interpreter may have in legal assignments, and describe the primary function an interpreter fulfills in each role. How would you prepare yourself for these different roles?

Activities

1. Conduct a review of the requirements and qualifications needed to work as a legal interpreter in your state as well as three other states. Develop a visual comparison of the requirements, and write a one- to two-page reaction paper explaining your findings. Consider both what is required and what is not required, and discuss the impact this has on the interpreters and the Deaf community at large.

2. In this chapter, the document *Toward Effective Practice: Specialist Competencies of the Interpreter Practicing within Court and Legal Settings* is discussed in detail. The document can be found online by searching for it by its title. Access the document, and carefully review the 41 competencies presented across the five domains. As you review them, consider your own knowledge, skills, and experiences and create a three-column list, where you divide the competencies into three categories, based on your considerations regarding your own skills and knowledge: Unfamiliar, Somewhat familiar, Very familiar. Use this list to gain an understanding of where you are now with respect to developing the knowledge and skills to be a competent legal interpreter.

3. There is no better way to understand the work of a legal interpreter than to observe her, or him, in action. Contact a local, nationally certified interpreter who works in legal settings and ask if you could observe her or him during an assignment. This would need to be arranged ahead of time, of course, and would need to be cleared by everyone involved. Alternatively, you could reach out to a local court and ask if there would be any upcoming legal proceedings that are open for observations with an interpreter. Take the time to fully observe everything about the setting, such as environmental demands, the people involved, the roles of each person involved, space management, time management, and the role of the interpreter during the proceedings. Be prepared to share your observation with others.

4. There is an excellent video series available on YouTube that was produced by a federal grant project that focuses on the work of Deaf interpreters. Search YouTube for "Deaf Interpreters at Work, Mock Trial," and you will easily find the series. For this activity, view the trial as well as the interview with the interpreters. Consider what you have learned in this chapter and what you see in the videos, and be prepared to discuss what applications of what you have learned can be made to the work of the interpreters in the video. Also, consider whether there are differences in the work, process, or competency requirements observed in the video, as compared with what was presented in this chapter.

CHAPTER 8. INTERPRETING FOR PEOPLE WHO ARE DEAFBLIND, SHERRY SHAW

Objectives:

After studying this chapter, students will be able to do the following:

1. Describe the expanded role of interpreters.
2. Describe the role and responsibilities of support service providers.
3. Discuss the importance of providing visual/environmental information.
4. Describe various communication methods and when each would be used.

5. Reflect on conditions, adjustments, isolation, and other aspects of a consumer's "lived reality" that impact the interpreter's role and responsibilities.

Keywords

DeafBlind, support service provider, communication, tactile signed language, haptics, Pro-Tactile, backchanneling, sighted guide, adventitious, congenital

Discussion Questions

1. Why is it more important to focus on a person's communication needs than conditions that cause a person to be DeafBlind?
2. What are the characteristics of an effective interpreter for people who are DeafBlind?
3. What additional responsibilities are involved in interpreting for people who are DeafBlind?
4. Discuss the many ways touch keeps a person connected to the environment.
5. How does the cause and onset of vision and hearing changes affect the communication modes used by a person who is DeafBlind?
6. What psychological adjustments might result from a person who has a degenerative condition that results in progressive vision or hearing loss?
7. Describe the cultural and social movement known as *Pro-Tactile*.

Activities

1. Watch presentations about *Pro-Tactile: The DeafBlind Way* online, and discuss how Pro-Tactile contributes to dynamic conversations and total involvement in meetings.
2. Use vision simulators (occluders) to work in teams, to practice various methods of interpreting and guiding a person.
3. Interview a DeafBlind person to learn more about the person's *lived reality*.
4. Volunteer at a local event within the DeafBlind community.

5. Demonstrate the use of touch signals to inform a person about the layout of a room.

6. Conduct a community assessment of services and resources available to DeafBlind people in your area.

7. Investigate the availability of SSP training through the local or state DeafBlind association (or other organization).

8. Take advantage of an SSP training or a call for volunteers from the DeafBlind community.

9. Practice Print on Palm, tactile communication, tracking, and communicating in a restricted field (small space).

10. Practice describing the visual environment (indoors and outdoors, in a busy restaurant, at the mall, at a sporting event, etc.).

11. Conduct a personal assessment of the skill sets needed to work within the DeafBlind population. Objectively evaluate your open-mindedness, flexibility, stamina, motivation, energy, and desire to specialize in DeafBlind interpreting.

12. Practice guiding a person on a flat terrain, ascending and descending stairs, and negotiating narrow spaces, uneven terrain, doorways, and crowded areas.

CHAPTER 9: CREDENTIALING AND REGULATION OF SIGNED LANGUAGE INTERPRETERS, ANNA WITTER-MERITHEW

Objectives

After studying this chapter, you will be able to do the following:

1. Define what it means to be a qualified interpreter.

2. Identify the primary purposes of professional regulation.

3. Identify key differences between certification, licensure, and specialty endorsement.

4. Discuss key strengths and key challenges associated with certification, licensure, and/or specialty endorsement.

5. Discuss the status of certification, licensure, and specialty endorsement of sign language interpreters in the United States.

Keywords

Certification, competency, competence, consumers, qualified, quality control, licensure, performance criteria, professional regulation, standards, specialty endorsements

Discussion Questions

1. What can master practitioners offer to new and entering practitioners, to support them in gaining the experience they need to solidify the skills necessary to gain certification?
2. What strategies can be employed to foster the willingness of Deaf consumers to allow novice interpreters to gain work experience prior to gaining certification or licensure?
3. What are the minimum standards a signed language interpreter should be prepared to meet as part of their entry into practice? Identify at least eight to 10. What is the source of your observations? What literature or resources exist that support your observations?
4. Discuss the value of certification from the perspective of a Deaf consumer, a practitioner, and a member of society who has the responsibility to hire interpreters in order to provide linguistic access. Why would certification be of value to each of these individuals? How does the value differ for each? Whose interest does certification serve?
5. Why would a state agency want to implement licensure if a national certification system already exists? What does licensure provide that certification cannot? What does certification offer that licensure does not? How is relying on national certification of benefit to state agencies that are responsible to regulate the work of interpreters.

Activities

1. Research the regulations governing interpreters in your state. Compare your findings on your state with the regulations in at least three surrounding states. Create a chart that delineates the various standards. Identify where there are similarities and differences.

2. Conduct interviews with at least three interpreters who engage in specialization. They can be three interpreters who specialize in the same area of specialization or different areas, depending on your interests and access to working interpreters. Develop a list of six to eight questions that you will ask. Sample questions can include inquiry into why they chose to specialize, what unique knowledge and skills are necessary to specialize in their area of expertise, how they acquired the specialized knowledge and skills, what they enjoy about specialization, and what they would recommend to a new interpreter wanting to specialize. Prepare a summary of your findings that addresses similarities and differences between the three interpreters and what you learned from the experience.

3. In collaboration with two or three peers, create a list of competencies you believe a working interpreter should possess. You can draw on existing literature to help you identify the competencies. The list should include at least 15 to 20 abilities an interpreter seeking endorsement through certification or licensure should possess and be able to demonstrate. Keep in mind that the competencies should encompass both ASL-to-English and English-to-ASL performance. Define each one of the competencies, so that it is clear to others what is involved. Then, work together to create a system for measuring the degree of fluency/ competence an interpreter possesses for each. You might use a Likert scale, a rubric, or a matrix. Prepare a rationale for why you chose the measurement system you used. Then, using a sample of interpreting performance (perhaps one that is available commercially or that one of the members of the peer group generated), each member of the peer group will apply the measurement system you collaboratively created to rate the performance. Compare your findings, and be prepared to share them with other groups.

CHAPTER 10. INTERNATIONAL PERSPECTIVES ON INTERPRETING: ISN'T EVERYTHING JUST LIKE AT HOME?, DEBRA RUSSELL

Objectives

After reviewing this chapter, you will be able to do the following:

1. Describe the stage of development of the interpreting profession in eight regions of the world.
2. Identify the major organizations that are working to develop interpreting at the international level.
3. List the key challenges facing interpreters and Deaf people in eight regions of the world.
4. Evaluate your skills and knowledge according to your readiness to work internationally, by contrasting them with the skills, knowledge, and attitudes needed for successful cross-cultural learning exchanges.
5. Contrast the information in this chapter to your understanding of the stage of development of interpreting in your local context.

Keywords

Signed languages, International Sign, emerging countries, memo of understanding (MOU), WASLI, WFD, FIT, video-relay service

Discussion Questions

1. What aspects of learning about international developments in the area of interpreting most interested you, and why? What region of the world would you like to learn more about, and why?
2. If you were to mobilize a group of interpreters in your community to undertake a fundraising project that could benefit an emerging country, what project could you manage, given your resources and experience with the Deaf and interpreter communities? What steps would you take to identify an association that would benefit from your efforts?
3. What are the potential problems associated with an interpreter providing training in a country, when she or he is unfamiliar with the languages and cultures of the country?

Activities

1. Conduct a self-assessment of your potential strengths and weakness as an interpreter who wants to work in an international setting. How will you address your weaknesses?

2. Review the WASLI Interpreter Education Guidelines, and summarize the key learning you take away from the four examples of countries that have developed interpreter training? Describe the three-phase model that WASLI is suggesting. Are there core subject areas you think could be added into a potential curriculum, and why do you think they are important?

3. As a class, divide into groups to identify the key components of the UNCRPD that make specific mention of the use of sign language and/or of supporting Deaf people. Then identify five countries that have ratified the convention, and contrast that with five countries that are signatories. Describe the differences between ratifying and being a signatory. Share your findings with the rest of the class.

4. Divide into groups of four. Each member will research one of the following websites: the World Federation of the Deaf (http://wfdeaf.org, the World Association of Sign Language Interpreters (http://wasli .org), the Federation of Interpreters and Translators (http://www.fit -ift.org/), or the website of a national interpreters association in a country outside your own. Report back on the following:
    a. When was the organization established?
    b. Who does it serve?
    c. What are the requirements to be a member?
    d. What programs and/or services does the organization offer?
    e. Are there resources on the site you would recommend to your peers?
    f. How might you use this website in the future?

5. Interview a Deaf and non-deaf interpreter educator that has worked in another country. Seek their experiences and advice for interpreters thinking about working in countries outside their own. Share your findings with the rest of the class.

INDEX

Figures and tables are indicated by "f" and "t" following page numbers.